ISIS Beyond the Spectacle

What is ISIS? A quasi-state? A terrorist group? A movement? An ideology? As ISIS has transformed and mutated, gained and lost territory, horrified the world and been its punch line, media have been central to understanding it. The changing, yet constant, relationship between ISIS and the media, as well as its adversaries' dependency on media to make sense of ISIS, is central to this book.

More than just the images of mutilated bodies that garnered ISIS its initial infamy, the book considers an ISIS media world that includes infographics, administrative reports, and various depictions of a post-racial utopia in which justice is swift and candy is bought and sold with its own currency. The book reveals that the efforts of ISIS and its adversaries to communicate and make sense of this world share modes of visual, aesthetic, and journalistic practice and expression. The short tumultuous history of ISIS does not allow for a single approach to understanding its relation to media. Thus, the book's contributions are to be read as contrapuntal analyses that productively connect and disconnect, providing a much-needed complex account of the ISIS-media relationship.

This book was originally published as a special issue of *Critical Studies in Media Communication*.

Mehdi Semati is Professor of Communication at Northern Illinois University, USA, and has published on media and terrorism, and Islamophobia.

Piotr M. Szpunar is Assistant Professor of Communication at Albany, State University of New York, USA, and is the author of *Homegrown: Identity and Difference in the American War on Terror* (2018).

Robert Alan Brookey is Professor of Telecommunications at Ball State University, USA, and has published on political economy and identity politics in new media and virtual environments.

NCA Studies in Communication

The National Communication Association (NCA) advances Communication as the discipline that studies all forms, modes, media, and consequences of communication through humanistic, social scientific, and aesthetic inquiry.

NCA serves the scholars, teachers, and practitioners who are its members by enabling and supporting their professional interests in research and teaching. Dedicated to fostering and promoting free and ethical communication, NCA promotes the widespread appreciation of the importance of communication in public and private life, the application of competent communication to improve the quality of human life and relationships, and the use of knowledge about communication to solve human problems.

NCA publishes 11 academic journals that provide the latest research in the discipline and showcase diverse perspectives on a range of scholarly topics. These journals are:

- *Communication and Critical/Cultural Studies*
- *Communication Education*
- *Communication Monographs*
- *Communication Teacher*
- *Critical Studies in Media Communication*
- *First Amendment Studies*
- *Journal of International and Intercultural Communication*
- *Journal of Applied Communication Research*
- *Quarterly Journal of Speech*
- *Review of Communication*
- *Text and Performance Quarterly*

The *NCA Studies in Communication* book series contains special issues from these journals, edited by leading scholars. The main aim of publishing these special issues as a series of books is to allow a wider audience of scholars from across multiple disciplines to engage with the work of the National Communication Association.

Available book titles in the series:

The Future of Internet Policy
Edited by Peter Decherney and Victor Pickard

Race(ing) Intercultural Communication
Edited by Dreama Moon and Michelle Holling

Teaching First-Year Communication Courses
Paradigms and Innovations
Edited by Pat J. Gehrke

Queer Technologies
Affordances, Affect, Ambivalence
Edited by Katherine Sender and Adrienne Shaw

Stuart Hall Lives: Cultural Studies in an Age of Digital Media
Edited by Peter Decherney and Katherine Sender

ISIS Beyond the Spectacle
Communication Media, Networked Publics, and Terrorism
Edited by Mehdi Semati, Piotr M. Szpunar and Robert Alan Brookey

ISIS Beyond the Spectacle
Communication Media, Networked Publics, and Terrorism

Edited by
Mehdi Semati, Piotr M. Szpunar and
Robert Alan Brookey

LONDON AND NEW YORK

First published 2019
by Routledge
2 Park Square, Milton Park, Abingdon, Oxon, OX14 4RN, UK

and by Routledge
711 Third Avenue, New York, NY 10017, USA

Routledge is an imprint of the Taylor & Francis Group, an informa business

© 2019 National Communication Association

All rights reserved. No part of this book may be reprinted or reproduced
or utilised in any form or by any electronic, mechanical, or other means,
now known or hereafter invented, including photocopying and recording,
or in any information storage or retrieval system, without permission in
writing from the publishers.

Trademark notice: Product or corporate names may be trademarks or
registered trademarks, and are used only for identification and
explanation without intent to infringe.

British Library Cataloguing in Publication Data
A catalogue record for this book is available from the British Library

ISBN 13: 978-1-138-60059-1

Typeset in Minion Pro
by RefineCatch Limited, Bungay, Suffolk

Publisher's Note
The publisher accepts responsibility for any inconsistencies that may have
arisen during the conversion of this book from journal articles to book chapters,
namely the possible inclusion of journal terminology.

Disclaimer
Every effort has been made to contact copyright holders for their permission to
reprint material in this book. The publishers would be grateful to hear from any
copyright holder who is not here acknowledged and will undertake to rectify
any errors or omissions in future editions of this book.

Contents

Citation Information	vii
Notes on Contributors	ix

Introduction – ISIS beyond the spectacle: communication media, networked
publics, terrorism   1
Mehdi Semati and Piotr M. Szpunar

Section I: Brand/Media/Visualization

1. The communication of horrorism: a typology of ISIS online death videos   8
    Lilie Chouliaraki and Angelos Kissas

2. One apostate run over, hundreds repented: excess, unthinkability, and infographics
    from the war with I.S.I.S.   24
    Rebecca A. Adelman

3. Apocalypse, later: a longitudinal study of the Islamic State brand   41
    Charlie Winter

Section II: Media Theory

4. Fun against fear in the Caliphate: Islamic State's spectacle and counter-spectacle   60
    Marwan M. Kraidy

5. The viral mediation of terror: ISIS, image, implosion   77
    Ryan E. Artrip and François Debrix

Section III: Journalism/Narratives/Interpretive Tiers

6. Cold War redux and the news: Islamic State and the US through each other's eyes   92
    Barbie Zelizer

7. Deflating the iconoclash: shifting the focus from Islamic State's iconoclasm to
    its realpolitik   108
    Ben O'Loughlin

8. Arguing with ISIS: web 2.0, open source journalism, and narrative disruption   122
    Matt Sienkiewicz

Index   137

Citation Information

The chapters in this book were originally published in *Critical Studies in Media Communication*, volume 35, issue 1 (March 2018). When citing this material, please use the original page numbering for each article, as follows:

Introduction
ISIS beyond the spectacle: communication media, networked publics, terrorism
Mehdi Semati and Piotr M. Szpunar
Critical Studies in Media Communication, volume 35, issue 1 (March 2018), pp. 1–7

Chapter 1
The communication of horrorism: a typology of ISIS online death videos
Lilie Chouliaraki and Angelos Kissas
Critical Studies in Media Communication, volume 35, issue 1 (March 2018), pp. 24–39

Chapter 2
One apostate run over, hundreds repented: excess, unthinkability, and infographics from the war with I.S.I.S.
Rebecca A. Adelman
Critical Studies in Media Communication, volume 35, issue 1 (March 2018), pp. 57–73

Chapter 3
Apocalypse, later: a longitudinal study of the Islamic State brand
Charlie Winter
Critical Studies in Media Communication, volume 35, issue 1 (March 2018), pp. 103–121

Chapter 4
Fun against fear in the Caliphate: Islamic State's spectacle and counter-spectacle
Marwan M. Kraidy
Critical Studies in Media Communication, volume 35, issue 1 (March 2018), pp. 40–56

Chapter 5
The viral mediation of terror: ISIS, image, implosion
Ryan E. Artrip and François Debrix
Critical Studies in Media Communication, volume 35, issue 1 (March 2018), pp. 74–88

CITATION INFORMATION

Chapter 6
Cold War redux and the news: Islamic State and the US through each other's eyes
Barbie Zelizer
Critical Studies in Media Communication, volume 35, issue 1 (March 2018), pp. 8–23

Chapter 7
Deflating the iconoclash: shifting the focus from Islamic State's iconoclasm to its realpolitik
Ben O'Loughlin
Critical Studies in Media Communication, volume 35, issue 1 (March 2018), pp. 89–102

Chapter 8
Arguing with ISIS: web 2.0, open source journalism, and narrative disruption
Matt Sienkiewicz
Critical Studies in Media Communication, volume 35, issue 1 (March 2018), pp. 122–135

For any permission-related enquiries please visit:
http://www.tandfonline.com/page/help/permissions

Notes on Contributors

Rebecca A. Adelman is Associate Professor of Media and Communication Studies at the University of Maryland, Baltimore County, USA. She specializes in visual culture, political theory, trauma studies, ethics, and cultural studies of war, terrorism, and militarization.

Ryan E. Artrip teaches in Philosophy and Political Science at Guilford College and Elon University, USA. He is currently completing a manuscript on the politics and theory of viral media culture.

Robert Alan Brookey is Professor of Telecommunications at Ball State University, USA, and has published on political economy and identity politics in new media and virtual environments.

Lilie Chouliaraki is Professor of Media and Communications in the Department of Media and Communications at the London School of Economics, UK. Her research focuses largely on mediated suffering (disaster news, aid and humanitarianism, migration, and war).

François Debrix is Director of the ASPECT program and Professor of Political Science at Virginia Tech University, USA. He is the author of *Global Powers of Horror* (2017).

Angelos Kissas is a PhD candidate in the Department of Media and Communications at the London School of Economics, UK. His research interest lies in transformations of ideology under conditions of mediatized politics.

Marwan M. Kraidy is the Anthony Shadid Chair in Global Media, Politics and Culture and the Director of the Center for Advanced Research in Global Communication at the Annenberg School for Communication, University of Pennsylvania, USA.

Ben O'Loughlin is Professor of International Relations and Co-Director of the New Political Communication Centre at Royal Holloway, University of London, UK. He was Specialist Advisor to the UK Parliamentary Committee on Soft Power and UK Influence.

Mehdi Semati is Professor of Communication at Northern Illinois University, USA, and has published on media and terrorism, and Islamophobia.

Matt Sienkiewicz is Associate Professor in the Department of Communication at Boston College, USA. His research focuses on the West's investment in Middle Eastern broadcasting initiatives as well as the politics of contemporary American comedy.

Piotr M. Szpunar is Assistant Professor of Communication at Albany, State University of New York, USA, and is the author of *Homegrown: Identity and Difference in the American War on Terror* (2018).

NOTES ON CONTRIBUTORS

Charlie Winter is a Senior Research Fellow at the International Centre for the Study of Radicalisation. He is currently studying for a PhD in War Studies at King's College London, UK, examining how propaganda articulates meaning and how militant groups cultivate creative approaches to governance and war.

Barbie Zelizer is the Raymond Williams Professor of Communication and Director of the Center for Media at Risk in the Annenberg School for Communication at the University of Pennsylvania, USA.

INTRODUCTION

ISIS beyond the spectacle: communication media, networked publics, terrorism

Mehdi Semati and Piotr M. Szpunar

October 1, 2017: A "gunman" uses automatic weapons and opens fire on a crowd of concert goers in Las Vegas, Nevada, killing 58 persons and injuring 546 people. ISIS's claim of responsibility for the violence that killed and injured hundreds of people in Las Vegas was received skeptically and interpreted as "somewhat of a joke among the rank-and-file of the international terrorist elite" and a "sign of desperation" (Smith, 2017). If the first day of October ushered in a time that ISIS was dismissed as a joke, the last day of the month changed the narrative.

October 31, 2017: Sayfullo Saipov, an Uzbek national with permanent residency in the U.S., uses a rented truck to crush pedestrians in a bike lane in Manhattan, New York. Upon the discovery of his religious identity and his ideological affiliation with ISIS he is immediately declared a terrorist. Although authorities could find no communication between him and the terrorist group, it became clear that "ISIS's propaganda was sufficient to animate Saipov to carry out the worst terrorist attack in New York since 9/11" (Wright, 2017). As Wright (2017) reported:

> According to the ten-page federal complaint filed against him, Saipov fell under the ISIS spell by viewing some ninety ISIS-related videos and almost four thousand images on his (at least two) cell phones. He was specifically inspired by issue No. 3 of the slick online magazine *Rumiyah*, which means "Rome," an allusion to an old prophecy foretelling the fall of the infidel West.

Although the act somehow seemed small and pathetic for all the grandiose claims of ISIS, and especially given "iconic stature" of New York as a target for the terrorist group, terrorism "inspired" by ISIS and their ideology is not going to disappear anytime soon.

The essays for this collection were proposed at the height of global panic caused by ISIS (the Islamic State of Iraq and Syria), also known as ISIL (the Islamic State of Iraq and the Levant) and DAESH (its Arabic acronym).[1] From 2014 to 2017 the group controlled territories in Syria and across central and northern Iraq. As we write these words by way of an introduction to the collection, we received the news that forces backed by the United States in Syria liberated the city of Raqqa, the self-declared capital of the "Islamic State." The group's claim of maintaining a "state" is now only an empty symbolic gesture, even if such a gesture had the ring of credibility to it at some point. That the group never posed an existential threat to any state but managed to project a threat on a global scale points to its ontological status as a creature, a byproduct and an effect of an assemblage, made up of vectors of communication media, spectacles of violence, technological agency, non-human agency and processes, bodies both mortal and capable of violence, and networked and affective publics. The essays in this collection examine various dimensions of this assemblage and the discourses that contribute to its stability and its permanency.

Where to being when discussing the Islamic State and communication media beyond the spectacle? Perhaps at the most recent episodes of violence, where claims of responsibility are met skeptically and ridiculed in one case only to be followed by another episode when a "radicalized" individual appears to have followed "instructions" from online sources such as YouTube videos and encrypted channels of mobile apps (e.g. Telegram) where ISIS and its followers thrive. Speculation, im/plausibility, mis/information and the proliferation of images give us the order of the day. This state of global communication recalls Baudrillard's (1995) statement about the "sticky and unintelligible event" of the first Persian Gulf War in 1991:

> Of course, this anxious interrogation increases the uncertainty with respect to its possible irruption. And this uncertainty invades our screens like a real oil slick, in the image of that blind sea bird stranded on a beach in the Gulf, which will remain the symbol-image of what we all are in front of our screens, in front of that sticky and unintelligible event (p. 32).

In this haze, in the uncertainty, speculation, and claim-making in the aftermath of violence, lies the import of examining the link between the Islamic State and communication media. The Islamic State's prowess and presence is tied to media—digital, social, broadcast, and beyond. The past few years have spawned countless academic and talking head musings about ISIS and social media, about encryption and security, about radicalization and virality. Yet, the communicative dimensions of the conflict with ISIS are often reduced to hypodermic needle models of communication that fail to address the complexity of not only media and mediation but geopolitics as well. At issue is not just content but mode of address, platforms, vectors and the infrastructures of mediation, remediation, and premediation in which the deterritorialized arm of ISIS circulates.

In a context permeated by communication technologies through which identities and conflicts circulate, where networked publics are formed and reformed around expressions of outrage and sentiments related to them, what would going beyond spectacle entail? Is it to analyze ISIS beyond its brutal violence? Is it to get past the images that dominate our news cycles? Beyond the image itself? What sort of reckoning is required to make sense of ISIS and communication media in a way that does not play into the cyclical obsession with terror and counterterror (Giroux, 2016)? Articles in this collection offer no singular answer but a variety of approaches and methods through which to better understand the emergence and persistence of the mediated phenomenon that is the Islamic State and other such groups that owe their existence and durability to infrastructures of global communication technologies and their affordances.

ISIS is a fundamentally mediated phenomenon, even if "it" was born out of specific geopolitical formations, and much of what we know about the group, we know through communication media. Yet the media to which the Islamic State is intricately tied is often accompanied by the adjective "Western." In 2010, commentators responded to al-Qaeda in the Arabian Peninsula's *Inspire* magazine with shock. It looks Western, it is "slick," and it speaks "our" language. Today, ISIS propaganda is met with similar commentary. The idea that the enemy might be like us, or exploit our media, is part of contemporary counterterrorism discourse (Szpunar, 2018). It is worth remembering that Baudrillard (2003) pointed out long ago that terrorists and counter-terrorist authorities do share affinities in their approaches: they "have assimilated everything of globalism and modernity, without changing their goal, which is to destroy that power" (p. 19).

Such expressions of disbelief that individuals outside the Global North might know how to use communication technologies or the grammar of audiovisual communication tell us more about the writers and their assumptions than the individuals who deploy media technologies in the Global South. However much modified in various contexts, the adeptness with which any group utilizes global media should perhaps not be so surprising in the age of global mediascapes and technoscapes. However, beyond the militarization of media in statements that claim that "they" have taken over "our" media, there is much to learn about media and ISIS through examining their relationship.

The epistemological view underpinning such thinking is captured to a large extent by Barbie Zelizer's notion of "Cold War Mindedness." She examines how both U.S. media (commercial and start-up) and ISIS propaganda share a journalistic style. "Cold War Mindedness" is a mode of reportage characterized by an uncritical dependence on media in the face of a conflict in which much remains unseen. She deploys a comparative approach in her study that examines how U.S. media and ISIS media cover each other. Her analysis reveals the re-emergence of a "Cold War Mindedness" in journalism practice that is shared between these adversarial media. This style frames the conflict in a simplistic us/ other binary, is part and parcel of "invisible war," and is built upon an assumption that equates media's reach with its impact or effect. The use of an us/other binary reveals that while the two media systems compared here are vastly different (i.e. one an arm of a quasi-state, the other an assemblage of commercial enterprises and networks), each participates in constructing a divide that one cannot cross, conscripted into the service of structuring conflict. In contrast to the hyper-visibility usually ascribed to ISIS, Zelizer argues that much of the conflict remains unseen, with any information gaps filled in through phantasmagorical, speculative, and imaginative registers. Along the same lines, the equation of media reach and impact underwrites the narratives of a battle for "hearts and minds," which provides a proxy gauge through which to assess which side of the binary is "winning." Zelizer does not suggest that the conflict does not inflict very real casualties, only that it is also fought on the plane of the informational at which journalism relies on very predictable modes of representation.

Rebecca Adelman also engages that epistemological view, as she examines a shared mode of informational war, namely, infographics. Adelman argues that infographics are used by "Western" media as a technology through which to locate and contain the phantom enemy of the war on terror. ISIS uses the same technology to preclude this diffusive function; its utilization of infographics communicates a calculating and able adversary, who—and Zelizer also points to this—does not seem so "other." Adelman starts her piece with a provocative question: What would 330 suicide car bombings look like? In relation to ISIS, it is a query that might bring to mind scenes of horror. Yet, Adelman, like various authors in this collection of essays, moves away from the violent and analyzes a seemingly more banal form of mediating violence: the infographic. Exploring the output of both ISIS and Western news media, Adelman identifies the unassuming infographic as a technology for "managing excess and unthinkability" that is integral to war efforts. For Western media, the infographic locates the phantom enemy, reducing its threatening nature by aiding its intelligibility; by placing the enemy, one might control it. However, ISIS weaponizes this sanitizing technique simply by incorporating it in its activities. In its use, ISIS reinforces anxieties concerning its viral ability to use media for its own ends.

In general, ISIS, "Western" news media, and other actors all operate within the same global media architecture. Through the lens of Situationist theory, Marwan Kraidy explores ISIS spectacles and the potential of counter-spectacles of satire produced by various Arab publics. Identifying the discursive connection between fear and fun, which binds ISIS and its adversaries, Kraidy argues that ISIS's diffuse spectacles present an aptitude to exploit global media architecture that precedes contemporary anxieties about "fake news." He utilizes Situationist theory to explore ISIS's use of non-violent spectacle in order to maintain power and presence. He also explores the potential of utilizing counter-spectacles against ISIS. Relying on the critical thought of Guy Debord, Kraidy makes sense of ISIS's concentrated spectacle, those used to consolidate rule within a given territory, through a productive comparison to similar practices utilized by Bashar al-Assad and Saddam Hussein. In ISIS's productions, its Caliph, al-Baghdadi, plays the role of the dictatorial personality. The group's concentrated spectacle is not only reinforced by violent images of meting out punishment but also by illustrating the "good life" within the territory of the Islamic State and its administrative prowess (e.g. in minting the Dinar). Kraidy also asserts that ISIS's "success," i.e. its position as the world's contemporary existential threat, replacing al-Qaeda, depends much on its ability to exploit the global media infrastructure. Therein, Kraidy finds not just fear as the driving force of ISIS's diffuse spectacles but also fun—militants pose with cats, complain about the lack of a particular brand of candy, and recite poetry. Similarly, various parties have created ("fun") satires of ISIS and therein Kraidy positions the conundrum of combating ISIS. In effect, the spectacle and counter-spectacle are not distinguished through fear and fun, but both inhabit a plane in which they are inextricably linked, circulating in global media networks.

That link and the conditions of its existence are addressed in the contribution by François Debrix and Ryan Artrip. They too attribute the aptitude to exploit global media to the fungibility of reality and non-reality that characterizes global media and the global networked infrastructure that make it all possible. They take this one step further and suggest that the continued tendency to demand that meaning be assigned might lead to the exhaustion and implosion of the very system of mediation on which ISIS and its adversaries depend. In contrast to narratives of ISIS's inhumanity and placement outside of the world system, Artrip and Debrix situate ISIS directly within global processes of circulation and mediation. By outlining the regulatory and productive potentials of contemporary media processes—focused not on truths, but simulation, saturation, circulation, fungibility, virality, up-votes, likes, etc.—the authors illustrate the vulnerabilities that allow ISIS to effectively circulate its own images. They end with the provocative proposition that the never-fading demand to assign meaning to the meaningless (or that which is beyond representation), ISIS's spectacles, as its own kind of terror, could bring about the implosion of the very system on which ISIS depends. Here, ISIS has perfected "Western" modalities of meaning to the point of bringing about their downfall.

However, this environment is not made up of simply news media, entertainment media, ISIS, and other purveyors of propaganda. Integral to the system is what Matt Sienkiewicz calls an "interpretive tier" that acts as an intermediary by obtaining and translating documents internal to the Islamic State. The documents, which reveal infighting within its ranks, not only serve to disrupt the narratives of the Islamic State but also those of Western media that reinforce and support governmental counterterrorism discourse. Here Sienkiewicz explores the intersection of open source journalism and counter-terrorism. Focusing on the case of Aymenn Jawad Al-Tamimi, Sienkiewicz examines the disruptive function of journalists who fall within the "interpretive tier." These journalists work within a black market in which ISIS's internal documents are traded and sold. They have, at times, exclusive access to such documentation and develop the skills with which to distinguish between authentic and fake documents (created for profit). In gathering and analyzing ISIS documents this interpretive tier reveals the infighting, dissent, and contention within ISIS's operational and governance structure. Such revelations not only disrupt ISIS's own narrative but those of Western media that uncritically reflect counterterrorism discourse. Using textual analysis and interviews with Al-Tamimi, Sienkiewicz situates this disruptive work in a complex web of entanglements which include the global media structure and the organizations that fund the work of the interpretive tier. His contribution is yet another interrogation of the epistemological universe in which ISIS and its adversaries engage each other.

In the cycles of mediation and remediation (and premediation), the insight that ISIS exploits global media structures, is adept at producing spectacles, and appropriates "Western" tropes is not to be taken in the vein of counter-terrorism discourse. Rather, the authors point to the idea that the frame of ISIS as an existential threat from without needs to be re-read as a product of these very systems. For Friedrich Kittler (2012), states create their own terrorists. "State" here has two meanings: the geopolitical state and the global media environment. Thus—and without taking a deterministic position—rather than marveling at the barbarians at the gate, the insights of these papers help us understand just how global media infrastructures facilitate ISIS's style and, just as important, how ISIS's media practice reveals much about "our" cultures of mediation and contemporary spheres of conflict, more generally.

In this context, one way to grapple with ISIS and conflict on a global scale is to think through the implications of the arguments made in this collection of articles for the conditions of geopolitics at the present conjuncture. Among the approaches that highlight such implications in international relations and allied fields is what Connolly (2013) characterizes as "new materialism." He defines this approach as:

> the most common name given to a series of movements in several fields that criticize anthropocentrism, rethink subjectivity by playing up the role of inhuman forces within the human, emphasize the self-organizing powers of several non-human processes, explore dissonant relations between those processes and cultural practice, rethink the sources of ethics, and comment on the need to fold a planetary dimension more actively and regularly into studies of global, interstate and state politics (p. 399).

Ben O'Loughlin's contribution effectively brings ISIS back to the orbit of realpolitik and geopolitics. He considers what tactics might be useful in countering ISIS propaganda in an age he calls the "Iconoclash." The Iconoclash is an environment in which conflict involves a tit-for-tat exchange of images: the beheading video, the drone strike, the angry cleric, etc. O'Loughlin argues that what makes ISIS particularly adept in its own iconoclasm is the religious modality that they have effectively appropriated. As a countermeasure, O'Loughlin sees hope not in illustrating how ISIS is not really about Islam. Rather, more effective, he argues, might be a strategy that highlights ISIS's own "secular realpolitik" found in its compromises with Turkey; in one instance ISIS gave free passage to Turkish troops and refrained from destroying what the group itself considers to be forbidden idols. O'Loughlin suggests that highlighting ISIS's realpolitik is not only about showing the complexities and compromises of operating a state but revealing how this actively goes against the "religious" principles that underpin the modality within which it has been able to exploit the Iconoclash.

In his contribution to this collection, Charlie Winter has created an archive of ISIS media output and thus provides a longitudinal account of the group's activity. Winter compares media output by ISIS in two distinct moments: mid-2015 and early 2017, the latter a time in which the Islamic State had lost about 30% of its territory. Winter reveals an important connection between geopolitics and ISIS media output, in that the destabilization of the Islamic State's territorial strongholds is correlated to a decrease in the volume of media production, the increased centralization of production, and a shift in thematic composition from utopianism and state-building to warfare and denial. Denying its geopolitical precarity, Winter argues that posturing and display become increasingly important to ISIS in maintaining its brand. Winter and O'Loughlin, in discussing posturing, display, and branding, effectively provide a context for the readers that exposes where prevailing epistemological views bump up against geopolitics and re-territorialization of various kinds on the global stage.

One of ISIS's achievements is that it is part of the news cycle. Most any public act of violence is met with speculation about whether or not it is an act of terror. Much of this is due to the fact that ISIS tells "us" either what we already know or what we want to hear. A quick perusal through *Dabiq* or *Rumiyah* and one can read therein a clash of civilizations narrative in which ISIS embraces the violent, vengeful adversary that seeks to usurp "Western" culture (ISIS uses this modifier just as often and problematically as any news report or academic article). It is the key frame for Western news stories as both Zelizer and Sienkiewicz point out. However, ISIS's position in the terror news cycle points to the importance of appearances and display. While ISIS's presence goes beyond brutal violence, which various authors in this collection stress, it is certainly the case that much of the attention ISIS has garnered has been the result of its violence. Lilie Chouliaraki and Angelos Kissas provide a typology of the functions of horror in this context.

Drawing on the work of Cavarero (2009) that distinguishes terrorism from horrorism, Chouliaraki and Kissas theorize the communicative logic of ISIS's death spectacle in terms of "regimes of horrorism" (grotesque, abject, and sublime horror), as experienced by distant spectators. Going beyond the literature in strategic communication and political communication, they explore how ISIS addresses the world through specific aesthetic practices. These practices invite a range of moral responses and in doing so articulate a specific ethico-political project that, borrowing from Murray (2006), they call thanatopolitics (i.e. "the use of death at the service of political life"). Chouliaraki and Kissas show dominant hierarchies of grievability are subverted in favor of thanatopolitics in the process of fusing Western and non-Western genres and narratives in the operation of horrorism. One of the advantages of their approach is that, by deploying the analytics of horrorism, they can address death in ISIS's videos not as an element of religiosity but as a deployment of Western cultural forms and secular rationalities. Ultimately, they show how ISIS unleashes on its worldwide spectators a "spectacular thanatopolitics" that, through the savaged body, renders their dedication to death into the new "norm of heroic subjectivity."

Mutilated bodies, infographics, various depictions of utopia, all circulating through various channels of global media, inflected by shared modes of journalistic, visual, and aesthetic practice and expression, trading in fear and fun, reality and nonreality, terror and horror, affected by the (mediated) boots of geopolitics, these are the many entangled vectors through which the ontological status of ISIS is revealed. It is within the interstices and connections laid out and suggested by the contributions in this special issue that ISIS's visual brutality is squared with its less violent claims—for example, that it constitutes a "transnational multiethnic state" that moves beyond racism in a way that America never could.[2] However, as stated earlier, the contributions to this collection do not offer a uniform or a singular approach, method or theoretical perspective. To the contrary, they offer a range of approaches, analytics, and theoretical orientations to problematize various aspects of the context in which a phenomenon like ISIS exists and to which it speaks and contributes. We invite our readers to engage these contributions, especially for the insights they offer for communication studies, media theories, and rhetorical criticism.

Notes

1. For the sake of convenience this collection of essays refers to this group by its commonly known names as "ISIS" or "IS."
2. Limitations of space prevent us from a more comprehensive treatment of terrorism and media, especially with respect to discussions of Muslim identity, racialization, and politics of representation. For an example of such a discussion see Semati (2010).

References

Baudrillard, J. (1995). *The Gulf war did not take place.* (P. Patton, Trans.). Bloomington, IN: Indiana University Press.

Baudrillard, J. (2003). *The spirit of terrorism.* London: Verso.

Cavarero, A. (2009). *Horrorism: Naming contemporary violence.* New York, NY: Columbia University Press.

Connolly, W. (2013). The "new materialism" and the fragility of things. *Millennium: Journal of International Studies, 41*(3), 399–412.

Giroux, H. (2016). *America's addition to terrorism.* New York, NY: Monthly Review Press.

Kittler, K. (2012). Of states and their terrorists. *Cultural Politics: An International Journal, 8*(3), 385–397.

Murray, S. (2006). Thanatopolitics: On the use of death for mobilizing political life. *Polygraph: An International Journal of Politics and Culture, 18,* 191–215.

Semati, M. (2010). Islamophobia, culture and race in the age of Empire. *Cultural Studies, 24*(2), 256–275.

Smith, S. (2017, October 3). Las Vegas Shooting: ISIS Claim of Responsibility Is Sign of Desperation. *NBC News.* Retrieved from https://www.nbcnews.com/storyline/las-vegas-shooting/las-vegas-shooting-isis-claim-responsibility-sign-desperation-say-experts-n807076

Szpunar, P. M. (2018). *Homegrown: Identity and difference in the American war on terror.* New York, NY: New York University Press.

Wright, R. (2017, November 2). What the New York Attack Says About ISIS Now. *The New Yorker.* Retrieved from https://www.newyorker.com/news/news-desk/what-the-new-york-attack-says-about-isis-now

The communication of horrorism: a typology of ISIS online death videos

Lilie Chouliaraki and Angelos Kissas ⓘ

ABSTRACT

In this article, the authors theorize the communicative logic of ISIS online death videos—from the burning and shooting of individual hostages to mass battleground executions. Drawing on Adriana Cavarero's reflections on contemporary violence, they demonstrate how ISIS' digital spectacles of the annihilated body confront Western viewers with horror— or rather with different "regimes of horrorism" (grotesque, abject and sublime horror). These spectacles of horror, the authors argue, mix Western with Islamic aesthetic practices and secular with religious moral claims so as to challenge dominant hierarchies of grievability (who is worthy of our grief) and norms of subjectivity. In so doing, the authors conclude, ISIS introduces into global spaces of publicity a "spectacular thanatopolitics"—a novel form of thanatopolitics that brings the spectacle of the savaged body, banished from display since the 19th century, back to the public stage, thereby turning the pursuit of death into the new norm of heroic subjectivity.

Introduction: horrorism and ISIS' aesthetics of death

[...] it is all about death, not only about the violent irruption of death in real time—"live", so to speak—but the irruption of a death which is far more than real: a death which is symbolic and sacrificial—that is to say, the absolute, irrevocable event. (Baudrillard, 2003, pp. 16–17)

ISIS digital communication is indeed "all about death" in that death is the trademark visual feature of ISIS online videos. This spectacle of death is, we argue, not the endpoint but, rather, the starting point of ISIS terrorist acts. It signals the moment when the annihilation of human life enters the symbolic realm and becomes "the absolute, irrevocable event." Our focus in this essay is on these digital messages of human annihilation through which ISIS addresses the world. Our aim is to explore ISIS' "death spectacles" as aesthetic practices that use the dying or dead body to invite a range of moral responses on behalf of their online publics in the Arab and Western worlds and, in so doing, to communicate a specific ethico-political project—what Murray (2006) calls thanatopolitics or the use of death at the service of political life.

Instrumental to our approach is Cavarero's (2009) distinction between terrorism and horrorism. Cavarero argues that, while terror is associated with proximity and addresses the eyewitness of violent death, horror is associated with mediated witnessing and addresses the distant spectator. Taking Medusa's gaze as its prototypical figure, Cavarero implies that horror operates in the "realm of the eye" and, as opposed to the effects of frantic movement incited by the instinct to survive a terror attack (terror as panicking fear), it bears the effects of physical paralysis at the sight of massacred bodies (horror as freezing disgust). There is, in her words, "an affinity between horror and vision" that turns us into passive viewers of the spectacle of corporeal destruction (ibid). Even though horror has indeed an irreducible corporeality that cannot be contained in its visual dimension, for our purposes, the key distinction here is between terror as lived experience and horror as a mediated one.

Pace Cavarero, however, our interest in the visuality of horror moves beyond her "instinctive disgust" towards analyzing how exactly the aesthetic practices of ISIS videos invest the dying or dead body in a range of normative engagements with death. Echoing Zelizer (2010), we argue that we cannot fully understand the ethico-political implications of ISIS' global communication, what she calls the image's "subjunctive" or normative mode, without analyzing how it visually performs violent death and how it invites us to relate to it. By this token, what matters in the realm of mediation, as Cynthia Weber has succinctly put it, "is not only that we encounter horrorism but *how* we encounter horrorism and what we do when we see it'" (2014, p. 254, emphasis added). What, then, are the aesthetic practices of death in ISIS' videos? How does the victim appear to die and what are the semantic fields within which their death acquires meaning? What normative assumptions about death and mourning do these videos communicate and what forms of subjectivity do they imagine for their publics?

We reflect on these questions by examining three cases of English-speaking atrocity videos released by ISIS in 2016: the burning of two Turkish soldiers (December 8, 2016); the shooting of five UK presumed intelligence agents (January 3, 2016); and mass battleground executions in the Syrian–Iraqi war zones (January 2, 2017). We show that, instead of a purely religious message, horrorism operates through a logic of recontextualization, which fuses Western with non-Western genres and narratives with a view to mirroring and ultimately subverting dominant hierarchies of grievability in favor of what we introduce as a spectacular thanatopolitics—"grotesque," "sublime" and "abject" spectacles/regimes of horrorism. We define ISIS' spectacular thanatopolitics as a distinct aesthetic and ethical project that re-introduces ferocious death spectacles (banned since the 19th century) into Western public spheres with a view to performing an anti-humanist politics of critique. And we discuss the nature of this politics as the performance of three communicative acts, namely: retribution (denouncing the enemy's way of war, in the grotesque); disgrace (humiliating the West, in the abject) and redemption (glorifying its own mythical subjectivities, in the sublime).

The value of this horroristic approach lies in enabling us to rethink ISIS' online communication in at least two new ways: (i) conceptualizing videos of violent death not only, as the dominant literature has it (see the next part of this essay), in terms of ISIS branding or visual propaganda, but as aesthetic performances that articulate meaning around the body and its mortal vulnerability and (ii) re-conceptualizing these aesthetic performances in terms of a logic of recontextualization that appropriates and harnesses Western genres to its own ends, namely to promote new norms of heroic subjectivity. These insights contribute to an enriched understanding of ISIS which, *pace* dominant perceptions of it as "medieval"/primitive or "evil"/transcendental[1] (Patruss, 2016 for criticisms), establishes that, while neo-fundamentalist religion is a key component of its message, ISIS *also* relies on Western popular culture and secular rationalities to legitimize the sanctification of violent death in the moral imagination of digital platforms.

Spectacles of death: strategic and political communication approaches

Contemporary literature across disciplines (media studies, sociology, political science and international relations) has engaged with terrorism and communication in terms of two analytical approaches: *strategic* communication, which is concerned with the instrumental value of terrorism as a means of propaganda and *political* communication, which looks into the broader political dynamics of the spectacle of terror.

The *strategic communication* approach relies on the claim that "communication and terrorism go hand in hand because communication is the oxygen of terrorist acts" (Wilkinson, 1997, p. 52). It explores the ways in which terrorist organizations use media as instruments of propaganda and recruitment in the context of the digital information economy (Nacos, 2016; Pattwell, Mitman, & Porpora, 2015). The first strand of this literature engages with what Ayalon, Popovich and Yarchi call the strategic use of "'imagefare'—'the use of images as substitutes for military means, namely fighting to establish their version of events or ideas as dominant'" (2016, p. 256). Given its state-building ambitions, emphasis here falls on ISIS' organizational narratives as platforms that voice the aspirations of disaffected Muslims to combat Western aggression and establish their own "universal" community, the "caliphate." "The group's narrative", as Farwell puts it, "portrays ISIS as an agent of change, the true apostle of a sovereign faith, [and] a champion of its own perverse notions of social justice" (2014, pp. 49–50). Despite controversy within terrorist networks around the value of atrocity videos (see Farwell, 2014), ISIS' platforms have successfully combined their terrorist message with global audiences' proclivity to spectacles of apocalyptic violence (Cohen-Almagor, 2005), rendering such spectacles instrumental in sustaining the organization's global "brand".

A second strand of research within strategic communication draws on cultural analysis to explore ISIS' savvy use of media platforms; as NYT journalist David Carr put it: "ISIS seems to understand that the same forces that carried the Ice Bucket Challenge's message of uplift ... can be used to spread fear and terror as well".[2] While some examine its rhetoric in terms of, for instance, video games' "flame, troll and engage" language (Al-Rawi, 2016), others look into visual genres, such as photographs, to show how ISIS' prolific use of "about to die" imagery "has transformed the online environment itself into a medium of terrorism" (Winkler, El Damanhoury, Dicker, & Lemieux, 2016, p. 15). What ISIS' communication strategies have produced, as Ingram (2015, p. 730) proposes, is a powerful "competitive system of meaning" that challenges mainstream ideas on justice, victimhood and friend/enemy relationships and proposes alternative versions of identity for Islamic populations across the globe.

Strategic communication research, in summary, indicates that violent death is not an additional component of ISIS' digital practice, but an essential part of it, co-nascent with the management of its image as a state-aspiring militant entity. This is a key insight that drives our own adoption of horrorism both as digital practice that "extend[s] the reach of violent abuse into the boundless sphere of digital networks" (Pötzsch, 2015, p. 12) and as symbolic practice that constructs the ISIS brand.

The *political communication* approach is not concerned with the instrumental goals of horrorism but with its socio-political implications. Images of annihilated bodies, this literature has it, participate in broader projects of ideological hegemony in global geopolitics. One strand of this literature focuses on the histories of Western interventionism in the Middle East as a cause for fundamentalist insurgency to gain ideological and military influence across the world (Mamdani, 2009)—paying extra attention on the role of religion in the formation of terrorist identities. While a large number of studies regards Islam as a key factor in the emergence of Middle Eastern militancy, including the emergence of its horrific death spectacles (Pelletier, Lundmark, Gardner, Scott Ligon, & Kilinc, 2016; Perlmutter, 2005), others problematize this privileging of religion as an inadequate or even misleading explanation (e.g. considering Islam as a coherent ideology which explains everything involving Muslims) for contemporary terrorism (Roy, 2004). We draw upon these criticisms to approach ISIS videos as relatively open texts that articulate a complex message, which includes but is not "exhausted to," religious fundamentalism.

The second relevant research strand of political communication draws on studies of the socio-cultural implications of ISIS' imagery. Giroux argues that spectacles of terror fuse the distinct logics of global consumerism, or "soft war," with global militarism, or "hard war," into one cultural experience, elevating violent death "to a new prominent feature of social and political power" (2014).[3] His argument confirms both Kellner (2004) and Boal, Clark, Matthews, and Watts (2005) who link terrorist spectacles to a wider trajectory of mediated violence in the neo-liberal entertainment industry of the West. This trajectory, they maintain, has undermined the idea of the "historical monopoly of the means of destruction by the state" (Boal et al., 2005, p. 17) and has contributed to trivializing the sanctity of human life—a core value of the liberal imaginary.

While the religion-based analysis of ISIS death spectacles emphasizes the distinctive non-and-anti-Western fundamentalism of ISIS ideology, the broader socio-cultural analysis of these spectacles points towards narrative continuities between ISIS and Western ideologies. In so doing, the latter problematizes ISIS' radical "othering" and forces us to see continuities between "us" and "them". In line with these two strands of research, our analysis is sensitized both towards commonalities in ISIS and Western tropes of representing death *and* towards the distinct moralities embedded in ISIS' spectacles of violent death.

In summary, strategic and political communication approaches have greatly contributed to clarifying the conceptual territory of digital horror either as a tool of ISIS branding or as a practice of power. Each of them nonetheless misses the whole picture. Strategic communication focuses on the message without attending to power; the broader ethico-political implications of digital spectacles of death "disappear" in the strategic analysis of terrorists' marketing campaigns. Political communication focuses on power but is not as attentive to the message; what disappears in this analysis is the detail of meaning-making practices through which power is articulated in particular digital spectacles. As a consequence, neither of the two approaches can offer insights in how death spectacles may produce ethico-political effects: how such spectacles may legitimize or challenge hierarchies of death and norms of subjectivity. What we aim to explore here is the co-articulation of the two, the message *and* power—horrorism being precisely an aesthetic logic of death at the service of a thanatopolitical project of power.

Analyzing horrorism: multi-modality and recontextualization

In its emphasis on the dead or dying body as both aesthetic object and ethico-political practice, we argue, horrorism is informed by a dialectical epistemology which attends both to the aesthetics of singular spectacles of death and to the global power relations in which ISIS seeks to intervene. Instead of prioritizing either message or power, horrorism approaches digital death as performative: as aesthetic micro-practices of corporeal destruction that, in the course of re-presentation, simultaneously produce macro-effects of power—they provisionally fix the objects and subjects of death in specific relationships of power, or "regimes of horrorism". Our methodological principle, it follows, similarly involves a two-dimensional conception of visual analysis that attends to the detail of ISIS' aesthetic representations while also interrogating the ethico-political implications such representations bear on their contexts.

Our starting point for this dialectical inquiry is the claim that ISIS operates on the basis of a "competitive system of meanings", (Ingram, 2015) which challenges *both* contemporary iconographies of Western publicity through, for instance, the introduction of graphic immolation videos *and* the normative boundaries of this space of publicity, namely whose death should legitimately be depicted as worthy of mourning and which identities we should endorse as desirable. Even though this synergetic relationship between imagery and norm has already been the focus of critical inquiry on Western visualities of death and their "orientalist" or "biopolitical" implications (for instance, Campbell, 2004; Chouliaraki, 2015), the focus on horrorism begs for an expansion of our analytical tools. Thus, while we borrow key insights from this literature, namely the focus on "multi-modality" so as to analyze the meaning-making articulations of image with sound in the videos, we further incorporate the concept of "recontextualization" in our analytical vocabulary.

The category of *"multi-modality"* offers the established categories of "frame sequencing" (how visual frames are edited in cohesive sequences) and "visual-verbal correspondence" (how language invests these frames in meaning) so as to "read" the dying or dead body as a visual grammar that produces meaning about humanity (Jewitt, 2009). The role of the body is instrumental in the production of horrorism insofar as the body that dies disfigured or dismembered, that is the body reduced into matter, challenges the very ontology of the human: "killing merely to kill is too little," as Caverero puts it; horrorism "aims to destroy the uniqueness of the body, tearing at its constitutive vulnerability" (2009, p. 8). Looking at the grammar of this corporeal "tearing" means, therefore, asking questions about how the human body figures within a filmic sequence, which semiotic resources are used in its aesthetic constitution and what moralizing function it comes to perform.

The category of *"recontextualization"* rests on the assumption that all story-telling is intertextually constituted through other stories. The concept is designed to identify the process by which each narrative selectively draws together genres, tropes and narratives of death, so as to re-situate and re-signify the body within different registers of moral evaluation (Chouliaraki & Fairclough, 1999; Kissas, 2017). Recontextualization, we claim, is an apt concept to explore the extent to which ISIS' "competitive system of meanings" intervenes in the global information landscape by *engaging with*, rather than opposing, the aesthetic tropes of death available in the West. While such engagements challenge Western rules of "taste and decency" (Campbell, 2004), they simultaneously mirror back and expose Western practices of death-at-war that largely remain invisible to its publics—for instance by confronting us with the forbidden imagery of the death of "our" soldiers in the battlefield. How and to what effect this recontextualization of death takes place in ISIS' videos are precisely the questions of our analysis.

Our analysis of horrorism differs thus from prior approaches in that it brackets abstract or top-down explanations (for instance, privileging religion) in order to re-construct the aesthetic logics of horror from the bottom up (multi-modality) and to re-describe the moral narratives that these logics privilege as desirable for their viewing publics (recontextualization)—see Chouliaraki (2006) for this "phronetic" approach in media research.

Regimes of horrorism in ISIS videos: grotesque, abject, sublime

ISIS' communicative strategy should be understood in the context of what Kaplan and Costa refer to as "fifth wave" terrorism—a mutation of Al Qaeda and the Islamic *Umah*, now developed into "a malign sectarian group of its own, whose dynamism and successes are attracting a global audience and support from Muslims in almost every country" (2015, p. 926). What, in their view, characterizes ISIS is, on the one hand, its "idiosyncratic ... ideological orientation" at the service of its state-building aspirations and, on the other, its expert use of social media that "integrates traditional propaganda channels with the twenty-first century tools" (2015, p. 936).

These uses of ISIS videos tactically fulfill many functions, including addressing their "polity," recruiting new martyrs and inspiring local attacks, as well as threatening Muslim and Western publics alike. Guided by the three videos, our analysis fully acknowl-edges ISIS' sectarian polemics against Muslim populations, yet focuses primarily on its relationship with the West: how these videos engage with Western aesthetic and moral practices, and, as we shall see in the conclusion, how they address Western audiences through normative understandings of death and subjectivity.

Our videos were selected for purposefully engaging with Western audiences in that they were deliberately released in English as well as Arabic, and in that they directly address Western figures (former U.K. PM David Cameron) and Western viewers at large. They were also selected because of their "paradigmatic" status (Flyvbjerg, 2006): their particular features both assert and transcend their particularity, standing for a broader category of aesthetic performativity that each example comes to typify. As particularities, these videos constitute three historically distinct events of violent death: the burning of two Turkish pilot prisoners in Al Bab ("The Shield of the Cross", released in Arabic on Decem-ber 22, 2016 and in English on January 2, 2017)[4], the shooting of five UK assumed spies (untitled, released in English on January 2, 2016)[5], and the large-scale atrocities across the Syria–Iraq war zones (The "Impenetrable Forces," released in Arabic on November 8, 2016 and in English December 8, 2016)[6]—though, because of space, we do not engage with the historical specifics of these stories. As generalities, the videos constitute an indicative typology of performativities of horrorism (grotesque, abject and sublime) that together exemplify ISIS' contribution to shaping an alternative moral imagination in the spaces of global publicity. Let us examine each in turn.

Grotesque horrorism

The burning of the Turkish pilots video, titled "The Shield of the Cross," refers to the "secular apostate state of Turkey" and consists of two parts: a long introductory sequence and the execution sequence itself. The first part narrates Turkey's involvement in the Syrian warfare. It is cast in the aesthetics of news documentary, in that it uses intertextual fragments of journalistic reports (news clips and photojournalism) so as to present "objective" evidence of the truth and make claims to authenticity. Turkey's President Erdogan appears together with anti-ISIS world leaders (Obama, Putin, Assad, and the Pope) in a briskly edited series of news images, which is followed by footage of Turkish airstrikes in Al-Bab zooming on civilian casualties. This collage acquires narrative coherence through voiceover, which blames Turkey as an "apostate"—a religious brother who turned against the faith.

This part is followed by the execution sequence that comes late into the video, consisting of edited frames of two chained soldiers on a leash, briefly address the camera before they are set on fire through petrol-soaked material wrapped around their chains. These about to die frames are juxtaposed by images of civilian death, while the voiceover is now replaced by a speaking militant, who disgraces the victims—"the blood of one them is as base and inferior as that of a dog." Written language is also used to control visual meaning; when the juxtaposition of about to die images with frames of civilian death is subtitled "The Crimes of the Turkish Army Against the Oppressed" or when a fullscreen frame of a Quran quote interrupts this visual juxtaposition: "And if you punish, then punish them with the like of that with which you were afflicted (An-Nahl, 116)." The presence of Islamic verses complicates the documentary aesthetic by mixing it with religious preaching and the prisoners' exhortation to their army to "leave the territories of the Islamic state."

The execution frames themselves contain unprecedentedly graphic scenes of corporeal annihilation. The camera records the process in full detail, from the moment the fire starts making its way up the soldiers' bodies to the moment they collapse unconscious, zooming into their foaming mouths and disfigured bodies. This visuality points to a grotesque aesthetic, a style that captures the excess of the human body in its distorted states— dismembered, burned or erupted, thereby highlighting the porous and often transgressive relationship of the body with nature (Russo, 1995). It is this intolerable visual intimacy of the grotesque, staged as an "intentional offence to the ontological dignity of the victim" (Cavarero, 2009, p. 9) that renders this spectacle horroristic par excellence. How is the story of this grotesque horrorism told? Which resources are brought together to recontextualize these deaths into ISIS' normative narratives?

If multi-modality is, as we saw, about the aesthetic rendering of the annihilation of the prisoners' bodies, recontextualization refers to their symbolic annihilation. In the context of Islamic moral norms, which forbid Muslims to harm innocent humanity, this symbolic annihilation takes places through the deployment of the animalization trope—itself an element of the grotesque. The Turkish pilots are presented as "dogs", through linguistic attribution (reference to "dogs") and through visual association (dragged on a leash), while their burned, disfigured bodies have lost all attributes of humanity. By reducing human to canine life and then to matter, this trope evokes archaic Arab symbolisms of impurity and miasma (El Fadl, 2004) and, in so doing, recontextualizes the prisoners' bodies from the realm of innocent humanity to that of the profane. While symbolic annihilation renders their killing ethically possible, however, the moral validation of the killing emerges from a further recontextualizing move that embeds animalization into a narrative structure of justification.

It is specifically the cut from civilian casualties to the burning scene that situates the prisoners' death into a visual arrangement of sectarian argumentative causality: "your" war against "us" leads to "your" death as just punishment, as retaliation. Recontextualization occurs here though the intertextual mix of documentary news and religious preaching, which locates the pilots' burning bodies within a justificatory system of both military retaliation and religious punishment. While the former produces evidence of the soldiers as enemies of the "state" ("The crimes of the Turkish state..."), the latter proclaims their religious fall from grace—"The shields of the cross." It is this hybrid logic of treason, both secular and religious, that legitimizes their physical annihilation as a consequence of disloyalty.[7]

In summary, the grotesque pushes the dying and dead body beyond the boundaries of the human, by way of amalgamating two aesthetic styles: the documentary, a journalistic genre that speaks the Western epistemology of objective truth, and religious preaching, which introduces a transcendental epistemology of truth as religious faith. As ethico-political practice, these styles work to recontextualize the annihilated body through tropes of rational justification and animalization. While the latter situates human bodies into the realm of the non-human and thus removes moral obstacles to physical annihilation, the former explains this act of annihilation through a retributive rationality that combines proportionate retaliation with spiritual vengeance ("if you punish, then punish them with the like of that with which you were afflicted"). In so doing, grotesque horrorism relies on a mix of Western and non-Western styles and secular/religious truth claims in order to perform the communicative act of denunciation against the "coalition's" deaths and to establish itself as a force of self-righteous justice in global spaces of publicity.

Abject horrorism

This spectacle of horror records the point blank shooting of five hostages accused of working for the British intelligence service. Similarly to the previous one, this video consists of two parts too: the introduction, which contextualizes the story, and the execution itself. Unlike the previous one, however, the multi-modality of this one establishes the truth of the dying and dead body by drawing on Western entertainment rather than news documentary genres. Echoing the television genre of *CSI*-type police dramas, the video's first sequence includes animation visuals of a gun targeted at the viewer, a screaming face in black background, the presentation of the actors/hostages featuring in this episode and a closing trailer of the next "episode" (scenes of the next execution video). This *CSI* style comes to claim the authenticity of death not on the basis of objective facticity, as the previous one, but of the aesthetic realism of its own representations—promising not the truth of events but the truth of mediation itself.

The second part consists of three sequences: talking head frames of the orange uniform-clad hostages reading out a scripted confession in Arabic before they kneel down in front of their respective executioners; then the frontal frame of a hooded executioner threatening in English the then British Prime Minister, David Cameron; and finally the line up of the now hooded hostages, each shot point blank behind the head, by their respective executioner. Two features stand out in this part. Firstly, multi-modality is organized around contrasting distributions of the visual-verbal components. The use of Arabic in the hostage's confession steers attention away from content and onto his face as a communicative medium, while, subsequently, the lack of visual contact with the hooded executioner invites us to focus on what is said—a glorification of ISIS (the "state of Allah") and a humiliation of the Western coalition ("imbecile" for the U.K. PM metonymically standing for Western arrogance and deception). A tenuous semantic field emerges from this juxtaposition whereby, on the one hand, the face close-ups invite us to scrutinize the face of indescribable agony of the about to die (the tense muscles and the agonizing gaze of fear) and, on the other, the focus on the executioner's language invites intense engagement with his speech acts (humiliation and threat).

Secondly, the final sequence of the execution is staged as a filmic choreography of carnage, as the camera, rather than flinching from, indulges in the five point blank shootings, following their successive occurrence in rhythmical repetition. Known as the "*CSI* shot*,*" this stylistic mannerism is about amplification; it enacts, what Allen calls, "the dynamic and visceral zooming into and through human bodies as they are punctured by knives and bullets" (2007, p. 6). The multi-modal properties of this video can therefore be said to represent the human body in its "abject" moment—the in-between moment suspended between life and death, when anguish is written on the body and the flesh is split apart by a bullet; "the abject," as Kristeva puts it, is "what disturbs identity, system, order. What does not respect borders, positions, rules" (1982, p. 4). Ultimately, like the grotesque, this is an aesthetic of excess that challenges Western norms of public visibility around death and, in so doing, further undermines the sacredness of human corporeality. How does the abject aesthetic participate in the recontextualization of the dead body in this video? What story is being told and which moral claims are inscribed in it?

The hybridity of the video recontextualizes death in two moves. In a first move, the *CSI* style works intertextually to re-position the body into a global register of media consumption, where it is the hyper-real effects of the camera that tell the truth of the victims' final moments. This is a kind of truth that in its magnification of the moment of death, deliberately highlights the all-too human fragility of dying. As opposed to the expressionless faces of the Turkish prisoners, which alluded to the sub-humanity of the "infidel," this proximity captures vulnerable humanity in its most liminal state—dread at the awareness of impending violent death.

In a second move, the executioner's language introduces into the video a structure of evaluation that recontextualizes death by reversing the hierarchies of grievability at play in the liberal West. This reversal is organized around a juxtaposition of emotions, between love of life for British people, and love of death for the fighters of the "state of Allah," but also around a respective contrast of moralities between Western hypocrisy —claiming love for life but letting its people die ("do you really think your government will care about you when you come into our hands?" …)—and Islamic protectionism ("where the people live under the justice and security of the Sharia"). While the first juxtaposition draws on religious (Sharia's view of death as martyrdom) and secular (masculinist conceptions of heroic soldiering) narratives so as to expose Western subjectivities as weak and incompetent ("fools who thought they could fight the Islamic State"), the second combines Sharia's tribal protectionism (Khouri, 2015) with a secular critique of Western geo-politics as hypocritical, so as to expose the West as evil and dishonest. Moving beyond the denunciation of the previous video, then, this one is a performance of disgrace and ultimately humiliation of ISIS' main enemy.

In summary, horrorism operates here through an abject aesthetic, where the liminal body of impending death becomes the site upon which a particular evaluation of Western subjectivity takes place. As aesthetic practice, the abject is recontextualized through the mixing of Western television drama conventions with religious preaching so as to portray this death in terms of "ecstatic" terror—magnifying the materiality of the act. As ethico-political practice, the abject operates as a structure of evaluation, which inserts this liminal moment in a hierarchy of thanatopolitical values: glorifying the love of death over the preservation of life. Organized around multi-modal juxtapositions, this hierarchy turns the abject into moral judgment by degrading both Western subjectivities as cowardly and weak and Western politics as hypocritical and callous.

Sublime horrorism

The "Impenetrable Fortress" video, in contrast to the previous two, focuses on celebrating the Islamic State amid the battle of Mosul, 2016–17 (for the significance of the city to ISIS see Gerges, 2016). The two-part collage structure of this video consists of battlefield footage and of talking head statements by ISIS militants. In contrast to the localized intensity of the previous video, the multi-modality of this first part capitalizes on the panoramic effect of the "neutral-reporter/observer" genre. Using visual editing, it tracks across space to show multiple battlefield deaths (suicide bombing, beheading, shooting, etc., of ISIS and its enemies, including Peshmerga Kurdish and Russian forces). It also tracks across time to tell the story of the birth of the Islamic State. News frames of the 2003 Iraqi Freedom operation ("largest Crusader campaign in the modern era," in the voiceover), cut to spectacular scenes from the 2014 "re-capturing" of the city by the Islamic State (a "great mission in the name of Allah"), and conclude with images of an anti-ISIS alliance of international leaders (the "collusion against the Islamic State"). The second part of the video is a series of "testimonials" by ISIS spokespersons and militants, who call its audiences to arms against the "infidels".

This collage hangs together through voiceover, which offers a historical narrative of ISIS; panoramic visuality resonates here with an epic narrative style, which frames the dead body in two ways. As documentary evidence, Muslim mass death relies on the "objective" truth of neutral observation to legitimize its call to jihad against the perpetrators—the "unholy alliance" of Crusaders. The documentary further establishes a contrast between two imaginations of death: ISIS' imagination is portrayed in the figure of a groomed "rested-in-peace" body kissed farewell by a child, while the enemy's one is presented in open-eyed, disfigured and infested faces, scattered in the battlefield. The grotesque, as we encountered it earlier, is again present albeit now thrown against the sublime: a style that beautifies ISIS' death (peaceful face, child's kiss) so as to both expose viewing publics to it and protect them from the scene of violence, thereby introducing an ambivalent element of horrific pleasure into the spectacle (Hills, 2005).

The sublime is further amplified in the second part of the video, as militant talking heads reiterate religious praise for the martyrs of the holy war; speaking to "his brothers in Mosul", an ISIS militant quotes the Quran: "[. .] little is the enjoyment of this world as compared to the hereafter" while another one exclaims: seeing His [Allah's] face is the most complete of pleasures for mankind. It is Jannah that is sweet, as well as, its bliss." How is the story of sublime horrorism told? Which resources are brought together to recontextualize these deaths in specific moral claims?

The imagery of mass death is doubly recontextualized so as to establish a hierarchy of grievability at the service of heroic subjectivity: while desecrating the hostile body, the video sanctifies the ISIS warrior. The sublime is the catalyst for the first recontextualization. It works through the contrast between exalted "us" and grotesque "them", which re-situates death within an implicit moral order: ISIS deaths deserve solemn grief as heroic but the Crusaders' deaths remain "unrepresentable" and undeserving of mourning. The second recontextualization is established through a structure of narrativization: these sublime visualities of death, framed by a voiceover of martyrdom, are themselves embedded in the mythical story telling of the Islamic State (e.g. in the reference to the death of the Prophet's grandson, Imam Husayn). Even though narrativization, an argumentative strategy that "recount[s] the past and treat[s] the present as part of a timeless and cherished tradition" (Thompson, 1990, p. 61), is a key component of all nationalist rhetoric, it is here used to put an apocalyptic religious discourse at the service of ISIS' "revolutionary statehood" (Walt, 2015). In this way, the brief trajectory of the Islamic State not only turns into Islam's end-of-history grand moment but also the imagery of the sublimated body of the ISIS warrior comes to stand as the norm of Islamic masculinity.

In summary, sublime horrorism turns the dead body into the site upon which ISIS' jihadist subjectivity is formed. As aesthetic practice, the hybridity of the video mixes, as before, the secular epistemology of objective truth with an epic religious eschatology, in ways that subordinate the grotesque to the sublime—to the pleasure-giving spectacle of heroic death. As ethico-political practice, then, the video operates through a structure of narrativization, which, on the one hand, situates death into a hierarchy of grievability that celebrates martyrdom, while, on the other, appropriates and inscribes this death into a sectarian narrative of Islamic eschatology that it claims for itself. In so doing, sublime horrorism intervenes in the global public sphere through a communicative act of glorification that renders death the master-signifier of Islamic masculinity.

The spectacular thanatopolitics of horrorism

In our opening quote, Baudrillard highlights the catalytic role that violent death plays in "the spirit of terrorism." Even though Baudrillard does not use the term "thanatopolitics," his focus away from actual death ("a death far more than real") and on the re-significations of such death in the media powerfully informs our argument on ISIS thanatopolitics. Against dominant understandings of the term as a subtle form of modern power that uses death to achieve political ends without speaking about it—"in the last two centuries we no longer properly speak about death" (Murray, 2006, p. 192), our own analysis sought to explore the new, visual grammar of ISIS counter-thanatopolitics—the grammar of the horroristic spectacle. Spectacular thanatopolitics, we argue with Baudrillard, is today more efficacious because it moves from the battlefield to the symbolic sphere, where, in his words, "the rule is that of challenge, reversion and outbidding'" (2003 p. 17). By inserting violent death in the sphere of aesthetic representation and digital narrativity, our aim has been to trace how ISIS performs this very symbolic struggle of "challenge, reversion and outbidding", through spectacles of corporeal destruction.

To this end, we drew on a definition of spectacles of violent death as regimes of horrorism, as meaning-making practices that recontextualize the dead or dying body within tactically selected ideas of the beautiful and the ugly (the aesthetic) or the fair and the evil (the moral) with a view to producing normative accounts of worthy and unworthy subjectivities (hierarchies of grievability). In so doing, we were able to produce a suggestive typology of horrorism, where "grotesque," "abject" and "sublime" deaths tell their own distinct, yet interrelated, stories about what ISIS stands for and how it addresses the world.

While all three aesthetic styles recontextualize death within Western and "non-Western" epistemologies of truth (journalistic objectivity or entertainment drama with religious faith), each regime relies on its own hybrid "truth" to propose distinct forms of desirable subjectivity. Grotesque horrorism fully dehumanizes the burning "infidels" and attaches their bodies to a sectarian logic of justification that treats their death as an act of retribution: secular and religious claims to revenge against the "apostates." Abject horrorism, in a paradoxical gesture of hyper-humanization (through various magnification effects), inserts the about to die body in a logic of evaluation that speaks of their execution as an act of disgrace: secular (nationalist) and religious (transcendental) claims that deprive ISIS' Western enemies of virtue and humiliate them as weak and dishonest. Finally, sublime horrorism relies on a moral contrast between dehumanization (grotesque "enemy") and hyper-humanization (sublime jihadist), so as to attach death in battle to a logic of redemption: a nationalist glorification of pious martyrdom as the new norm of heroic existence.

It is these hierarchies of grievability, articulated through distinct communicative acts, which make up the spectacular thanatopolitics of ISIS. Retribution, disgrace and redemption are not only particularities, local manifestations of aesthetic practice, but also, in line with our phronetic epistemology, generalities: structures of address that call up "competitive systems of meanings" (Ingram, 2015), wherein the savaged body, in its many variations, antagonizes the West's clean spectacles of the battlefield and challenges its humanitarian ethics of war—its "empathic civilization" (Rifkin, 2009). These thanatopolitical structures of address work, in line with relevant literature, both to promote the ISIS brand for purposes of global legitimacy and recruitment (glorifying ISIS through its Islamic legacy and sanctifying sacrificial soldiering) *and* participate in ISIS' sectarian and anti-Western struggle for ideological hegemony within and beyond the Arab world (threatening "infidels" or disgracing the West as evil and cowardly). Taking our lead on these insights, let us, in conclusion, reflect on two key features of these videos: narrative hybridity and the presence of the savaged body.

Hybridity and moral narratives

The first insight engages with the political communication literature. *Pace* accounts of ISIS as solely a neo-fundamentalist religious platform that renews Huntingtonian "clash of civilizations" scenarios, our videos cannot be reduced to Islamic fundamentalism. Instead, these digital spectacles of death bring together Western media genres with the Quran, religious fundamentalist with secular epistemologies (truth of facts and truth of faith) as well as sectarian logics of tribalism with aggressive nationalism (blood bonds of a specific Islamic tradition and territorial claims to statehood). While these are combined in various orders of horroristic meaning, the point here is that ISIS' structure of address is not reducible to its parts as religion is always-already found within state-driven narratives. It is, in Mamdani's words, both about "salvation and liberation" (2009, p. 148).

Our analytical focus on recontextualization was instrumental in identifying these hybrid constellations of meaning as aesthetic practices of death that serve a specific ethico-political project, in digital media networks. Recontextualization is, in this sense, not only a linguistic but, fundamentally, a moral process of attuning and re-configuring heterogeneous narratives into powerful myths of revenge and redemption. In line with scholarship that insists on seeing ISIS as a intricate historical and geopolitical reality with a complex trajectory of emergence (Gerges, 2016), it is important that critical research on ISIS continues to develop, on the one hand, conceptual tools sensitive to the hybridity of narratives but also, on the other, comprehensive designs that capture the technological connectivities of digital platforms and their various transnational appropriations. If the horroristic spectacle enjoys a broad appeal that, as Kaplan and Costa claim, "even ... the U.S. government openly admires and unsuccessfully seeks to emulate" (2015, p. 936), then visceral reactions to its brutal aesthetics of bodily excess should not be our only response. What techno-symbolic operations horrorism performs and how we can theorize and analyze these as aesthetic and ethical digital practices are not peripheral but central questions to comprehending ISIS as a platform of political communication.

Critique and the savaged body

The second and related insight engages with ISIS as propaganda and recruitment—the strategic communication literature. All three communicative practices of retribution, disgrace and redemption are part of a vocabulary of aggressive propaganda, nationalist (revenge and humiliation of the enemy) as well as sectarian/religious (martyrdom as promise of heaven). Simultaneously, however, these practices should be seen as performing the function of critique.[8] By showing both civilian deaths by, and soldier deaths of, the anti-ISIS coalition, the spectacular thanatopolitics of ISIS, let us recall, challenges the boundaries of visibility beyond Western economies of "taste and decency" and brings into focus the savagery of war deaths that is otherwise invisible to Western viewers. While this new visibility operates, in line with Joseph Conrad's "Heart of Darkness", as a mirror that reflects back on "us" the military implication of Western interests in the violent histories of Arab statehood (Cavarero, 2009), its critical mirroring nonetheless entails no life-affirming, positive promise. Instead of the humanist sensibility that informs radical critiques of the Western ways of war as industrial mass killing or as a biopolitical project that kills through saving lives (Pötzsch, 2015), the horroristic critique is profoundly anti-humanist. It savagely challenges the very core of common humanity, the integrity of the body, turning its brutal annihilation into theater and relishing the ferocious spectacle.

The aesthetics of the grotesque, the abject and the sublime enact, in this sense, three distinct practices of anti-humanist critique that, by focusing on corporeal destruction, mirror, problematize and ultimately replace the universal sanctity of bodily integrity with a sanctification of brutal killing and death—a counter thanatopolitics of the spectacle. In this light, our horroristic approach does not simply introduce and incorporate the visual dimension of violent death into current conceptions of thanatopolitics. It also, importantly, highlights ISIS' use of the gruesome fragility of the human flesh as a new privileged site of global propaganda. If, as Khouri puts it, one of the key features of ISIS recruits is political disenchantment in the West and the Arab worlds, particularly among the young, then its videos' proposals of heroic self-sacrifice for a noble cause engages with precisely this disenchanted youth in their "search for order, meaning, and fulfilment" (2015, p. 14). In this sense, Farwell's claim that ISIS has today effectively branded itself as "the true apostle of a sovereign faith [and] a champion of its own perverse notions of social justice" (2014, pp. 49–50) is indeed fully reflected in our analysis. But we need to go further than this. We must persist in asking the crucial questions of *how* it achieves its ideological goals, what kinds of communicative practices it performs and how its normative imaginations and identities are put together in its own brutal narratives of faith and justice. How, ultimately, it manages to globalize its spectacular thanatopolitics as a dystopian manifesto that reverses Western norms of 'humanitarian' militarism and invisible death so as to celebrate the inevitable horrorism of all warfare.

Notes

1. Cameron D. (2014, September 1) "PM statement on European Council and tackling extremism". Retrieved from https://www.gov.uk/government/speeches/pm-statement-on-european-council-and-tackling-extremism; Obama B. (2014, September 24) "Remarks to the United Nations General Assembly in New York City", Public Papers. Retrieved from https://obamawhitehouse.archives.gov/the-press-office/2014/09/24/remarks-president-obama-address-united-nations-general-assembly. See also The Editorial Board, *New York Times* (2014, October 2). Retrieved from https://www.nytimes.com/2014/10/03/opinion/the-fundamental-horror-of-isis.html; Boyle, M. (2014, August 23) 'The problem with "evil"'. Retrieved from https://www.nytimes.com/2014/08/23/opinion/the-moral-hazard-of-calling-isis-a-cancer.html
2. https://www.nytimes.com/2014/09/08/business/media/with-videos-of-killings-isis-hones-social-media-as-a-weapon.html?mcubz=0&_r=0
3. "ISIS and the spectacle of terrorism. Resisting mainstream workstations of fear" (2014, October 7). Retrieved from https://philosophersforchange.org/2014/10/07/isis-and-the-spectacle-of-terrorism-resisting-mainstream-workstations-of-fear/ (accessed June 15th, 2017)
4. The video is available on different websites; indicatively see here: http://heavy.com/news/2017/01/isis-islamic-state-amaq-news-the-cross-of-the-shield-turkey-turkish-soldiers-burned-to-death-execution-wilayat-halab-aleppo-syria-english-translation-subtitles-video/
5. This video is available online at: http://heavy.com/news/2016/01/new-isis-islamic-state-news-pictures-videos-united-kingdom-english-england-invade-imbecile-execute-spies-full-uncensored-youtube/
6. This video is available online at: http://heavy.com/news/2016/12/new-isis-islamic-state-amaq-news-agency-wilayat-al-khayr-deir-ez-zor-syria-syrian-arab-army-saa-pkk-peshmerga-ypg-russia-forces-war-executions-footage-full-uncensored-mp4-video-english-subtitles/
7. For the fluid boundaries of the categories religious/secular and Western/non-Western used throughout the analysis, see also Asad, Brown, Butler, and Mahmood (2009).
8. Critique is here understood, in Wendy Brown's terms, as "polemical rejection" (2009, p. 9).

ORCID

Angelos Kissas ⓘ http://orcid.org/0000-0002-0289-0495

References

Allen, M. (Ed.). (2007). *Reading "CSI": Television under the microscope*. London: Palgrave.
Al-Rawi, A. (2016). Video games, terrorism, and ISIS's jihad 3.0. *Terrorism and Political Violence*, 1–21. doi:10.1080/09546553.2016.1207633
Asad, T., Brown, W., Butler, J., & Mahmood, S. (Eds.). (2009). Is critique secular? Blasphemy, injury and free speech. *The Townsent Papers in the Humanities*. Rerieved from http://escholarship.org/uc/item/84q9c6ft
Ayalon, A., Popovich, E., & Yarchi, M. (2016). From warfare to imagefare: How states should manage asymmetric conflicts with extensive media coverage. *Terrorism and Political Violence*, *28*(2), 254–273. doi:10.1080/09546553.2014.897622
Baudrillard, J. (2003). *The spirit of terrorism and other essays*. London: Verso.
Boal, I., Clark, T. J., Matthews, J., & Watts, M. (2005). *Afflicted powers: Capital and spectacle in a new age of war*. London: Vesro.
Brown, W. (2009). Blasphemy, injury, and free speech. In T. Asad et al. (Eds), *Is critique secular. The townsent papers in the humanities* (pp. 177–217). London, CA: University of California Press. Retrieved from http://escholarship.org/uc/item/84q9c6ft
Campbell, D. (2004). Horrific blindness: Images of death in contemporary media. *Journal for Cultural Research*, *8*(1), 55–74. doi:10.1080/14797580420001969971
Cavarero, A. (2009). *Horrorism: Naming contemporary violence*. New York: Columbia University Press.
Chouliaraki, L. (2006). *The spectatorship of suffering*. London: Sage.
Chouliaraki, L. (2015). Digital witnessing in conflict zones: The politics of remediation. *Information Communication and Society*, *18*(11), 1362–1377. doi:10.1080/1369118X.2015.1070890
Chouliaraki, L., & Fairclough, N. (1999). *Discourse in late modernity. Rethinking critical discourse analysis*. Edinburgh, Scotland: Edinburgh University Press.
Cohen-Almagor, R. (2005). Media coverage of acts of terrorism: Troubling episodes and suggested guidelines. *Canadian Journal of Communication*, *30*(3), 383–409. Retrieved from http://www.cjc-online.ca/index.php/journal/article/view/1579/1734
El Fadl, K. (2004). *Dogs in the Islamic Tradition and Nature*. New York: Continuum International. Retrieved from http://www.scholarofthehouse.org/dinistrandna.html
Farwell, J. P. (2014). The media strategy of ISIS. *Survival. Global Politics and Strategy*, *56*(6), 49–55. doi:10.1080/00396338.2014.985436
Flyvbjerg, B. (2006). Five misunderstandings about case-study research. *Qualitative Inquiry*, *12*(2), 219–245. doi:10.1177/1077800405284363
Gerges, F. (2016). *A history. ISIS*. Princeton, NJ: Princeton University Press.
Giroux, H. (2014). ISIS and the spectacle of terrorism: resisting mainstream workstations of fear. *Truthout*. Retrieved from: http://www.truth-out.org/news/item/26519-isis-and-the-spectacle-of-terrorism-resisting-mainstream-workstations-of-fear.

Hills, M. (2005). *The pleasures of horror*. London: Continuum.

Ingram, H. (2015). The strategic logic of Islamic State information operations. *Australian Journal of International Affairs, 69*(6), 729–752. doi:10.1080/10357718.2015.1059799

Jewitt, C. (Ed.). (2009). *The Routledge handbook of multimodal research*. London: Routledge.

Kaplan, J., & Costa, C. (2015). The Islamic state and the new tribalism. *Terrorism and Political Violence, 27*(5), 926–969. doi:10.1080/09546553.2015.1094306

Kellner, D. (2004). 9/11, spectacles of terror and media manipulation. *Critical Discourse Studies, 1* (1), 41–64. doi:10.1080/17405900410001674515

Khouri, R. (2015). ISIS is about the past not the future Michael Van Dusen Lecture series. *Wilson Center Publication*. Retrieved from https://www.wilsoncenter.org/sites/default/files/isis_is_ about_the_arab_past_not_the_future.pdf

Kissas, A. (2017). Ideology in the age of mediatized politics: From "belief systems" to the re-contextualizing principle of discourse. *Journal of Political Ideologies, 22*(2), 197–215. doi:10.1080/ 13569317.2017.1306958

Kristeva, J. (1982). *Powers of horror. An essay on abjection*. New York, NY: Columbia University Press.

Mamdani, M. (2009). *Saviors and survivors; darfur, politics and the war or terror*. London: Verso.

Murray, S. (2006). Thanatopolitics: On the use of death for mobilizing political life. *Polygraph: An International Journal of Politics and Culture, 18*(2006), 191–215. Retrieved from http://www. duke.edu/web/polygraph/index.html

Nacos, B. (2016). *Mass-mediated terrorism: Mainstream and digita media in terrorism and counter-terrorissm*. Lanham, MD: Rowman & Littlefield.

Patruss, K. (2016). "The face of evil". The discourse on ISIS and the visual complexities in the ISIS beheading videos. *Politik, 19*(4), 67–87.

Pattwell, A., Mitman, Z., & Porpora, D. (2015). Terrorism as failed political communication. *International Journal of Communication, 9*(2015), 1120–1139. Retrieved from: from http:// ijoc.org/index.php/ijoc/article/view/2247/1359

Pelletier, I. R., Lundmark, L., Gardner, R., Scott Ligon, G., & Kilinc, R. (2016). Why ISIS's message resonates: Leveraging islam, sociopolitical catalysts, and adaptive messaging. *Studies in Conflict and Terrorism, 39*(10), 871–899. doi:10.1080/1057610X.2016.1139373

Perlmutter, D. D. (2005). Photojournalism and foreign affairs. *Wilson Web*. Retrieved from: http:// www.davidperlmutter-research.com/wp-content/uploads/2013/09/2005.-Perlmutter.- PHOTOJOURNALISM-AND-FOREIGN-AFFAIRS-Orbis.-49-1-2005.pdf

Pötzsch, H. (2015). The emergence of iWar: Changing practices and perceptions of military engagement in a digital era. *New Media and Society, 17*(1), 78–95. doi:10.1177/1461444813516834

Rifkin, J. (2009). *The empathic civilization: The race to global consciousness in a world in crisis*. London: Penguin.

Roy, O. (2004). *Globalized Islam. The search for a new ummah*. New York: Columbia University Press.

Russo, M. (1995). *The female grotesque. Risk, excess and modernity*. London: Routledge.

Thompson, J. B. (1990). *Ideology and modern culture. Social theory in the era of mass communication*. Cambridge, UK: Polity.

Walt, S. M. (2015). ISIS as revolutionary state: New twist on an old story. *Foreign Affairs*. Retrieved from https://www.foreignaffairs.com/articles/middle-east/isis-revolutionary-state

Weber, C. (2014). Encountering violence: Terrorism and horrorism in war and citizenship. *International Political Sociology, 8*(3), 237–255. doi:10.1111/ips.12056

Wilkinson, I. (1997). The media and terrorism: A reassessment. *Terrorism and Political Violence, 9* (2), 51–64. doi:10.1080/09546559708427402

Winkler, C. K., El Damanhoury, K., Dicker, A., & Lemieux, A. F. (2016). The medium is terrorism: Transformation of the about to die trope in Dabiq. *Terrorism and Political Violence*, 1–20. doi:10. 1080/09546553.2016.1211526

Zelizer, B. (2010). *About to die: How news images move the public*. Oxford, UK: Oxford University Press.

One apostate run over, hundreds repented: excess, unthinkability, and infographics from the war with I.S.I.S.

Rebecca A. Adelman

ABSTRACT
Compared to the more spectacular elements of its media repertoire—the slick recruitment campaigns on social media, the artfully composed battlefield footage, the grisly executions—I.S.I.S.'s infographics may seem dull, even trivial. Indeed, these data visualizations have gone largely unremarked, eliciting more bemusement than serious consideration. Against the tendency to discount these images, however, I argue that when I.S.I.S. turns toward charts and diagrams to represent its operations, it launches a stealthy but substantial epistemological challenge to media outlets that depict it as backward and irrational and rely on command of information as an index of Western power. Comparing infographics produced about I.S.I.S. and those produced by the group, I demonstrate that, despite their obvious differences, both types of infographics evince common preoccupations. Like Western news sources, I.S.I.S. creates infographics to map attacks, plot territorial gains, tally and categorize casualties, and track the types of weapons deployed. News media and I.S.I.S. infographics diverge primarily in their affective resonance, as similar information signifies in radically different ways. Ultimately, by producing and circulating these infographics, I.S.I.S. renders simultaneously renders itself more and less intelligible to outsiders: encapsulating its story while confounding prevailing representations as it weaponizes information.

What would 330 suicide car bombings look like? Even if we have seen countless news reports about individual attacks, the imaginative work required to multiply those grisly scenes out by the hundreds is almost unbearable. Three hundred thirty car bombs might look like an endless reel of horrific scenes: blood, charred vehicles, victims, survivors. Or they might look like a clip-art pickup truck with a cartoony blast shooting out of its bed, a cloud of debris behind it and the number "330" floating above in a textbox, all contained in just a few square inches. It is the latter form of representation that concerns me here, as this little picture appeared in an infographic that I.S.I.S. (Islamic State of Iraq and Syria) produced within its 2014 annual report, along with similar tallies of improvised explosive devices (I.E.D.s) (3412), assassinations (633), and remote bike bombs (22) (Matthews, 2014) (Figure 1).

Figure 1. An infographic from I.S.I.S.'s annual report, published in March 2014.

Graphics like this, largely sanitized of gore, contrast sharply with predominant depictions of I.S.I.S., which has, by many measures, achieved far more than al-Qaeda and spiked American fears of terrorism to levels similar to the period after September 11 (Byman, 2016, p. 128). Compared with the more spectacular elements of its media repertoire—the slick recruitment campaigns on social media, the artfully composed battlefield footage, the grisly executions—I.S.I.S.'s infographics may seem dull, even trivial. With the attention of news media and audiences alike trained on the group's suicide bombings, beheadings, abductions, internet hacks, and destroyed antiquities, these data visualizations have gone largely unremarked, eliciting more bemusement than serious consideration. Against the tendency to discount these images, however, I argue that when I.S.I.S. turns to charts and diagrams to represent its operations it launches a stealthy but substantial epistemological challenge to Western media outlets that depict it as backward and irrational and rely on command of information as an index of power.

Essentially, infographics are tools for managing excess and unthinkability. They make voluminous data about complex social, cultural, and political phenomena accessible by condensing and organizing it into a comprehensible, digestible visual narrative. Consequently, Western news sources rely heavily on infographics to describe and explain I.S.I.S. and the multiplying conflicts in which it is involved. These graphics vary in their levels of detail and interactivity, but work to locate I.S.I.S. geopolitically, cartographically, and ideologically, giving a coherent visual shape to the otherwise frighteningly amorphous entity of the "terror network." In this way, they attempt to exercise a degree of epistemological control over the threat. Against the pervasive and terrifying idea that I.S.I.S. is uncontainable, such infographics position it logically in space and time, reassuringly emplotting the mysterious enemy through, and as, data points. When I.S.I.S. itself turns to infographics, the group coopts this epistemological strategy, reinvigorating the threat that infographics might otherwise have helped to defuse. Carlos Galli (2009) has theorized that enemies are frightening not because they are foreign but because they are uncannily familiar, and so I.S.I.S. may be even more unnerving when it parrots recognizable forms of communication than when it broadcasts dramatic scenes of violence or destruction.[1]

Here, I consider two sorts of infographics: those produced about I.S.I.S. by Western news media and those produced by I.S.I.S. for strategic and promotional ends. My goal is not so much the analysis of specific infographics; rather, I develop a catalog of each party's infographic visual practice. Elsewhere, I have argued that close reading as a methodology is of radically limited utility for analyzing visual representations of terrorism, because terrorism traffics in the unrepresentable (Adelman, 2014). What, after all, would 3,412 I.E.D.s look like? Instead, I proposed an alternative approach, the analysis of visual practices: querying who is using the visual, how, for what purposes, and with what consequences. Informed by visual culture studies and political theory, I orient my analysis of selected infographics similarly. Specifically, I chart the epistemological assurances and instabilities they generate within this sprawling conflict.

Answers and reassurances: a brief history of infographic visual practice

Infographics are ways of imagining the world around us; they are predicated on the conceit that its constituent mechanisms can be identified, classified, and known. Infographics can take a variety of forms, which Robin Featherstone describes as "rebranded knowledge assemblages for an information age" (2014, p. 147). Generally, information visualization is "the use of interactive visual representations of data to amplify cognition" so that it can be "mapped to screen space." This data can be either qualitative or quantitative, though "data visualization" typically refers to the schematic representation of quantitative data (Lengler & Eppler, n.d.). Infographics enable their creators to "presen[t] deep data in a concise, highly visual format" and then offer their viewers efficient modes for obtaining and presumably processing that information (Štrok, 2015). Data drive this visual economy. Orit Halpern (2014) writes that, since the Enlightenment, data have become "the site of value to emerge from the seeming informational abundance once assumed to be the province of nature." Over time, "data visualization became a democratic virtue and a moral good" (pp. 15–16), while the meaning of "visualization" shifted to encompass "bringing that which is not already present into sight" (p. 21). Although the design literature about infographics generally treats them as presentations of extant information, infographics often work to construct the very reality they appear only to portray (Drucker, 2014, p. 2). All images, in Pasi Väliaho's (2014, p. 11) terms, "establish shared ways of sensing, feeling, and making sense;" infographics aspire primarily to the third objective. Johanna Drucker argues that "most information visualizations are acts of interpretation masquerading as presentation" (2014, p. 8). The practices of both creating and consuming infographics are shot through with this tension.

Loosely defined, the history of infographics might begin in 30,000 B.C.E., with the first cave paintings depicting animals (Visually, n.d.). A stricter interpretation might place their origins 27,000 years later, in ancient Egyptian hieroglyphics (Visually, n.d.; Friendly, 2006). The first maps, and hence the first data visualizations, appeared roughly 8,000 years ago (Thompson, 2016, p. 24). Whether designed to aid in earthly navigation or chart the positions of celestial bodies, such documents are direct, if remote, predecessors of the infographics we have today. Prior to the nineteenth century, "data visualization was rare because," as Clive Thompson (2016, p. 24) notes, "data was rare." Even in conditions of relative scarcity, however, infographic visual practices were beginning to take shape. By the early Enlightenment, as Drucker (2014, p. 68) notes, "visuality and knowledge provided mutual guarantees," cementing a positivist approach to the world. The first atlas was produced in 1570 in Europe, and the seventeenth century preoccupation with measurement yielded analytic geometry and coordinate systems (Friendly, 2006). The first efforts at the "thematic mapping of geologic, economic, and medical data" were underway by the end of the eighteenth century (Friendly, 2006, p. 7). Around the turn of the nineteenth century, William Playfair, a Scottish engineer and political economist, invented the rudiments of most contemporary graphical forms, like the line graph, bar chart, and circle chart (Friendly, 2006, p. 9).

Infographics promise to manage complexity and excess by synthesizing unwieldy masses of data about perplexing phenomena. Epidemiologists were some of the earliest infographers, and their approaches were quickly adapted to other vexing social and cultural problems like illiteracy and crime across Europe (Friendly, 2006, pp. 10–12). By augmenting human capacities to acquire, store, and manage information, infographics prevent cognitive overload. While they long preceded the advent of digital technology, infographics are now largely unthinkable without it. Digital technologies generate and acquire data at an unprecedented rate, making infographics seem all the more necessary. Michael Betancourt has described the tantalizing promises of the digital format in terms of informational plenitude and boundless capacity (2006); infographics corral and organize this surplus. Prior to the late twentieth century, information visualization was largely the purview of experts, whether in subject matter or technique. Today, complex visualizations still require advanced knowledge of design, but the easy availability of user-friendly and low-cost visualization tools has prompted a D.I.Y. turn (Rogers, 2011).

Basic infographics can only present summaries of the data from which they are drawn, but more complex visualizations aspire and promise to illuminate solutions for otherwise impossible problems. Michael Friendly (2006, p. 30) argues that practical necessity often drove innovation in data visualization. As the graphically driven rise of social science begot a new kind of citizen used to thinking in terms of statistics and trends, infographics acquired the power to shape public policy; a key exemplar of this was Florence Nightingale's "coxcomb" graphics demonstrating that disease killed more British soldiers in the Crimea than combat injuries did (Friendly, 2006, pp. 14–15; Thompson, 2016, pp. 26–27). Once infographics proved that they *could* reveal otherwise inaccessible answers, their proponents quickly arrived at the consensus that they *should* be used for these purposes.

Now, infographics abound, and their applications seem limitless. The U.S. military, for example, has enthusiastically seized on the infographic form to clarify its objectives, plot its strategies, or outline its challenges, with mixed success. Some of the resultant images are lethally effective enhancements of military decision-making about how to prioritize, target, and eliminate enemies (Ford, 2014). Others are visual boondoggles, like the much-maligned "spaghetti Powerpoint," an impenetrable tangle meant to illustrate the U.S. strategy in Afghanistan (Bumiller, 2010). Critics of the Powerpointization of the U.S. military claim that overreliance on this tool backfires by adding rather than reducing complexity, while also requiring an unreasonable investment of time on the part of its users. Rather than concede that some geopolitical phenomena are irreducible to data that can be rendered in two dimensions, the debate hinges on the conceit that better design would succeed where lousy images had failed.

Infographic visual practice rests on the tantalizing promise that sophisticated visualization can remake the world into a more manageable form. Infographics assure us that there is, or can be, order where we might only see chaos. Whatever its content, the infographic model insists that anything can be made intelligible or predictable. From that vantage, information is never misleading, unwieldy, overwhelming, or alarming; with the proper skill, it can always be fashioned into an answer and a reassurance. Given this, infographics' appeal for the architects of U.S. foreign policy is obvious, particularly in the confrontation with an enemy that seems so unknowable, or becomes knowable only too late, in the aftermath of yet another surprise attack.

Singularly grisly, uncannily familiar: I.S.I.S.'s visual media

So much about I.S.I.S. is flummoxing: its methods, its wantonness, its effectiveness. Philipe-Joseph Salazar (2016, pp. 343–344) faults Western intellectuals and governments, for misrecognizing the group's aims and its cultural underpinnings, invoking mental illness or shadowy processes of "radicalization" to explain its appeal to young people. Likewise, outsiders struggle to understand the group's communication strategy, and to reconcile its fluency in the characteristic platforms and styles of our contemporary media landscape with its apparently retrograde ideology and practice.

Besides being singular in their grisliness, many of I.S.I.S.'s visual productions are also uncanny in their utilization of visual forms that are seemingly the purview of Western media, a juxtaposition that often confounds Western observers. This is not simply "celluloid barbarism" (Evans & Giroux, 2015, p. 202). Instead, I.S.I.S. relies on tools like social media to preserve its legitimacy, to both amplify and offset its "brute force" (Farwell,

2015). And it employs agile propagandists who smooth over contradictions between theology and practicality (Byman, 2016, p. 140). I.S.I.S. does all of this while deploying what Cori Dauber and Mark Robinson describe as a "Hollywood visual style" (2015) with a facility unparalleled in the universe of jihadist media production. Although I consistently describe I.S.I.S. as utilizing a Western-inspired visual style, I do not mean to suggest that there is a clear or dichotomous separation between "us" and "them." Indeed, the globalized nature of mass media means that disparate audiences often consume the same texts. But I.S.I.S.'s deliberate incorporation of stylistic features prevalent in media from cultures they define as apostate is significant. These aesthetic choices are a calculated appeal to viewers, both domestic and foreign, "accustomed to a European or North American industry standard" (Dauber & Robinson, 2015). I.S.I.S. videos attend to visual details like color palette and depth of field, and the group compresses them carefully so that the images may circulate widely with only minimal loss of quality. Such techniques are not ancillary to I.S.I.S.'s overall objectives, they are essential elements of its visual brand. And I.S.I.S.'s ability to both recognize and replicate these stylistic features belies Western narratives of their absolute difference.

Their strategy is expressly digital. Leveraging the ubiquity and interactivity of digital forms, and embedding their messages in familiar genres like music videos (Franz, 2015, p. 9), I.S.I.S. tailors both content and delivery. These techniques enable them to reach and recruit millennials (Salazar, 2016, p. 349). Young recruits, in turn, help ensure that the group stays cutting-edge (Byman, 2016, p. 148). Today, most jihadi groups use platforms like YouTube and Twitter (Lassalle & Akgül, 2016, p. 62); al-Qaeda pioneered this strategy, but I.S.I.S. has perfected it. From its inception, I.S.I.S.—under the founding guidance of Abu Musab al-Zarqawi—developed a repertoire that was both flashier and more versatile than al-Qaeda's. Whereas al-Qaeda's videos often featured "tedious sermonizing," I.S.I.S.'s showcase a "mix of ultraviolence and good governance practices" (Byman, 2016, p. 147). In general, "disseminating acts of spectacular violence is a way of fomenting divisions, weakening the enemy, and recruiting," but I.S.I.S. also utilizes social media to gauge popular sentiment about its actions (Byman, 2016, pp. 147–148). I.S.I.S. carefully cultivates its media profile, harmonizing a corporate sensibility about marketing with its tactical decentralization, which effectively outsources promotional work to adherents all over the world.

In this way, the group both draws on al-Qaeda's influence and diverges from it. This bifurcated relationship parallels the similarities and differences between the groups in ambition and organization (Lassalle & Akgül, 2016, pp. 42–43). Like al-Qaeda, I.S.I.S. is prolific. U.S. raids have uncovered terabytes worth of content that al-Qaeda created but never circulated (Winkler & Dauber, 2014, p. 3), and I.S.I.S. too generates content at an astonishing rate. I.S.I.S. has also apparently adopted al-Qaeda's penchant for branding. Dauber (2014, pp. 137–138) argues that after September 11 al-Qaeda became less an entity than a brand, relying on standardized logos and animations to distinguish itself in an increasingly crowded jihadi field. Likewise, I.S.I.S. maintains a fairly coherent visual identity, even without exercising direct creative control over its scattered network of promoters. This coherence is evidenced in a stock image that the group frequently recycles—"two rows of fighters, one in the black 'ninja' outfit, the other row dressed in white, both marching in unison, shot in slow motion and from below"—which is so compelling and identifiable that many news organizations have incorporated it into their reporting (Dauber & Robinson, 2015). In this way, I.S.I.S. dictates the terms of its representation both internally and externally.

Al-Qaeda set the pattern for jihadi media engagement, but I.S.I.S. has refined and expanded it. Aesthetically, I.S.I.S. is much more careful than al-Qaeda (Dauber & Robinson, 2015), and the group has integrated media production much more deeply into its operations. Its heavy reliance on social media has inspired the U.S. to respond, albeit belatedly and sometimes clumsily, with countermessaging via the same platforms (Fernandez, 2015). This dexterous and consistent use of social media sets I.S.I.S. apart from similar groups. The combination of its social media following and the viewers it draws through mainstream media coverage yields a huge combined audience (Farwell, 2015, pp. 49–50). Though I.S.I.S. operatives rely on encrypted messaging services to orchestrate attacks, the group otherwise courts publicity and visibility, and does not seem overly concerned about the risk of exposure entailed by social media use (Farwell, 2015, p. 50). Indeed, because the group often operates in places it has made prohibitively dangerous for journalists, its own content frequently supplants traditional news reportage. Ultimately, despite the various ways that al-Qaeda familiarized Western audiences with jihadi media, most observers still seem exercised or perplexed by I.S.I.S.'s ability to marshal these technologies.

Thus far, most scholarship on I.S.I.S.'s media production has focused on its video and social media strategies, and nearly all accounts emphasize that I.S.I.S. has far surpassed al-Qaeda in the polish and efficacy of its communication. I.S.I.S.'s production of infographics conforms to this general trend. Their use of infographics and generation of comprehensive annual reports bespeak an advanced media strategy, although most (but not all) of its infographic productions are fairly basic, even clunky, compared with much of their other visual work. Practically, these graphics endeavor to disseminate facts about their operations and achievements in a way that is efficient and eye-catching. But they also represent a much deeper challenge to mechanisms that Western institutions often rely upon for managing and understanding the same type of information.

Against unthinkability: infographics about I.S.I.S.

Terrorist acts are exercises in unthinkability; they are terrifying largely because they are incomprehensible, as they seem to obliterate what is rational or predictable. Increasingly, we are confronted with forms of violence that seem more awful even than terrorism. Adriana Cavarero (2011) has described this condition as "horrorism," while Steven Miller (2014) has developed an inventory of forms of violence that do not stop at killing victims. In such a context, infographics, with their promises of sense-making and revelation, acquire new valences of both urgency and comfort, despite the mismatch between the smallness of the infographic and the magnitude of what it depicts. Arguably one of the first American efforts to represent the threat of terrorism graphically was the ill-fated Terror Alert System, which "neatly juxtaposed the realms of the seen and unseen, transforming the invisible enemy into a vivid block of color" (Barkun, 2011, p. 110). Throughout the 16 years of the war on terror, the visual has been central to state and popular efforts to assess and contain the threat of terrorism (Adelman, 2014); infographics are a new addition to this repertoire.

Despite its hypervisibility, much about I.S.I.S. remains unknown, including the size and composition of its membership or confusing (Franz, 2015, p. 6), like its organizational nature and its ambit (Byman, 2016, p. 129). In general, news outlets worldwide endeavor to fit I.S.I.S. into recognizable narrative frames (Xhang & Hellmueller, 2016) or rely on well-worn stereotypes about Muslims.[2] Yet the difficulty in representing I.S.I.S. is a function of more than its shocking tactics; the group amplifies the representational difficulties provoked by any enemy, particularly in its capacity to insinuate itself into spaces previously thought safe. Indeed, Islam has served as an exemplary enemy for the West since the Middle Ages, and Galli (2009, pp. 199–200) writes that, while external enemies are representable, internal enemies tend to be the opposite, appearing often as "a shadow, a phantom." In an effort to rout out invisible threats, through "obvious compensative and defensive practices, the enemy is actually *hyperrepresented*" (Galli, 2009, p. 197). This tendency manifests across the spectrum of Western media, and is made apparent in the profusion of infographics about the group.

The turn toward data visualization, with its fundamental promise to reveal patterns between seemingly disconnected fragments, is consonant with the increased reliance of Western governments on data to manage risks of terrorism (Amoore, 2013). Whether in the form of algorithms or biometrics or infographics, such initiatives are updated versions of the efforts that the U.S. began undertaking in the mid-twentieth century to "model, game, intuit, and access" the enemy mind (Masco, 2014, p. 16). In this environment, an increased "sense of threat" drives a voracious "appetite for information" (Barkun, 2011, p. 134). Theoretically, when governments confront non-state actors like terrorist organizations, data visualization for mapping networks should help identify connections and leaders (Lima, 2011, p. 142).

Yet I.S.I.S. defies this potential twice over. First, the protean and shadowy structure of the organization itself refuses straightforward translation into orderly infographics. Consequently, most graphics about I.S.I.S. personnel (e.g. Thompson, Greene, & Torre, 2014) focus on individual biographies rather than mapping connections between them. And the vaunted "heat map" of I.S.I.S. influence (Osborne, 2016) that purports to track the spread of the network plots this as territorial gains instead. Second, when I.S.I.S. turns to the production of infographics, the group perverts the format's promise to help make terrorist organizations more visible, comprehensible, and hence more vulnerable to defeat.

From the outset, news organizations have utilized infographics for the descriptive tasks of explaining what I.S.I.S. is and how it operates. By the fall of 2014, with I.S.I.S. firmly in control of major Iraqi cities like Fallujah and Mosul, the *New York Times* (Aisch et al., 2014) and C.N.N. (Thompson et al., 2014) had both taken to infographics to explicate the nature of this new enemy to bewildered publics, promising comprehensive knowledge. C.N.N. described its own infographic as "everything you need to know," combining maps of territory and the origins of its fighters with an organizational chart and a brief video montage. These graphics aimed at demystification and marked the inauguration of a multifaceted infographic practice.

Some of the conceptual difficulty around I.S.I.S. arises from its connections to the multi-sided conflict in Syria, with its countless reversals of fortune and shifting alliances. This has elicited some elaborate visualizations, like the *New York Times's* five-year retrospective of the war, with text-heavy explanations alongside a collection of maps and timelines (Barnard, Samaan, & Watkins, 2016). Others are much simpler, like *Slate's* Middle

East Friendship Chart, which plots the various parties to the war on a grid and uses color-coded emoji faces to classify relationships as "friends," "enemies," or "it's complicated" (Keating & Kirk, 2015). In these graphics, the emphasis on mapping intergroup dynamics simplifies associations for audiences who might be unable to comprehend such fractured or crowded political landscapes.

Maps are central to the practice of producing infographics about I.S.I.S.. The very earliest maps were intended for use in navigation and way finding but also the more abstract demarcation of property ownership (Drucker, 2014, p. 77), and maps serve similar purposes in this conflict. Because I.S.I.S. is fundamentally concerned with establishing a trans-state caliphate, territorial expansion is at the core of its mission, and innumerable maps track its encroachments across the Middle East. Whether by pinning its various affiliate groups to specific countries (Leigh, French, & Juan, 2016) or visualizing the "spread" of I.S.I.S. around the world (Osborne, 2016), such graphics represent an uncontainable threat but then stabilize it by arranging it onto the familiar backdrop of the map, where borders between countries are reassuringly impermeable. Before and after maps and satellite photos can be arranged to show either I.S.I.S.'s expansion or its contraction (Almukhtar, Wallace, & Watkins, 2016) and so plot the group's history in manageable linearity. Mapping the expansion of I.S.I.S. requires confronting not only the nature of this threat but also the design challenge of rendering change over time, which is notoriously difficult to convey in static infographics (Lima, 2011, p. 84). Digital media have resolved the technical problems, and interactive timelines enable users to track the history of I.S.I.S. (John, 2015). Such infographics enable their users to exercise a degree of control over this history by dictating the speed at which it progresses as they scroll.

Other infographics undertake a grim accounting, tallying up casualties or developing censuses of its fighters. Because I.S.I.S. is planetary in its scope and composition, maps of the world figure heavily in these graphics as well and become the scaffolds for other types of data. There are, for example, linked timelines and maps of I.S.I.S. attacks, with each strike represented by a small red circle (Yourish et al., 2016), or graphics that track the countries of origin of foreign I.S.I.S. fighters (McCarthy, 2015). Among the most ambitious are those that endeavor to account for all American I.S.I.S. recruits, which often match capsule bibliographies with data like birthplace, citizenship, and family arrangements (Goldman, Yang, & Muyskens, 2017; Yourish & Lee, 2016). Such graphics reveal a faith in the power of infographics to render these transformations comprehensible when they directly contradict so many of our assumptions about the identity of the nation and its enemies. Infographics that I.S.I.S. produces, by contrast, trouble these assumptions anew by their demonstrated efficiency with and repurposing of the Western-style infographic form.

The weaponization of information: I.S.I.S.'s infographic production

Overall, in its infographics, I.S.I.S. portrays itself as lethally rational. Thus, the graphics grate against Western notions that the group is irrational or amodern because it is fervently religious (Walzer, 2015). In these images, I.S.I.S. appears as almost actuarial in its sensibility, and methodically expansive in its reach and ambition. Compared with those produced by their Western counterparts, I.S.I.S.'s infographics are generally (but not always) less conceptually elaborate, technically involved, and aesthetically sophisticated. Unsurprisingly, there are differences in content as well; some infographics in Western news sources try to humanize the victims of I.S.I.S. attacks by providing personal photos and biographies, while I.S.I.S. tracks things like the number of "apostates" it has inspired to "repent." And given its strong propagandistic impulse, I.S.I.S. may not always prize accuracy or verifiability in its data production. Despite these differences, however, both types of infographics evince many common focal points. Like Western news sources, I.S.I.S. creates infographics to map attacks, mark territorial gains, tally and categorize casualties, and track the types of weapons deployed. The two types of infographics diverge primarily in their affective resonance, as similar information signifies in radically different ways. Ultimately, by producing and circulating these infographics, I.S.I.S. simultaneously renders itself more and less intelligible to outsiders, confounding prevailing representations by weaponizing information. I.S.I.S.'s production of infographics grates against outsiders' visions of the group, as the painstaking creative work of design contrasts starkly to the wild forms of violence that it otherwise prefers.

Western news sources produce infographics about I.S.I.S. in an effort to make otherwise incomprehensible phenomena seem accessible, while I.S.I.S. engages in a cognate visual practice to emphasize the magnitude and imminence of the threat that they pose. They are triumphalist. Drucker (2014, p. 128) argues that all "data" are actually "capta," information that is constructed rather than found. In this context, I.S.I.S.'s content fills the informational void created by the impossibility of access for outsiders. Indeed, in its 2014 annual report, as Alex Bilger (2014) notes, "I.S.I.S. is claiming credit for significant battlefield effects, including some that are not readily observable in open source reporting" (p. 2). This means that outsiders' analyses, both scholarly (Lassalle & Akgül, 2016, p. 43) and journalistic, of I.S.I.S.'s prospects must depend, at least in some measure, on the group's own, and occasionally preposterous, data.

Like their Western counterparts, I.S.I.S.'s infographics tend toward redundancy, as they rehash similar types of data from various time periods and operations. While they are clearly meant to appeal to their audiences, none of the infographics I have found so far is interactive. Some of them rely on a cartoonish visual style; others borrow from the visual rhetoric of corporate communication. The group and its affiliates release infographics in both English and Arabic, sometimes simultaneously. Unlike Western-produced infographics, which primarily target Western audiences, I.S.I.S. is speaking to multiple, and mutually exclusive, constituencies: its allies and its enemies. To outsiders, I.S.I.S.'s infographics are decipherable because they adopt the conventions of Western-produced visualizations.

For its adherents, I.S.I.S.'s infographics offer a morale boost, confirming accomplishments and asserting the inevitability of victory. For its enemies, infographics afford a rare, and often troubling, opportunity to see how the group represents itself, beyond the hypervisibility of their violence. Hugh Gusterson (2012) has argued that Western media accounts of insurgency in the Middle East systematically erase actual insurgents; figured as "medieval, brutal, fanatical, tyrannical, and misogynistic," they are essential for "securing American identity" by contrast. In such a media economy, insurgents are "fundamentally unknowable and must be so" (p. 85). Reflecting on the conditions of enemy visibility more generally, Galli argues (2009, p. 209) that:

> In order to warn of the danger the enemy embodies, and in order to prevent it from camou-
> flaging itself in, and mingling itself with, the genuine substance of politics, the enemy will be
> represented in the mode of a caricature, with grotesque traits and glaring marks announcing
> its lack of humanity.

The enemy, he contends, is at its most fearsome when it is appears as "mimetic, one that takes our own appearance" (p. 216). Besides the much-vaunted threat of homegrown I.S.I.S. operatives, who may look like "us" but kill like "them," there is also something unsettling about I.S.I.S.'s dexterity with the infographic visual style, its capacity to mimic this increasingly trusted and ubiquitous form of communication.[3] Unlike the videos of beheadings or immolations that invite visceral responses rather than rational evaluation, infographics urge their audiences to sustained consideration, compelling reflection both on what I.S.I.S. has done and on how it has broadcasted these feats.[4]

Although media coverage of I.S.I.S.'s infographic production has been fairly scant compared with that dedicated to its more spectacular visual releases, I.S.I.S. infographics are relatively easy to find with a quick internet search; they are not secrets. Still, researching I.S.I.S. infographics entails some challenges. Infographics in general can be difficult to locate, as they are often embedded in other documents, and because they are "borndigital" they can frequently be "too ephemeral to capture" (Featherstone, 2014, p. 149; Lima, 2011, p. 16). These problems are magnified when working with I.S.I.S. infographics—they may be posted on Twitter accounts that subsequently disappear, or buried in materials that remain obscure to uninitiated seekers. Despite these obstacles, however, it is possible to discern salient patterns in the group's infographic visual practice, particularly as the group continues to expand this lexicon.

The production of infographics is part of the group's general managerial approach, elsewhere evidenced in its publication of corporate-looking annual reports, its emphasis on metrics, and its provision of "basic state-like services" in the territories it controls (Byman, 2016, p. 141). As with the rest of its media production, some of these infographics are produced by I.S.I.S. itself, while others are produced by affiliate groups (S.I.T.E., 2016). They bespeak a regularization or banalization of violence (Hariman & Lucaites, 2012) integrated with seemingly unexceptional routines. I.S.I.S.'s infographics first elicited attention with the group's release of a 410-page annual report in 2014. According to Bilger (2014, p. 1), this document revealed, to allies and enemies alike, that "I.S.I.S. in Iraq is willing and able to organize centralized reporting procedures and to publish the results of its performance to achieve organizational effects," like acquiring financial support. Taken together, these artifacts showcase I.S.I.S.'s effort to construct and communicate a narrative about its place in the world.

Typically, when I.S.I.S. makes a map, it does so to graph the locations of its attacks. For example, the A.M.A.Q. News Agency, I.S.I.S.'s quasi-official mouthpiece, generated a series of infographics that listed and mapped clusters of attacks. Some of these are grouped by cities, like Baghdad, or regions; significantly, in the latter category, the group depicts Iraq and Syria as a unified territory. Other infographics focus on specific enemies, mapping operations against "crusader Russia," or take the fight to a planetary scale, pinpointing the locations of attacks on a flattened world map. In one (Aronheim, 2016), all of the land is black (one of I.S.I.S.'s trademark colors) and the boundaries between nations have disappeared. Here, as in maps produced by Western media sources, attacks are marked with tiny red icons, reflecting a shared visual language deployed for very different ends.

I.S.I.S. also displays a penchant for totting up operational statistics. Some of these aggregate different types of attacks, divided by the type of weapons employed. Often, these are represented by cartoon graphics of things like mortars, I.E.D.s, incendiary vests, and vehicles (e.g. Matthews, 2014). In an especially lavish release from early 2017, the group focused specifically on the outcomes of a series of its drone attacks, illustrated with both a graphic silhouette of a drone and a photo of a masked fighter preparing to launch a handheld unmanned aerial vehicle (U.A.V.) (Middle East Media Research Institute [M.E.M.R.I.], 2017). The group also produced dedicated infographics for "martyrdom operations." Such suicide missions, as scholars like Talal Asad (2007) and Ghassan Hage (2003) have argued, are uniquely unthinkable to outsiders; they are also difficult to understand, because those with the most intimate knowledge of them, the bombers themselves, perish in the execution. In these instances, too, the attacks are illustrated by the types of weapons involved, the actual bombers remaining unrepresented (Aronheim, 2016), simultaneously memorialized in and eclipsed by the infographic. Thus, the image declines to provide outside audiences with any information about what such an attacker might look like, and hence how such threats might be detected.

Casualties also figure prominently in I.S.I.S.'s infographic practice; Figure 2 combines this accounting with a cartography of attacks. Typically, I.S.I.S. represents these people as aggregate figures, usually identifying them either by place of death or by national affiliation. Notably, the group reserves its most graphic illustrations for these numbers, appending, for example, images of splattered blood and viscera or thumbnail images of piled bodies in combat fatigues (Aronheim, 2016). While the group relishes its tallies of apostates killed, it also tracks among its outcomes the number of those who have "repented" or been forced to atone. In the 2014 annual report, for example, the group claims more than 100 such "forced atonements," and also notes in a separate section that one apostate was "run over" (Bilger, 2014, p. 10). On the signature infographic from the report, the symbol for apostates repented is indecipherable, just an oblong black smudge.

We cannot know what audiences friendly to I.S.I.S. think about their infographics, but for alarmed outsiders these images confront, and ultimately upend, the founding promise of infographics to make the world a safer and more comprehensible place. In this way, the accuracy of the information—we can safely assume that I.S.I.S. is juking its numbers, even if we cannot know by exactly how much—matters less than its presentation as such. I.S.I.S. severs the data-driven episteme of the infographic from the Enlightenment promises on which it is founded. The threat of I.S.I.S.'s excess is captured in these images and intensified rather than defused.

Epistemic threat multipliers

The production of infographics about I.S.I.S. is underpinned by a hope that the group, if fully comprehended, can be more readily defeated. For example, a series of graphics published by the Canadian newsmagazine *Maclean's* visualize the impact of Canada's armed forces in the fight (Shendruk, 2015). With graphs, a timeline and map of airstrikes, and accountings of personnel and aircraft, these images hint that the war can be, is being, won. Focusing tightly on Canadian military capacity, the graphics offer no comparable

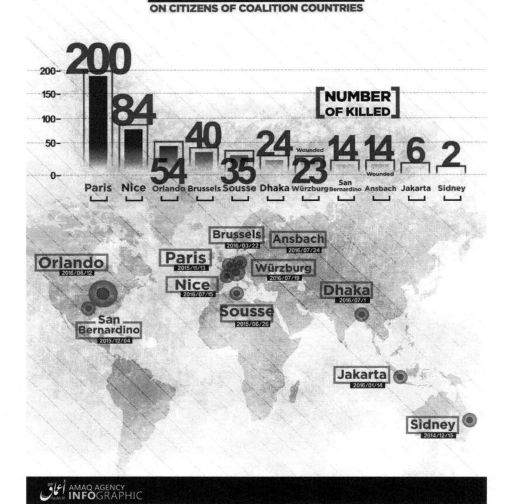

Figure 2. A June 2016 infographic published by A.M.A.Q., an I.S.I.S. news agency.

data on I.S.I.S., conjuring an outcome in which I.S.I.S. is vanquished because it is invisible. Roughly ten years after the group's formation, and three since it became a viable threat, I.S.I.S. has drawn its enemies into a conflict that is stochastic, unbounded, and seemingly intractable. For those who feel threatened by I.S.I.S., infographics give the enemy a shape, and the practices of constructing and consuming such images offer an illusion of control. But only temporarily.

As I.S.I.S. accelerates its infographic production, it demonstrates a growing capacity to use these images as threat multipliers, launching epistemic assaults on its Western adversaries. Infographics have the capacity to impose order on seemingly random events, but the patterns shaped in I.S.I.S.'s infographics hint at a creeping entropy in the geopolitical order. The boundaries of the infographic form suggest the containment of the otherwise unwieldy phenomena it documents; by contrast, I.S.I.S.'s infographics suggest a grinding sprawl, moving onto new terrestrial and digital fronts. Infographics appeal because they promise solutions, but the profusion of I.S.I.S. infographics, released from shadowy corners of the internet at unpredictable frequencies and full of staggering numbers, hint that the fight will continue indefinitely, while neither data nor technological sophistication guarantees victory for Western powers. I.S.I.S. infographics subvert the sense-making promise of the infographic form itself, while swiping at the foundations of U.S. foreign policy and its presumptions about how American dominance can be assured. I.S.I.S. infographics contain a different type of threat than that posed by the grislier elements of its visual repertoire, like beheadings, which are chilling but easily dismissed as a sign of the group's barbarism and incompatibility with contemporary ways of life. Their infographics issue a warning that is subtler but more profound.

`Lately, I.S.I.S. affiliates have become more ambitious in their infographic practice. In December 2016, its Yaqeen Media foundation released a two-and-a-half-minute animated infographic detailing the "Battle of Mosul" (M.E.M.R.I., 2016). In a C.G.I.-style evocative of video games, the graphic includes diegetic battle noises and English-language text. It opens in a small I.S.I.S. redoubt: a wooden table sheltered by a scrubby tree and

Figure 3. Scenes from a two-and-a-half-minute animated infographic published by the pro-I.S.I.S. Al-Yaqeen Media Center in December 2016.

marked with a flagpole flying I.S.I.S.'s colors. The table features a map of Iraq, and floating text explicates the fight, accompanied by a graphic of the flags from the nations allied against it, including the U.S., U.K., and Canada. The remainder of the video consists primarily of a three-dimensional accounting of enemy equipment destroyed or captured, as tanks and other armored vehicles appear with a beeping red bullseye on their side. It also claims that I.S.I.S. destroyed 21 drones and killed 4,909 fighters, a number illustrated with a stacked pile of camouflaged bodies. The video ends abruptly after boasting of 209 martyrdom operations, with a tower of flame visible in the background behind a rigged vehicle (Figure 3). In terms of showiness, Yaqeen has here outdone all of its Western media competitors with this video. Practically, there was no need to create this kind of simulation; the same information could have been just as readily, and more efficiently, conveyed in text or a single-page infographic. But that is beside the point. As an artifact, this video serves primarily to demonstrate I.S.I.S.'s visual prowess, and its capacity to use imaging technology to conjure a scene in which the clearest landmark is its black flag, unfurled in the wind over an otherwise empty space.

Notes

1. Szpunar (2016) argues that increasingly, terrorists do not appear as the "Other" but rather as a "Double."
2. For more on the geopolitical lives of these stereotypes, see Alsultany (2013) and McAlister (2005).
3. The group engaged in a similar form of mimesis when it coerced British journalist John Cantlie to "report" on I.S.I.S. successes, relying on the familiar visual trappings of on-location battlefield reporting.
4. "We see the knife," Salazar (2016, p. 345) writes, but "we don't see what makes the knife so eloquent."

References

Adelman, R. (2014). *Beyond the checkpoint: Visual practices in America's global war on terror*. Boston: University of Massachusetts Press.

Aisch, G., et al. (2014, September 16). How ISIS works. *New York Times*. Retrieved from http://www.nytimes.com/interactive/2014/09/16/world/middleeast/how-isis-works.html

Almukhtar, S., Wallace, T., & Watkins, D. (2016, June 18). ISIS has lost many of the key places it once controlled. *New York Times*. Retrieved from https://www.nytimes.com/interactive/2016/06/18/world/middleeast/isis-control-places-cities.html

Alsultany, E. (2013). Arabs and Muslims in the Media after 9/11: Representational strategies for a "Postrace" Era. *American Quarterly, 65*(1), 161–169.

Amoore, L. (2013). *The politics of possibility: Risk and security beyond probability*. Durham: Duke University Press.

Aronheim, A. (@AAhronheim) (2016, April–October). *Twitter*. Retrieved from https://twitter.com/aahronheim/status/749123835857891328

Asad, T. (2007). *On suicide bombing*. New York: Columbia University Press.

Barkun, M. (2011). *Chasing phantoms: Reality, imagination, and homeland security since 9/11*. Chapel Hill: University of North Carolina Press.

Barnard, A., Samaan, M., & Watkins, D. (2016, March 12). Signs of hope five years after start of Syria's war. *New York Times*. Retrieved from http://www.nytimes.com/interactive/2016/03/13/world/middleeast/syria-control-isis-maps-cease-fire-civil-war-five-years.html

Betancourt, M. (2006, September 5). The Aura of the digital. CT Theory. Retrieved from: http://www.ctheory.net/articles.aspx?id=519

Bilger, A. (2014, May 22). *ISIS annual reports reveal a metrics-driven miltiary command.* Institute for the Study of War. Retrieved from http://www.understandingwar.org/sites/default/files/ISWBackgrounder_ISIS_Annual_Reports_0.pdf

Bumiller, E. (2010, April 26). We have met the enemy and he is Powerpoint. *New York Times.* Retrieved from http://www.nytimes.com/2010/04/27/world/27powerpoint.html

Byman, D. (2016). Understanding the Islamic state—A review essay. *International Security, 40*(4), 127–165.

Cavarero, A. (2011). *Horrorism: Naming contemporary violence.* (W. McCuaig, Trans.). New York: Columbia University Press.

Dauber, C. E. (2014). The branding of violent jihadism. In Carol K. Winkler & Cori E. Dauber (Eds.), *Visual propaganda and extremism in the online environment* (pp. 137–163). Carlisle, PA: The U.S. Army War College Strategic Studies Institute.

Dauber, C. E., & Robinson, M. (2015, July 9). Isis and the Hollywood visual style. *Jihadology.* Retrieved from: http://jihadology.net/2015/07/06/guest-post-isis-and-the-hollywood-visual-style/

Drucker, J. (2014). *Graphesis: Visual forms of knowledge production.* Cambridge: Harvard University Press.

Evans, B., & Giroux, H. A. (2015). Intolerable violence. *symplokē, 23*(1/2), 201–223.

Farwell, J. P. (2015). The media strategy of ISIS. *Survival: Global Politics and Strategy, 56*(6), 49–55.

Featherstone, R. M. (2014). Visual research data: An infographics primer. *Journal of the Canadian Health Libraries Association / Journal de L'Association des Bibliothèques de la Santé du Canada, 35*(3), 147–150.

Fernandez, A. (2015). "Contesting the space": Adversarial online engagement as a tool for combating violent extremism. *Soundings: An Interdisciplinary Journal, 98*(4), 488–500.

Ford, P. (2014, May 14). Amazing military Infographics: An appreciation. *Medium.* Retrieved from https://medium.com/message/amazing-military-infographics-1ba60bdc32e7#.m9vfqbvmo

Franz, B. (2015, June). Popjihadism: Why young European Muslims are joining the Islamic state. *Mediterranean Quarterly, 26*(2), 5–20.

Friendly, M. (2006, March 21). *A brief history of data visualization. Datavis.* Retrieved from http://www.datavis.ca/papers/hbook.pdf

Galli, C. (2009). On war and on the enemy. *CR: The New Centennial Review, 9*(2), 195–219.

Goldman, A., Yang, J. L., & Muyskens, J. (2017, February 22). The Islamic state's suspected inroads into America. *Washington Post.* Retrieved from https://www.washingtonpost.com/graphics/national/isis-suspects/

Gusterson, H. (2012). Can the insurgent speak? In F. Barkawi & K. Stenski (Eds.), *Orientalism and war* (pp. 83–104). London: Hurst and Co.

Hage, G. (2003). "Comes a time we are all enthusiasm": Understanding Palestinian suicide bombers in times of exighophobia. *Public Culture, 15*, 65–89.

Halpern, O. (2014). *Beautiful data: A history of vision and reason since 1945.* Durham: Duke University Press.

Hariman, R., & Lucaites, J. (2012, January). The banality of violence. *Flow,* n.p. *Flow Journal.* Retrieved from http://flowtv.org/2012/01/banality-of-violence

John, T. (2015, October 9). Timeline: The rise of ISIS. *Time.* Retrieved from http://time.com/4030714/isis-timeline-islamic-state/

Keating, J., & Kirk, C. (2015, October 6). A guide to who is fighting whom in Syria. *Slate.* Retrieved from http://www.slate.com/blogs/the_slatest/2015/10/06/syrian_conflict_relationships_explained.html

Lassalle, K. E., & Akgül, B. (2016). "Light years ahead": Differences and similarities between Al-Qaeda and Islamic state's approach to the global jihad. *Review of International Law & Politics, 12*(2), 41–74.

Leigh, K., French, J., & Juan, J. (2016). The Islamic state and its affiliates. *The Wall Street Journal.* Retrieved from http://graphics.wsj.com/islamic-state-and-its-affiliates/

Lengler, R., & Eppler, M. J. (n.d.). *A periodic table of visualization methods. Visual Literacy.* Retrieved from http://www.visual-literacy.org/periodic_table/periodic_table.html

Lima, M. (2011). *Visual complexity: Mapping patterns of information*. New York: Princeton Architectural Press.

Masco, J. (2014). *The theater of operations: National security affect from the cold war to the war on terror*. Durham: Duke University Press.

Matthews, D. (2014, June 24). The surreal Infographics that ISIS is producing, translated. *Vox*. Retrieved from http://www.vox.com/2014/6/24/5834068/theiraqirebelsmakeannualreportswithinfographicswetranslated

McAlister, M. (2005). *Epic encounters: Culture, media, and U.S. interests in the Middle East since 1945*. Berkeley: University of California Press.

McCarthy, N. (2015, October 8). Where Syria & Iraq's foreign fighters come from. *Forbes*. Retrieved from https://www.forbes.com/sites/niallmccarthy/2015/10/08/where-syria-iraqs-foreign-fighters-come-from-infographic/#293ba30674e1

MEMRI. (2016, December 20). *Pro-ISIS Al-Yaqeen media foundation releases Infographic video touting accomplishments during battle for Mosul*. Retrieved from https://vimeo.com/196338558

MEMRI. (2017, March 2). *ISIS Infographic Details ISIS Drone Attacks in the Past Month*. Cyber & Jihad Lab. Retrieved from http://cjlab.memri.org/lab-projects/tracking-jihadi-terrorist-use-of-social-media/isis-infographic-details-isis-drone-attacks-in-past-month/

Miller, S. (2014). *War after death: On violence and its limits*. New York: New York University Press.

Osborne, S. (2016, August 3). Terrorism "heat map" shows Isis network spreading across the world. *The Independent*. Retrieved from http://www.independent.co.uk/news/world/middle-east/isis-terrorism-terror-groups-al-qaeda-al-shabaab-security-attacks-counterterrorism-a7169516.html

Rogers, S. (2011, October 17). In defence of bad graphics. *The Guardian Datablog*. Retrieved from https://www.theguardian.com/news/datablog/2011/oct/17/data-visualisation-visualization

Salazar, G. (2016). A caliphate of culture? ISIS's rhetorical power. *Philosophy and Rhetoric, 49*(3), 343–354.

Shendruk, A. (2015, November 22). Infographics: What Canada is doing in Iraq and Syria. *Maclean's* . Retrieved from http://www.macleans.ca/news/canada/infographics-what-canada-is-doing-in-iraq-and-syria-isis/

SITE. (2016, July 17). Pro-IS group publishes Infographic on IS-Claimed attacks in France. SITE Intelligence Group. Retrieved from https://news.siteintelgroup.com/Jihadist-News/pro-is-group-publishes-infographic-on-is-claimed-attacks-in-france.html

Štrok, J. (2015, June 10). The history of Infographics. *Tech Infographics*. Retrieved from https://techinfographics.com/the-history-of-infographics/

Thompson, C. (2016, July-August). How data won the west. *Smithsonian*, 23–27.

Thompson, N., Greene, R. A., & Torre, I. (2014, September). ISIS: Everything you need to know about the rise of the militant group. *CNN*. Retrieved from http://www.cnn.com/interactive/2014/09/world/isis-explained/

Väliaho, P. (2014). *Biopolitical screens: Image, power, and the neoliberal brain*. Cambridge: The MIT Press.

Visually. (n.d.). *History of Infographics. Visual.ly*. Retrieved February 6, 2017, from https://visual.ly/history-of-infographics

Walzer, M. (2015, Winter). Islamism and the left. *Dissent, 62*(1), 107–117.

Winkler, C. K., & Dauber, C. E. (2014). Radical visual propaganda in the online environment: An Introduction. In C. K. Winkler & C. E. Dauber (Eds.), *Visual propaganda and extremism in the online environment* (pp. 1–30). Carlisle, PA: The U.S. Army War College Strategic Studies Institute.

Xhang, Z., & Hellmueller, L. (2016). Transnational media coverage of the ISIS threat: A global perspective? *International Journal of Communication, 10*, 766–785.

Yourish, K., & Lee, J. C. (2016, July 6). What the Americans drawn to ISIS had in common. *The New York Times*. Retrieved from https://www.nytimes.com/interactive/2016/07/06/us/isis-in-america.html

Yourish, K., Watkins, D., Giratikanon, T., & Lee, J. C. (2016, March 25). How many people have been killed in ISIS attacks around the world. *New York Times*. Retrieved from https://www.nytimes.com/interactive/2016/03/25/world/map-isis-attacks-around-the-world.html

Apocalypse, later: a longitudinal study of the Islamic State brand

Charlie Winter

ABSTRACT

This article compares two universes of official Islamic State media that were compiled 18 months apart. It explores the nuances of the group's worldview and illustrates the extent to which external and internal situational exigencies impacted the Islamic State's brand during its formative years as caliphate. It finds that the organization's media infrastructure was about half as productive in early 2017 as it had been in mid-2015. The data also show that, even though the group had internationalized its theater of terrorist operations during the time period in question, the brand itself actually contracted to become markedly less globalized in 2016. Finally, the data indicate a substantial thematic rearrangement in the organization's propaganda, one that saw its story shifting away from the millenarian "utopia" towards military denialism. In sum, the data indicate that the Islamic State propagandists were far less productive by January 2017, and that their aggregate product was less international and less utopian but more militant and more defiant, a shift that suggested a new phase in their political marketing operations, one focused on framing the caliphate as an embattled but still defiant pseudo-state struggling to maintain past momentum.

Introduction

More than any other, 2014 was the year in which Salafi-jihadist propaganda went mainstream, largely due to the violent and professional media output of the self-proclaimed Islamic State. The group's brand became an international fixation that year, appearing in newspapers, on network television, and across social media. In the avalanche of attention that began in June 2014, when it captured Mosul and declared a caliphate, countless misconceptions emerged regarding even the most superficial aspects of the organization. Pundits and politicians declared that the Islamic State was a "death cult" and "wholly nihilistic" (Johnson, 2015; Safi, 2015), falling into traps carefully laid by its media officials. What these same commentators failed to take into account was that they were only exposed to a tiny portion of its propaganda—ultraviolent videos calibrated with a view to eliciting this very response. The Islamic State *wanted* to become an international pariah; it *wanted* non-Muslim statesmen and women to challenge it on matters of religion; it *wanted* headlines and air time. This strategy of provocation through flagrant brutality paid off and as a direct result of it, the Islamic State was able to raise its profile from "jayvee team" to "existential threat" in a matter of months, pushing rivals such as al-Qa'ida into relative obscurity (Fox News, 2014; Remnick, 2014).

Certainly, the menace it presented was formidable. While the Islamic State was at the height of its insurgency in 2014 and much of 2015, cities in Iraq and Syria fell like dominoes to its armies, and it obtained affiliated "provinces" from West Africa to South Asia. However, despite its best efforts, it was not destined to enjoy this position for long. As intelligence assets matured and understanding of its asymmetric secrets grew, the group was forced onto the back foot such that, by the end of 2016, its territory had shrunk by 33 percent, it had lost control of almost half the city of Mosul, and its supranational presence had contracted to be but a shadow of its former self (IHS Conflict Monitor, 2017; Winter & Clarke, 2017).

In an attempt to map this decline, the present article looks to the group's propaganda. By comparing two universes of official Islamic State media that were compiled 18 months apart, I explore the nuances of the caliphate worldview and illustrate how the group was marketing itself after the tumultuous events of the year and a half preceding January 2017. Not only does this approach allow for a granular level of analysis, it enables one to gauge the extent to which external and internal situational exigencies impacted the Islamic State brand during its formative years as caliphate—a pursuit that will become all the more important as its pseudo-state continues to crumble in years to come.

To this end, I adopt a longitudinal framework, using a propaganda archive compiled in mid-2015 as a baseline comparison for an identically structured propaganda archive I compiled in January 2017. The 2015 study, which was entitled "Documenting the Virtual 'Caliphate'," offered a window into the Islamic State brand at the height of its political, economic, and military influence—a visceral picture of utopia that was far removed from the irrational "death cult" image being peddled by politicians and mainstream media organizations at the time (Winter, 2015). In the following pages, I compare the results of this study with a more recent snapshot of the Islamic State's official media, demonstrating that, 18 months after its 2015 zenith, the Islamic State brand appeared to be crashing towards its nadir, for the most part resorting to martial posturing and military denialism.

The article will proceed as follows: after reviewing the literature on propaganda, Salafi-jihadism, and the Islamic State, I explain the data collection methodology and set out my coding process; next, I explore the archives, comparing and contrasting the Islamic State worldview according to each; I then speculate as to the causes and effects of the organization's marketing volte-face; and conclude with some thoughts relating to the broader theoretical questions raised by this research.

Propaganda, Salafi-jihadism, and the Islamic State

There is a rich tapestry of studies into how terrorists communicate, especially online. When one narrows the focus to Salafi-jihadism, a particularly useful contribution that has withstood the test of time is that of Bockstette (2008), who determined that Salafi-jihadists communicate for three main reasons: to enlarge their movement, to legitimize their cause, and, finally, to intimidate adversaries (p. 5). Lia (2015) came to a similar conclusion: that much of what Salafi-jihadists do—whether it is terrorism, warfighting, or governance

—is a communicative endeavor geared towards winning credibility in a world of scarce supporters. In the context of the Islamic State, Lia's contention is particularly apt.

Complementing more theoretical studies on the topic are a number of data-based forays into Salafi-jihadist marketing schemes. Research by Kimmage (2008) was perhaps the first such study, involving an archive of official Islamic State in Iraq propaganda gathered in July 2007 from two jihadist forums: al-Ikhlas and al-Fallujah. Just nine years on, the digital landscape it mapped is largely extinct. In any case, the rise of Abu Bakr al-Baghdadi's Islamic State—arguably history's most communicative terrorist organization—allowed a number of scholars to follow in Kimmage's steps and use data analysis to rummage beneath the surface of this often sensationalized issue. Fisher (2015), for example, put forth a number of important assertions regarding the Islamic State "swarmcast" using social network analysis. These assessments were both complemented and challenged by Berger and Morgan (2015), who evaluated the group's Twitter operations through big data. Focusing more at the individual level were Carter, Maher, and Neumann (2014), who investigated the focal figures of contemporary Salafi-jihadist "pop culture," culminating in a study that, coupled with Klausen's (2015) more recent effort, provided useful insight into the shape of the Salafi-jihadist sympathizer community in the age of digital communication.

When it comes to the specific issue of Islamic State propaganda, the works of Winter (2015), Zelin (2015), and Milton (2016) have offered detailed explorations into the way that the Islamic State wants to be understood. In isolation of each other, these studies are individually valuable. Taken together, they present a fairly detailed picture of the Islamic State brand. However, as synchronic studies assessing the organization's political language at a single moment in time, they were structurally limited to presenting tactical glimpses of its strategic communication rather than comparison-informed analyses. There has, as yet, been no longitudinal comparative assessment of the Islamic State brand. Using the aggregated findings of Winter's (2015) aforementioned study as a control, this article attempts to patch this gap in the research, thereby allowing for a more nuanced understanding not only of how the Islamic State was communicating with its supporters and adversaries in early 2017, but of how it used branding to navigate its way through the collapse of its "state," an entity that many believed was the sole source of its appeal.

Before proceeding, it is worth noting that the Islamic State has revolutionized many aspects of insurgent strategic communication and, indeed, propaganda more generally. Its media operations—which have been geared just as much towards radicalizing and recruiting would-be supporters online as they have been towards coercing and maintaining morale offline in the caliphate heartlands—have been unparalleled in their scope and sophistication. Already, other insurgents from across the ideological spectrum are following suit, devoting more time, energy, and manpower to the information space. Hence, the findings presented here are not just relevant to the growing body of literature on the Islamic State and terrorism, but to academic thought on communication, insurgency, and information warfare in general.

Methodology

Prior to setting out the data collection methodology I used to build the 2017 archive, I will summarize the methods used to create the 2015 baseline archive (hereinafter referred to as

"Control"). In mid-2015, the Islamic State disseminated all of its official propaganda through Twitter, while the Amaq News Agency also uploaded materials onto its Tumblr website. Although certain Islamic State social media users offered an almost complete picture, due to Twitter's suspension policy at the time, one could not be sure that any given disseminator was managing to republish all Islamic State propaganda before being taken offline. For that reason, the Control archive was compiled using a series of the Islamic State's officially designated Twitter hashtags—which could not be suspended— to identify and gather a full universe of its output for the Islamic month of Shawwal in the year 1436, which equates to 17 July 2015 to 15 August 2015 (Winter, 2015, pp. 10–14).

The resultant archive contained just under a thousand unique data points, ranging from radio bulletins and electronic magazines to videos and photographic essays. Once compiled, the 892 propaganda products were translated and coded into six themes—*Brutality*, *Mercy*, *Belonging*, *Victimhood*, *War*, and *Utopia*. The last two contained the vast majority of the dataset, so these themes—*War* and *Utopia*—were divided into 13 subcategories: for the theme of *War*, there were six subthemes: *Preparation*, *Offensive*, *Defensive*, *Attrition*, *Eulogy*, and *Summary*; for the theme of *Utopia*, there were seven: *Economics*, *Expansion*, *Governance*, *Justice*, *Religious Life*, *Social Life*, and *Nature and Landscape* (Winter, 2015, pp. 17–37). Through this analysis, it was possible to assemble a nuanced picture of how the Islamic State communicated its brand to both supporters and adversaries. As I discuss below in greater detail, the most striking finding of the study was that the Islamic State's media output was disproportionately weighted towards depicting the minutiae of its state-building project, which were, of course, gloriously exaggerated.

In the 18 months that followed Shawwal 1436, the Islamic State's virtual prospects declined. On Twitter, its support base contracted, as many thousands abandoned the platform because of the difficulties associated with avoiding its increasingly aggressive suspension policy. Taking Twitter's place was Telegram, a Russian-owned social media platform that was, in many ways, an ideal locus for terrorist information sharing. While it, too, followed a trajectory of mounting hostility towards the Islamic State in 2016, the platform was still the foremost arena for the organization's media dissemination at the beginning of 2017, hosting no fewer than six of its secretive official feeds.

To assemble the second archive (hereinafter referred to as "Test"), which comprised all Islamic State media released in the Islamic month of Rabi'a al-Thani in the year 1438— that is, 31 December 2016 to 29 January 2017—I followed those official feeds, adopting the same technical parameters as those set out above for the Control archive.

I determined that for the purpose of comparing the two archives, the Islamic State brand was best distilled into three thematic groups—not six, as used in Winter (2015). Therefore, I reorganized the aggregated Control data so that both archives would only feature the following three principal themes: *Victimhood*, *Utopia*, and *Warfare*. To this end, I moved media products originally coded under the theme *Belonging* to the *Social Life* subtheme of *Utopia*. I also reassigned media coded under the themes *Mercy* and *Brutality* to the *Aftermath* and *Deterrence and Provocation* subthemes of *Warfare* propaganda. Likewise, I moved propaganda products originally coded under the theme *Attrition* to the *Offensive* subtheme. After the above adjustments had been made, both the Control and Test data were identically structured, allowing me to proceed with a like-for-like comparative analysis.

The data

In this section, I compare and contrast the structural and thematic composition of 2015's Control archive and 2017's Test archive. First, I explore how the Islamic State's supranational brand became both more parochial and less prolific between 2015 and 2017. Next, I turn to the content itself, examining how the thematic composition of the Islamic State narrative changed over the 18 months between the data collection periods. To this end, I individually examine each constituent theme of the brand—*Victimhood*, *Utopia*, and *Warfare*—tracking how they matured with time.

Productivity

It is apparent from even a cursory glance at the data that the Islamic State's media momentum collapsed between late summer 2015 and January 2017 (see Figure 1). In the Control archive, there were 892 unique propaganda events produced by 38 individual outlets, with media ranging from documentary feature films, short battlefield clips, and photographic reports to audio statements, magazines, books, and pamphlets. In 2017's Test archive, though, there were only 463 items of propaganda—in other words, there was a 48 percent drop in productivity from roughly 30 media products a day to just 15. Moreover, while the Test archive comprised a similarly broad range of media, there were significantly fewer high-quality videos produced by the Islamic State's provincial media offices—just 9 in the Test data versus 54 in the Control data (Winter, 2015). Making up for this disparity were a large number of shorter, cruder video clips that were compiled by the Amaq News Agency.

It is clear that the Islamic State was producing much less propaganda in early 2017 than it was at its height in 2015. However, besides high-quality videos, there are few significant differences in the structural composition of each archive in terms of *what* the group was producing (see Figure 2). Indeed, in both the Control and Test data, the vast majority of propaganda was photographic, not video or text. That photographs remained the most prominent medium used is unsurprising; the Islamic State brand has long been heavily reliant on visuals and, while videos are an effective way to transmit messages, photographs are lower cost, less time-consuming, and more efficient for tactical communications.

Deglobalization

Besides the above, the data also show that the Islamic State brand was markedly less globalized in 2017 than in 2015 (see Figure 3). In the Control data, there were nearly a thousand propaganda events, originating from no fewer than nine states—in ascending order: Algeria, Saudi Arabia, Nigeria, Afghanistan, Yemen, Egypt, Libya, Syria, and Iraq (Winter, 2015, p. 12). The Test archive contained a much smaller amount of propaganda, and it originated from only five states—in ascending order: Afghanistan, Yemen, Egypt, Syria, and Iraq. This is particularly important to note because it starkly contrasts with the group's contemporaneous attempts to establish a more international presence for itself through the direction and inspiration of overseas terrorist operations.

In any case, when broken down on a province-by-province basis, the disparity between the two archives is even more apparent. The 2015 Control data held propaganda from 29

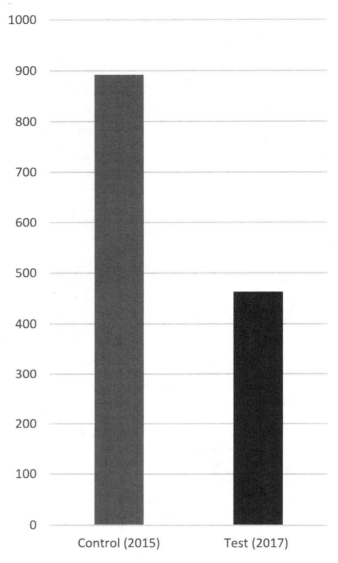

Figure 1. Total Islamic State propaganda production.

provincial media offices, whereas the 2017 Test archive held propaganda from only 22 provincial offices (Winter, 2015, p. 17). Moreover, almost all of the offices active in the Test archive were much less productive in 2017 than in 2015. The only significant exception was the Islamic State's Nineveh Province Media Office, which was a third more productive in the Test archive than in the Control archive, a trend that arose because of the Islamic State's need to communicate its way through the Iraqi government's campaign to recapture Mosul, launched in October 2016.

Though there was an almost across-the-board collapse in the activity of provincial outlets, the Islamic State's central media offices—the Al Hayat Media Center, Bayan Radio, Himma Library, Naba Newspaper, and Amaq News Agency—were similarly productive across both the Control and Test archives. This meant that, by early 2017, they had

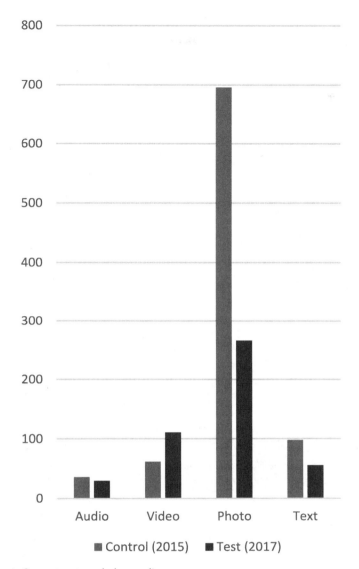

Figure 2. Islamic State propaganda by medium.

significantly increased their total share of the marketing operation, producing no less than 41 percent of all propaganda in that month, versus 16 percent in the Control sample. Of the central outlets, the Amaq News Agency was by far the most active in 2017, constituting more than 25 percent of the entire Test archive.

The brand

Between the summer of 2015 and early 2017, the Islamic State underwent something of a branding volte-face. Previously, it had a uniquely comprehensive approach towards marketing that afforded more prominence to ecstatic depictions of civilian life within its borders than military operations or Sunni Muslim victimization. Instead of framing its

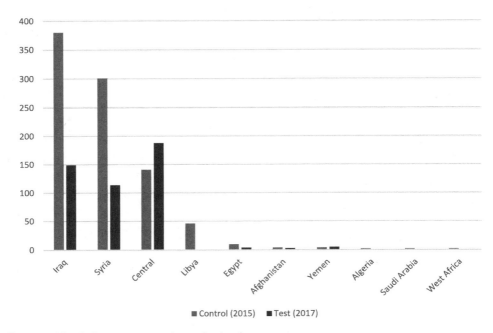

Figure 3. Islamic State propaganda production by state.

project with simple militarism, like other Salafi-jihadists, the Islamic State sought to offer itself to would-be supporters as a lifestyle choice, a utopian alternative within which new adherents would be blessed as founding fathers and mothers (Winter, 2015, pp. 30–37). To this end, its promise was holistic, covering many aspects of civilian existence, no matter how mundane—from schooling, street-cleaning, and social welfare to wild bird conservation, fishing excursions, and grape agriculture (Winter, 2015). With its rapid and steady flow of *Utopia* propaganda, the group was able to appeal across gender, nationality, and socioeconomics. However, as the present data demonstrate, this millenarian promise was diluted with time, such that, by early 2017, it was no longer as central to the Islamic State brand as it once was.

Victimhood

As Figure 4 shows, the proportional representation of the *Victimhood* trope was almost identical across both the 2015 Control archive and 2017 Test archive, comprising around 7 percent of each and appearing in the form of news articles, photo reports, and video clips (Winter, 2015, pp. 22–24). The only significant difference was that, in the Test archive, the Amaq News Agency was responsible for 91 percent of all *Victimhood* media and, in the Control archive, most *Victimhood* propaganda emanated from provincial media offices.

Broadly speaking, the Islamic State's *Victimhood* media is composed of two elements. The first is human collateral—dead or dying civilians lying maimed on hospital beds or in the bombed-out shells of buildings.[1] In both the Control and Test archives, this imagery formed the bulk of *Victimhood* propaganda. The second element is infrastructural damage, and these scenes were more prominent in the 2017 Test archive—a trend that

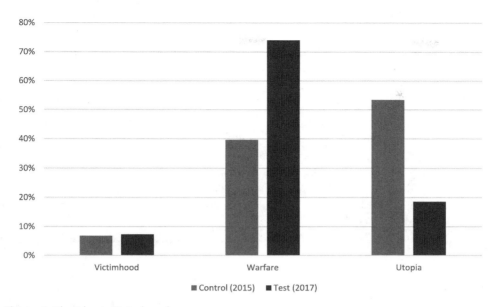

Figure 4. The Islamic State brand.

could be seen as a relatively accurate reflection of the evolution of the war against the Islamic State.[2] After all, in 2014 and the first half of 2015, much of the international coalition's efforts were focused on striking overtly military targets—personnel, convoys, artillery positions, and so on. However, in the second half of 2015 and 2016, the Islamic State began to present a less obvious foe to coalition bombers. The targeting metrics shifted accordingly and infrastructural assets that the group was using to facilitate and preserve its insurgency—bridges, roads, media kiosks, oil infrastructure, and so on—were prioritized (Michaels, 2016). As this gradual recalibration took place, the Islamic State's media team tracked it closely, making sure to hyperactively communicate whenever the coalition had struck and destroyed infrastructure that could be framed as civilian.

That the idea of _Victimhood_ was equally as prominent in 2017's Test archive as it was in 2015's Control archive is, besides anything else, demonstrative of its long-term strategic value to Salafi-jihadists. Just as it does for al-Qa'ida (Ingram, 2016a, 2016b)—and, for that matter, countless other extremist political movements—an urgent sense of injustice underpins the Islamic State ideology. Indeed, for the self-proclaimed caliphate, it is particularly intense. Its _Victimhood_ propaganda tells a story of existential and excessive warfare in which Sunni Muslim civilians are said to be the principal targets. The very idea of victimization thereby serves as a strategic legitimizer for the Islamic State, a facilitator of its ideology. Among other things, it relativizes the promise of utopia; depictions of peaceful life inside the Islamic State are all the more powerful when juxtaposed with stark images documenting collateral damage caused by the so-called "Crusader enemy." In this sense, civilian suffering is a source of momentum for the Islamic State, an emotive trope that it co-opts to frame itself as a populist Sunni Muslim vanguard. Hence, even if it is not the most prominent theme in either the Control or Test archive, _Victimhood_ propaganda is always present in the background, a thematic atmosphere within which the Islamic State idea better operates (Winter, 2015).

Utopia

Arguably the greatest political marketing innovation of the Islamic State was its recognition that, in order to create a sustainably appealing brand, it had to do more than simply criticize the status quo, which is what likeminded rivals (e.g. al-Qa'ida) had been doing for decades. This calculation paid off: it was no coincidence that tens of thousands of volunteers from around the world joined the Islamic State rather than other Salafi-jihadist groups in Syria and Iraq in the 2010s. As researchers like Sheikh (2016) have shown, this was largely because it was not just offering supporters a place where they could die as martyrs, it was also offering a place where they could live as heroes.

As Figure 5 demonstrates, *Utopia* propaganda depicting civilian life in the caliphate was the most prominent part of the Islamic State brand in late summer 2015. Of the 892 media products published in Shawwal 1436, no less than 53 percent were overtly utopian in nature. Twenty-nine percent of the time, *Utopia* propaganda in the Control archive depicted the Islamic State's *Governance* in action—a mixture of education, roadworks, public gardens, media operations, and policing. Twenty-four percent of the time, *Utopia* media was geared towards depicting *Religious life* in the Islamic State—from

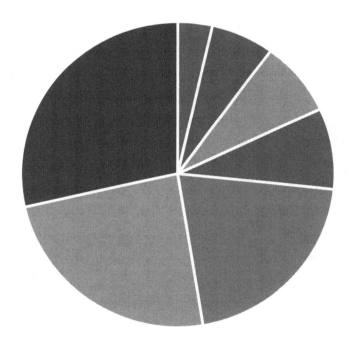

- Combination
- Social Life
- Economics
- Governance
- Landscape and Nature
- Justice
- Religious Life

Figure 5. *Utopia* media, Control (2015).

people praying in mosques, to almsgiving, and Qur'an memorization. Twenty-one percent of the time, the focus was on *Economics*, with reports showing bustling marketplaces, fertile farmland, and industrial-scale factories. Nine percent of the Control archive's *Utopia* media depicted the Islamic State's *Justice* in action, primarily in form of photo reports showing the implementation of *hudud* punishments, public spectacles at which "thieves" were dismembered, "bandits" decapitated, and "murderers" shot. Eight percent depicted *Social Life* in the caliphate—children playing in fair grounds, foreign fighters relaxing with each other, and tribal families meeting for lunch—and a further 6 percent documented scenes of *Nature and Landscape*, primarily focusing on lightning storms and sunsets. The remaining 4 percent was a combination of two or more of the above subthemes (Winter, 2015, pp. 30–37).

The sheer scope of the operation attests to the fact that the Islamic State was never telling as simplistic a story as often suggested. Foreigners and locals rarely joined the group simply to fulfill violent aspirations; rather, the Islamic State "*jihad*" attracted adherents because it had millenarian underpinnings and promised a blissful alternative to the status quo, one that offered redemption and empowerment in equal measure. As the group's own policy documents on propaganda assert, media operatives understood that they had to "paint a brighter picture of *jihad*" in order to forge a way forward in the crowded Salafi-jihadist marketplace of 2014—and that is precisely what they did (Winter, 2017).

With this in mind, it is striking indeed that the organization's emphasis on *Utopia* was significantly more restrained at the beginning of 2017 than previously (see Figure 4). Indeed, just 19 percent of its total media output was *Utopia*-themed in the Test archive —less than half what it had been 18 months earlier. That said, as Figures 5 and 6 illustrate, while its proportionate share of the brand had collapsed, the composite parts of the *Utopia* promise were much the same, with issues of *Governance* appearing 29 percent of the time, *Religious Life* 24 percent of the time, and *Economics* 21 percent of the time. What's more, each of these subthemes continued to be conveyed using the same or similar motifs—roadworks, gardening, mosque attendance, Qur'an memorization, marketplaces, factories, and so on.[3] The remaining 26 percent of the Test archive's *Utopia* propaganda was less varied than that of the Control data: while there was more attention paid to *Nature and Landscapes* (14 percent),[4] there was just one depiction of *Justice* (corporal or capital punishments),[5] and one video portraying *Social Life* in the Islamic State.[6] That being said, there was an 8 percent increase in propaganda bringing together two or more *Utopia* subthemes, some of which did include passing reference to caliphal society.[7]

In any case, by the beginning of 2017, the data show that the *Utopia* theme was playing a much lesser role in the Islamic State's propaganda than 18 months earlier. While it remained an intrinsic part of the caliphate brand, it was less than half as prominent as it once was.

Warfare

Propaganda regarding the Islamic State's military operations has long been central to the organization's appeal. However, in early 2017 it played a significantly greater role than it did in 2015. That the organization's reliance on *Warfare* media increased in the 18 months between the two data collection periods is unsurprising. As its territories hemorrhaged and

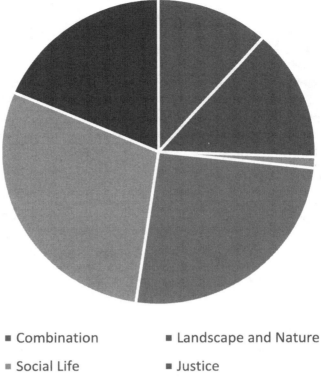

- Combination
- Social Life
- Economics
- Governance
- Landscape and Nature
- Justice
- Religious Life

Figure 6. *Utopia* media, Test (2017).

its leadership disintegrated, the Islamic State was at pains to prove to supporters that it remained a potent and, broadly speaking, winning force (Gartenstein-Ross, Barr, & Moreng, 2016). Hence, instead of looking the other way as its military prospects dwindled, an approach that other organizations might have preferred, its propagandists embraced the battlefield even more, seemingly hoping to communicate through the realities they were up against.

At the height of its insurgency in the summer of 2015, *Warfare* media took up 40 percent of the Islamic State's storytelling operation (see Figure 5). Thirty-seven percent of the time, *Warfare* media focused on the Islamic State's *Offensive* operations, whether individual raids or attrition-orientated attacks. Next most regular, appearing 24 percent of the time, was *Summary* propaganda, which was almost entirely delivered in the form of daily news reports detailing the previous 24 hours' operations. Fourteen percent of *Warfare* media in the Control archive comprised *Eulogy* propaganda celebrating the "heroism" of dead fighters, doctors, and propagandists. Ten percent of the time, the Islamic State's *Warfare* media depicted the carefully staged *Aftermath* of military operations—enemy soldiers would be shown repenting or being executed while fighters surveyed piles of newly seized ammunition and weaponry. Eight percent of the Islamic

State's _Warfare_ media in mid-2015 depicted the war machine in _Preparation_, be it in the form of photographic reports from training camps, frontline garrisons, or food halls. In spite of the disproportionate emphasis placed upon it by the media, just five percent of the organization's _Warfare_ propaganda was "characteristically" brutal, focusing internally on the _Deterrence_ of informers and externally on the _Provocation_ of global consternation. Just 2 percent of the Control archive's _Warfare_ media depicted the Islamic State's _Defensive_ operations (Winter, 2015, pp. 24–29).

Few significant differences emerged when contrasting the composition of _Warfare_ propaganda in the Control archive with _Warfare_ propaganda in the Test archive (see Figures 7 and 8). Both in early 2017 and in the summer of 2015, the most commonly occurring subtheme was _Offensive_ operations (45 percent).[8] Next most prominent were _Eulogy_ reports, which made up 21 percent of the total body of _Warfare_ media.[9] When it came to this subtheme, there was a 7 percent increase in the Test data compared to that of the Control archive. Close in third was _Summary_ media, which comprised 19 percent of the _Warfare_ theme.[10] The proportion of the _Aftermath_ subtheme remained about the same, falling to 8 percent as compared with 10 percent 18 months earlier.[11] According to 2017's Test archive, the propagandists spent very little time depicting the Islamic State's _Defensive_ operations, which proportionately increased just 1 percent on the Control data, from 2 percent to 3 percent.[12] _Deterrence and provocation_

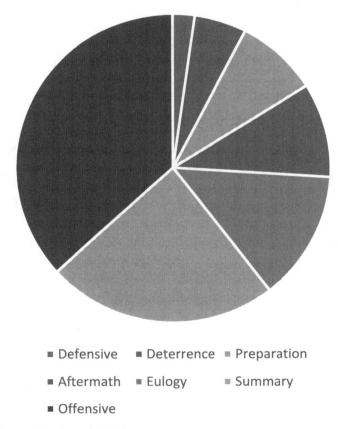

Figure 7. _Warfare_ media, Control (2015).

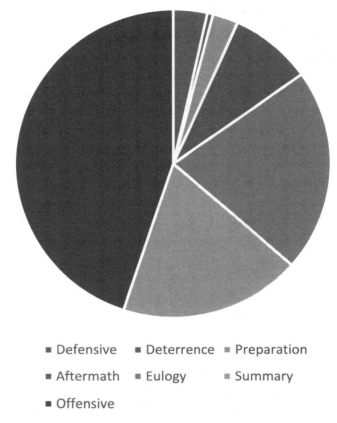

- Defensive
- Deterrence
- Preparation
- Aftermath
- Eulogy
- Summary
- Offensive

Figure 8. *Warfare* media, Test (2017).

propaganda fell from 5 percent to just 1 percent by 2017[13] and, witnessing a similar drop, propaganda on military *Preparation* fell from 8 percent of all *Warfare* media to just 3 percent.[14]

Despite a small number of insignificant statistical shifts, the Islamic State's *Warfare* media in the 2017 Test archive was strikingly similar to its *Warfare* media in the 2015 Control archive.

* * *

Easily the most striking thematic change between the two archives was the narrative shift away from *Utopia*, towards *Warfare*. While the former theme still played an important role in the Islamic State brand, it was less than half as prominent in early 2017 as it had been in the summer of 2015. In its place, *Warfare* media, which appeared nearly twice as often as it had 18 months earlier, took on the lion's share of the branding operation. At first glance, this is counterintuitive. After all, the Islamic State's chief appeal in 2015 was its civilian state. However, as the tides against it changed, so too did its propagandists recalibrate their strategic parameters, and they began focusing more on sustaining the morale of true believers than attracting new adherents.

Discussion

There are three main areas of divergence when comparing the 2015 Control archive with its 2017 counterpart. Two pertain to structural aspects, and the last to the content itself. Firstly, the data offer incontrovertible evidence that the Islamic State's media infrastructure was about half as productive in early 2017 as it had been in mid-2015. This finding is consistent with Milton (2016), which noted an across-the-board propaganda deceleration in 2015 and 2016. Given the fact that it was hemorrhaging territory and recruits across 2016 and early 2017, this trend is intuitive. Secondly, the data show that the Islamic State's brand contracted to become less global, even as its operational influence expanded. The geographic spread of the Test archive was significantly smaller than that of the Control archive, with the overall brand in early 2017 relying almost entirely on media originating in Iraq or Syria. This finding is also consistent with past research into the issue (Winter & Clarke, 2017). Third, the data are indicative of a substantial thematic rearrangement in the organization's propaganda, one that saw its story shifting away from *Utopia* towards *Warfare*. In sum, the data indicate that, in the Islamic month of Rabi'a al-Thani in the year 1438, the Islamic State propagandists were far less productive, and were portraying a less globalized and less utopian state of affairs, instead presenting their caliphate as an embattled but still defiant pseudo-state struggling to maintain past momentum.

The Islamic State is highly secretive when it comes to its media operations, so one can only speculate about what caused this transformation. However, given the group's recent history (Whiteside, 2016) and stated position on information warfare (Winter, 2017), the decline most likely did not come about by strategic choice. Rather, it was more likely the gradual outcome of external pressures the group faced in 2016 which, broadly speaking, took three forms: territorial loss, intelligence-led coalition operations, and cyber warfare.

In regard to the first factor, there is little doubt that the Islamic State's dwindling insurgent prospects had a direct impact upon its ability to propagandize. Its territorial control is intrinsically tied to its information operations, especially those focused on conveying the *Utopia* narrative. After all, it needs to be in control of territory—and administering said territory—in order to make propaganda about it, not to mention the fact that it requires space within which to compile, post-produce, and disseminate media. In 2016, as coalition-backed forces encroached on its heartlands in Iraq and Syria, a number of media nerve centers were captured and dismantled, something that was certain to obstruct the Islamic State propagandists' most basic capabilities (Choi, 2016). Wedded to the challenges presented by territorial loss is the next causative factor—human and signals intelligence-led operations. In the autumn of 2016 alone, three figures believed to be central to the smooth running of the Islamic State's media apparatus—Abu Muhammad al-Furqan, Abu Muhammad al-Adnani, and Abu al-Harith al-Lami—were killed in coalition airstrikes that were only possible because of top-level intelligence breakthroughs (BBC, 2016; RBSS, 2016; Wright, 2016). These were just three of many high-profile deaths; as indicated by the group's own propaganda, dozens more of the Islamic State's media cadres were struck down between 2015 and 2017.[15] Given the importance of technical expertise in the field of media, there can be little doubt that depleting human capital adversely affected the group's ability to produce propaganda. The last factor pertains to the virtual world. Simply put, the Islamic State's Internet ecosystem in early 2017 barely resembled its 2015 counterpart and, while still an undeniably potent force, the group's virtual operatives were not as ubiquitous as they once were. As Internet corporations became savvier and cyber teams began to enter the arena, the online landscape transformed faster than the propagandists could adapt (Turkel, 2016).

There is, of course, no way to know with certainty exactly what factors resulted in the Islamic State's 2015–2017 media decline. However, by taking into account the specificities of the deceleration noted above, one is left with a relatively high degree of confidence that it came as a result of confluence of these three elements. Whatever caused it, the implications of these deceleration and deglobalization trends suggest that the Islamic State brand had entered a new phase by the beginning of 2017. No more was it attempting to appeal to supporters primarily through the promise of utopia—instead, the focus of its political appeal was grounded almost uniquely in the fact that it could still pose a threat to its enemies.

Conclusion

This article compared two universes of Islamic State propaganda gathered 18 months apart to explore the group's insurgent decline. While it only took into account propaganda from the first and last 30 days of the 18 month period in question, the structural and thematic shifts it identified are consistent with broader trends in the Islamic State's propaganda trajectory. The organization's strategic communication policy is gradualist; almost all of its changes are imperceptible unless considered longitudinally. Hence, this data-informed approach was uniquely able to map not only how the group's brand contracted, but also how its supranational millenarianism weakened with time. At the same time, and perhaps more importantly, it allowed for a better understanding of how the Islamic State recalibrated its ideological priorities in order to navigate through the seemingly existential challenges it faced across 2016 and 2017. Moving forward, it would serve policymakers and practitioners alike to develop a better awareness of narrative acrobatics like this—namely, how insurgent groups use propaganda in the battle of ideas to defend themselves against the very real challenges they face in the physical world.

Two issues arise from this study that deserve further enquiry. First, one is left asking for whom the Islamic State is actually generating all this media. Even in its diminished 2017 state, the group was producing hundreds of propaganda products a month for a virtual audience that seemed to be increasingly disengaged. Indeed, much of the time online, its media drifted into almost immediate obscurity, the rate of consumption slowing to a trickle. Notwithstanding this, the propaganda flood was kept up, a result of the fact that for the Islamic State, propaganda is more important as a strategic lever of control within the caliphate itself. Indeed, by 2017, its role in helping to enlist foreign supporters was only a secondary function. Instead, Islamic State media was directed at civilian and military supporters in Iraq and Syria more than any other audience (see Winter, 2016). If one takes this into account, the group's branding transition from *Utopia* and towards *Warfare* over the course of 2016 is more logical, because the latter propaganda is more appropriate for sustaining internal morale than attracting external support. A better understanding of the offline application of insurgent propaganda is crucial, for it lies at the heart of the Islamic State's approach to strategic communication and will only become more relevant in the future.

A closely linked issue that merits further attention is how the Islamic State's desired ideological trajectory was used to deny reality. It would appear that, in the context of the Islamic State—as in other totalitarian contexts—propaganda is a lens through which to refract undesirable developments such that they satisfy the fancies of true believers rather than derail them. Propaganda becomes, in that sense, more important than reality itself. Notwithstanding the massive losses it faced between 2015 and 2017, the Islamic State was unwavering in its denialist approach towards communicating defeat. This is a useful, current, and rare example of wartime totalitarian propaganda that could usefully be scrutinized on a comparative basis.

Notes

1. For example: Aleppo Province Media Office (2017, January 1), Casualties caused by bombardment from the apostate Turkish Army in the town of Tadif [Photo essay], *The Islamic State*; Raqqa Province Media Office. (2017, January 22), Damage and casualties as a result of international coalition aerial bombardment on the city of Tabqa west of Raqqa [Photo essay], *The Islamic State*.
2. For example: Amaq News Agency (2017, January 2), Remains of the bombardment on the Euphrates Dam in the Raqqa countryside [Video], *The Islamic State*; Amaq News Agency (2017, January 26), Damage left behind by the aerial bombardment from American planes on living areas in the Ayman quarter of the city of Mosul [Video], *The Islamic State*.
3. For example: Raqqa Province Media Office (2017, January 8), Aspect of the work of the services office in the city of Raqqa [Photo report], *The Islamic State*; Raqqa Province Media Office (2017, January 14), The public gardens in the city of Raqqa [Photo report], *The Islamic State*; Nineveh Province Media Office (2017, January 21), Mosques in the city of Mosul—al-Sawwaf Mosque [Photo report], *The Islamic State*; Amaq News Agency (2017, January 4), Qur'an memorisation sessions and education in the mosques of the city of Mosul [Video], *The Islamic State*; Raqqa Province Media Office (2017, January 10), One of the local markets in the al-Karamah district in the east of the province [Photo report], *The Islamic State*; Euphrates Province Media Office (2017, January 12), The manufacture of water pipes in the city of Albu Kamal [Photo report], *The Islamic State*.
4. For example: Kirkuk Province Media Office (2017, January 24), Photographs from the countryside around the city of al-Hawijah [Photo report], *The Islamic State*; Kirkuk Province Media Office (2017, January 22), The banks of the Tigris river in west al-Hawija [Photo report], *The Islamic State*.
5. Nineveh Province Media Office (2017, January 10), Aspect of the work of the Hisbah centre in the city of Mosul—Implementation of the Hadd upon he who commits that of the people of Lut [Photo report], *The Islamic State*.
6. Amaq News Agency (2017, January 21), Renewal of allegiance to Shaykh Abu Bakr al-Baghdadi undertaken by the tribes in the al-Safsafah region west of Raqqa [Video], *The Islamic State*.
7. For example: Khayr Province Media Office (2017, January 22), Tour in the villages of the Shu'aytat [Photo report], *The Islamic State*; Jazira Province Media Office (2017, January 24), A tour of the village of al-'Aluliyya east of the city of Tal'afar [Photo report], *The Islamic State*.
8. For example: Amaq News Agency (2017, January 7), Surprise attack by the soldiers of the Islamic State north of Raqqa [News report], *The Islamic State*; Khayr Province Media Office (2017, January 15), Photographs from clashes with the Nusayri Army in the city of al-Khayr with multiple types of weapon [Photo report], *The Islamic State*.
9. For example: Nineveh Province Media Office (2017, January 8), The brother Abu Bakr al-Muslawi—may God accept him—One of the operatives of the martyrdom-seeking operations

on the gathering of the Rafidah Army and its militias in the outskirts of Shaqqaq al-Hadaba' in north east Mosul [Photo report], *The Islamic State*.

10. For example: Bayan Radio (2017, January 12), News broadcast for the Islamic State on Thursday 13 Rabi'a al-Akhr, 1438 [Audio bulletin], *The Islamic State*; Bayan Radio (2017, January 13), News broadcast for the Islamic State on Friday 14 Rabi'a al-Akhr, 1438 [Audio bulletin], *The Islamic State*.

11. For example: Diyala Province Media Office (2017, January 16), Aspect of the booty bestowed upon the mujahidin by God in the region of al-Nada [Photo report], *The Islamic State*;

12. For example: Aleppo Province Media Office.(2017, January 7), The repelling of an attempted advance by the awakening councils and the Turkish Army on the villages in the countryside around the city of al-Bab [Photo report], *The Islamic State*.

13. For example: Khayr Province Media Office (2017, January 8) Revived by his blood [Video], *The Islamic State*; Kirkuk Province Media Office (2017, January 17) Penalty for the traitors [Video], *The Islamic State*.

14. For example: Amaq News Agency (2017, January 8), Witnessing the deployment of the Islamic State fighters in Shaqqaq al-Hadaba' in north east Mosul [Video], *The Islamic State*; Damascus Province Media Office (2017, January 28), A camp for the cubs of the caliphate in al-Hajr al-Aswad in Damascus [Photo report], *The Islamic State*.

15. In January 2017 alone, the deaths of four mid-level media operatives were commemorated.

References

BBC. (2016, October 11). IS confirms death of propaganda chief Abu Mohammed al-Furqan. Retrieved from http://www.bbc.co.uk/news/world-middle-east-37619225

Berger, J. M., & Morgan, J. (2015). The ISIS twitter census: Defining and describing the population of ISIS supporters on twitter. *The Brookings Project on U.S. Relations with the Islamic World*. Paper no. 20. Retrieved from www.brookings.edu/~/media/research/files/papers/2015/03/isis-twitter-census-berger-morgan/isis_twitter_census_berger_morgan.pdf.

Bockstette, C. (2008). Jihadist use of strategic communication management techniques. *George C. Marshall European Center for Security Studies*. Paper no. 20. Retrieved from http://www.marshallcenter.org/mcpublicweb/MCDocs/files/College/F_Publications/occPapers/occ-paper_20-en.pdf

Carter, J. A., Maher, S., & Neumann, P. R. (2014). #Greenbirds: Measuring importance and influence in Syrian foreign fighter networks. *The International Centre for the Study of Radicalisation and Political Violence*.

Choi, D. (2016, August 19). ISIS is losing territory on all fronts—here's what the group leaves behind. *Business Insider*. Retrieved from http://www.businessinsider.in/ISIS-is-losing-territory-on-all-fronts-heres-what-the-group-leaves-behind/Heres-what-else-remained-at-the-ISIS-media-center-inside-the-Hammam-in-Manbij-/slideshow/53776999.cms

Fisher, A. (2015). Swarmcast: How jihadist networks maintain a persistent online presence. *Perspectives on Terrorism, 9*(3), 3–20.

Fox News. (2014, August 10). Is President Obama doing too little or too much in Iraq? Retrieved from http://www.foxnews.com/on-air/fox-news-sunday-chris-wallace/2014/08/10/president-obama-doing-too-little-or-too-much-iraq

Gartenstein-Ross, D., Barr, N., & Moreng, B. (2016). The Islamic State's global propaganda strategy. *The International Centre for Counter Terrorism*. Retrieved from https://www.icct.nl/wp-content/uploads/2016/03/ICCT-Gartenstein-Ross-IS-Global-Propaganda-Strategy-March 2016.pdf

IHS Conflict Monitor. (2017, January 18). Islamic State territorial losses between January 2015 and 31 December 2016. Retrieved from http://news.ihsmarkit.com/press-release/aerospace-defense-security/islamic-state-lost-almost-quarter-its-territory-2016-ihs-ma

Ingram, H. J. (2016a). An analysis of *inspire* and *dabiq*: Lessons from AQAP and Islamic State's propaganda war. *Studies in Conflict and Terrorism, 40*(5), 357–375.

Ingram, H. J. (2016b). *A linkage-based approach to combating militant Islamist propaganda: A two-tiered framework for practitioners.* The Hague: The International Center for Counter-Terrorism. Retrieved from https://icct.nl/wp-content/uploads/2016/11/ICCT-Ingram-A-Linkage-Based-Approach-Nov2016.pdf

Johnson, B. (2015, November 14). ISIS Is a sick, narcissistic death cult but we will defeat them. *The Daily Mail.* Retrieved from http://www.dailymail.co.uk/news/article-3318892/ISIS-sick-narcissistic-death-cult-defect-writes-Boris-Johnson.html

Kimmage, D. (2008). The al-Qaeda media nexus: The virtual network behind the global message. *RFE/RL.* Retrieved from http://docs.rferl.org/en-US/AQ_Media_Nexus.pdf

Klausen, J. (2015). Tweeting the jihad: Social media networks of Western foreign fighters in Syria and Iraq. *Studies in Conflict and Terrorism, 38*(1), 1–22.

Lia, B. (2015). Understanding jihadi proto-states. *Perspectives on Terrorism, 9*(4), 31–41.

Michaels, J. (2016, April 18). ISIS cash, oil under attack by U.S.-led air campaign. *Airforce Times.* Retrieved from http://www.airforcetimes.com/story/military/2016/04/18/isis-cash-oil-under-attack-us-led-air-campaign/83177114/

Milton, D. (2016). Communication breakdown: Unravelling the Islamic State's media efforts. *Combating Terrorism Center at West Point.* Retrieved from https://www.ctc.usma.edu/v2/wp-content/uploads/2016/10/ISMedia_Online.pdf

Raqqa Is Being Slaughtered Silently. [Raqqa_SL]. (2016, September 22). 3-on Sep 6 2016 "Abu Harith al-Lami" he is responsible for #ISIS propaganda and media in #Syria and #Iraq killed By Drone strike [Tweet]. Retrieved from https://twitter.com/raqqa_sl/status/7790542233130 35265?lang=en

Remnick, D. (2014, January 27). Going the distance. *The New Yorker.* Retrieved from http://www.newyorker.com/magazine/2014/01/27/going-the-distance-david-remnick

Safi, M. (2015, June 11). Tony Abbott opens summit on countering terrorist propaganda. *The Guardian.* Retrieved from https://www.theguardian.com/australia-news/2015/jun/11/sydney-summit-to-share-ideas-on-challenging-terrorist-propaganda

Sheikh, J. (2016). "I just said it. The state": Examining motivations for Danish foreign fighting in Syria. *Perspectives on Terrorism, 10*(6), 59–67.

Turkel, D. (2016). The US military has a new plan to fight ISIS—and it starts with making the group "extremely paranoid." *Business* Insider. Retrieved from http://uk.businessinsider.com/new-us-cyber-war-against-isis-2016-4?r=US&IR=T

Whiteside, C. (2016). *Lighting the path: The evolution of the Islamic State media enterprise (2003-2016).* The Hague: The International Center for Counter-Terrorism. Retrieved from https://icct.nl/publication/lighting-the-path-the-evolution-of-the-islamic-state-media-enterprise-2003-2016/

Winter, C. (2015). Documenting the virtual "caliphate." *The Quilliam Foundation.*

Winter, C. (2016). ISIS's offline propaganda strategy. *The Brookings Institution Markaz.* Retrieved from https://www.brookings.edu/blog/markaz/2016/03/31/isis-offline-propaganda-strategy/

Winter, C. (2017). Media jihad: The Islamic State's doctrine for information warfare. *The International Centre for the Study of Radicalisation.* Retrieved from http://icsr.info/wp-content/uploads/2017/02/Media-jihad_web.pdf

Winter, C., & Clarke, C. P. (2017, January 31). Is ISIS breaking apart? What its media operations suggest. *Foreign Affairs.* Retrieved from https://www.foreignaffairs.com/articles/2017-01-31/isis-breaking-apart

Wright, R. (2016, August 30). Abu Muhammad al-Adnani, the voice of ISIS, is dead. *The New Yorker.* Retrieved from http://www.newyorker.com/news/news-desk/abu-muhammad-al-adnani-the-voice-of-isis-is-dead

Zelin, A. Y. (2015). Picture or it didn't happen: A snapshot of the Islamic State's official media output. *Perspectives on Terrorism, 9*(4), 85–97.

Fun against fear in the Caliphate: Islamic State's spectacle and counter-spectacle

Marwan M. Kraidy

ABSTRACT
This article focuses on non-violent spectacular images produced and circulated by Islamic State (I.S.). These include I.S.'s declaration of the Caliphate, the group's peculiar depiction of the good life, and its presumptive currency, the dinar. I.S.'s spectacle is explored through Situationist theory. Using the case study of the declaration of the Caliphate in June 2014, I explain how I.S. uses spectacle as a technology of rule. Then I move on to what I call the "counter-spectacle," focusing on one case study, a program on Iraqi television al-Iraqiyya, *Dawlat al-Khurafa* (The Apocryphal State), that parodies I.S. as an entity. Probing ontological connections between "fear" and "fun" in the I.S. spectacle, the article concludes with a discussion of the im/possibility of countering spectacle, and the argument that the "success" of I.S.'s global spectacle rests on grafting I.S.'s own concentrated spectacle of rule onto the diffuse spectacle of a global commercial media discourse preoccupied with "Islam" as the main Other to a putative "Western" identity.

The rise of the group that calls itself "the Islamic State" (I.S.) constitutes a major international crisis and one of the most pressing geopolitical challenges to the global state order. I.S.'s media capacities and practices have attracted intense attention from policymakers, think-tank analysts, academics, and the public at large. Breathless public discourse has depicted I.S.'s use of digital media as a reverse image of dissenting digital communication in the Arab Spring: whereas in 2011 "digitally enabled activists" wielded Facebook and Twitter as technologies of emancipation, in 2014 I.S.'s cyber-soldiers deployed them as tools of terror, recruiting European teenage girls via mobile devices and spreading ultra-violence online. At the same time, I.S. online magazines and videos were described as "slick," "sophisticated," and "professional quality" products of an evil, media-savvy enemy.

Though I.S. achieved infamy with videos of beheadings, immolations, and bombings, most I.S. visuals are not videos: of 9,000 official images I.S. released between January 2015 and August 2016, approximately 10% were videos (Milton, 2016, p. 22). The majority of I.S. videos do not depict violence, "civil society" being a dominant theme in addition to "ultraviolence" (Stern & Berger, 2015, p. 72). Elsewhere I have written about I.S.'s deployment of ultra-violent images and videos to propagate fear globally (Kraidy, 2016, 2017a,

2017c), and shown how the early 2000s screed *Edarat al-Tawahhush* (The administration of savagery) (Naji, 2004) was a blueprint for I.S.'s spectacular visual warfare based on what I called the "projectilic image" (Kraidy, 2017c). In this article, I focus on non-violent spectacular images, which include I.S.'s declaration of the Caliphate, the group's peculiar depiction of the good life, and its putative currency, the dinar. I first describe and analyze I.S.'s spectacle via Situationist theory. Using the case study of the declaration of the Caliphate in June 2014, I explain how I.S. uses spectacle as a technology of rule. Then I move on to what I call the "counter-spectacle," focusing on one case study, a program on Iraqi television al-Iraqiyya, *Dawlat al-Khurafa* ("The Mythical State"—or "The Apocryphal State"), that parodies I.S. as an entity—"Dawlat al-Khilafa" means "The Caliphate State"—based on a close reading of the title sequence and early episodes, and an interview with the show's creator and lead screenwriter (T. Swadi, personal communication, June 12 2017). The article concludes with a discussion of the im/possibility of countering spectacle, and the argument that the "success" of I.S.'s global spectacle rests on grafting I.S.'s own *concentrated* spectacle of rule onto the *diffuse* spectacle of a global commercial media discourse preoccupied with "Islam" as the main Other to a putative "Western" identity, fueling xenophobic populism and various anti-Islam political and intellectual entrepreneurs.

The Islamic State spectacle

Guy Debord's (1967) authoritative critique of consumer capitalism is useful to understanding I.S. Debord led the Situationists, a 1950s European artistic–philosophical–political movement, and penned their manifesto, *La société du spectacle* (Debord, 1967). Inspired by Surrealism, Dada, and Lettrism, the Situationists later prioritized politics, participating in the May 1968 Paris protests. Debord (1967) opens his classic book thus: "the entire life of societies where modern conditions of production prevail is turning into an immense accumulation of *spectacles*. All that was directly lived has moved away into a representation" (p. 15). A system of social control under advanced capitalism in which representation dominates social life and images mediate human relations, "spectacle is the affirmation of appearances and the affirmation of all human, meaning social, life, as mere appearance" (Debord, 1967, p. 19).[1]

A Marxist and primarily a social critic rather than a theorist of images, Debord rejected both North Atlantic bourgeois capitalism and Soviet bureaucratic communism. He believed that spectacle dominated all societies—a truly *global* phenomenon. Debord (1967) identified two kinds of spectacle, concentrated and diffuse. In *concentrated* spectacle, commodity production and consumption are less developed than the advanced, media-driven consumerism of the *diffuse* spectacle. Concentrated spectacular societies arise under strong states, often autocracies. Neoliberal democracies spawn diffuse spectacles. Later Debord (1988) argued that between the publication of *La société du spectacle* (1967) and *Commentaires sur la société du spectacle* (1988), " the spectacle … reinforced itself … expanded … increase its density" (p. 15) as its concentrated and diffuse kinds fused in "a third form … the integrated spectacular, which tends to impose itself worldwide" (Debord, 1988, p. 21).

I.S. arose after the 2003 U.S.–U.K. invasion of Iraq and the Syrian Uprising. For decades, dictators ruled Syria and Iraq, instituting personality cults atop police states. Iraq wallowed under a U.S.-led sanctions regime until the ouster of Saddam Hussein, when an anti-occupation insurgency arose and the country descended into sectarian chaos. Bashar al-Assad had since 2000 initiated an oligarchic neoliberal economic order in Syria (Al-Ghazzi, 2013; Wedeen, 2013), disrupted when a 2011 popular uprising morphed into a civil/global proxy war. In Debordian terms, both Iraq and Syria were *concentrated spectacular societies*, "forwarding ideology epitomized by a dictatorial personality" (Debord, 1988, p. 21). This was particularly true in Iraq and Syria, where Baath Party ideology was so "fused with an exalted idealization of the leader" that the leader's personality "cult *replaced* ideology" (Sassoon, 2016, p. 201, emphasis added). Alienated individuals related to leaders—ubiquitously represented as strongmen—as master images at the center of national spectacles, and individuals related to one another through the image of the leader. The spectacle is enforced by coercion: "The dictatorship of the bureaucratic economy," Debord (1967) writes, "is accompanied by permanent violence. The imposed image of the good, in its spectacle, collects the totality of what officially exists, and normally focuses on one man, who is the guarantor of its totalitarian cohesion" (p. 59). Debord adds, "Everyone must magically identify with this absolute star ... the heroic image of an acceptable meaning for the absolute exploitation that primitive accumulation, accelerated by terror, is" (Debord, 1967, p. 59). Born in the wake of Assad's, and particularly Hussein's, police states (see Gerges, 2016, for I.S.'s Baathist genesis), I.S. coupled physical violence as technique of rule with graphic violence as technology of display, showing that, "[w]here the concentrated spectacular rules, so does the police" (Debord, 1967, p. 59).

Indeed, I.S.'s use of media for self-display echoes Neale's (1979) definition of spectacle—grounded in Nazi propaganda—as "a system which is essentially concerned ... to *display* the visibility of the visible" (emphasis in original, p. 66). The official declaration of the Caliphate, an impeccably choreographed event, epitomizes the logic of display at the heart of I.S.'s spectacle. In spring 2014, I.S.'s cybersoldiers flooded social media with propaganda (Atwan, 2015a), "seemingly rising up as a populist mass to tweet, 'We demand Shekh Al Baghdady declare the caliphate'" (Stern & Berger, 2015, p. 69). This systematic campaign was coordinated with I.S.'s military advance on Mosul, which it took in June. On June 29, an audio message by Abu Muhammad al-Adnani, an I.S. commander and spokesperson, announced the birth of "The Islamic State," calling al-Baghdadi "the sheikh, the fighter, the scholar who practices what he preaches, the worshipper, the leader, the warrior, the reviver, descendant from the family of the Prophet, the slave of God" and beseeching Muslims to "gather around your caliph, so that you may return as you once were for ages, kings of the earth and knights of war" (Aljazeera, 2014).

Though I.S. social media warriors built excitement for three months before al-Adnani's statement, his announcement was a preview of the main event. On July 4 2014, a middle-aged man with a black beard, a black robe, and a black turban climbed up the pulpit of the al-Nuri Mosque in Mosul, Iraq's second-largest city, which I.S. had recently conquered. Turning toward male believers, he intoned, "We praise God, and beseech him to aid us and forgive us." The camera zooms out to reveal a large I.S. flag on the wall. In the official I.S. video streamed online the following day, the I.S. leader is sitting, cleaning his teeth with a wooden twig known as a *miswak*, then stands up, speaking through a microphone, and declares the Caliphate. The *miswak*, known to be used by the Prophet Muhammad, underscored the new caliph's legitimacy, bolstering the message sent by al-Baghdadi's black turban, which marked him as a descendent of the Prophet. Indeed, al-Baghadi hails from the Bobadri clan, which include Muhammad's Quraysh tribe, and his full name is Ibrahim Bin Awwad Bin Ibrahim al-Badri *al-Qurayshi* (Atwan, 2015b). Stemming from a family of religious teachers and leaders, he obtained a doctorate from the Islamic University of Baghdad. Al-Baghdadi's religious symbolism emulated that of Assad and Hussein, ostensibly secular dictators: Hafiz al-Assad's cult cast him as "sacred" and "immortal" (Wedeen, 1999) and Hussein's cult emphasized his origins in the Prophet Muhammad's tribe and insisted that "those who swear allegiance to Saddam are swearing allegiance to God" (Woods & Lacey, 2007, quoted in Sassoon, 2016, p. 203). But al-Baghdadi went further: invoking historical, tribal, familial, and religious credentials, al-Baghdadi declared himself Caliph Ibrahim, commanding Muslims worldwide to obey him in the name of God (Atwan, 2015b) (Figure 1).

Al-Baghdadi declared a new, shorter, more ambitious name—*The* Islamic State tout court—as opposed to the geographically bounded Islamic State in Iraq and Syria (I.S.I.S.), asserting the new Caliphate's global ambitions. As usual when I.S. released major news, social media amplified the event with a new #IS hashtag on Twitter, and videos of celebration circulated on Facebook and YouTube (Vick, 2014). Immediately after the announcement, the famous Sykes–Picot—the secret 1916 agreement that carved the Middle East into British and French spheres of influence—video emerged, displaying I.S.'s obliteration of colonial borders (Tran & Weaver, 2014). I.S. also released its first issue of the online English-language magazine *Dabiq* to coincide with the Caliph's speech (Stern & Berger, 2015, p. 119). This was typical I.S. spectacle: a drum roll (a sustained social media campaign) building excitement, followed by a preview (Adnani's audio-recording) of the main affair, before the momentous event itself (the self-unveiling of the Caliph in the Grand Mosque), amplified by a post-event social media offensive (see Kraidy, 2017c). Coordinated military, political, and media campaigns, building a *crescendo* toward the capture of Mosul and reaching their climax with the declaration of the Caliphate, reflect an effective organization with tight command-and-control lines and the ability to execute an integrated and spectacular campaign culminating in a historic state-making claim.

This official, solemn, ceremonial spectacle bespoke power. As a momentous, state-birthing declaration, during an exceedingly rare—and only video—appearance of al-Baghdadi, the speech was spectacular—a "display" of "the visibility of the visible" (Neale, 1979).

Figure 1. Declaration of the Caliphate and unveiling of the Caliph.

It made I.S., for a moment, *hypervisible*. Unlike Bin Laden, whose turbaned head and gangly body were hypervisible on global screens in the decade after the 9/11 attacks (see Donghi, 2014), there are only two or three visual depictions of al-Baghdadi. Known as "the ghost" or the "invisible shaykh," he is so secretive that he conceals his face with a black balaclava when speaking with his commanders (Atwan, 2015b). His magisterial appearance—or *apparition*—at the mosque can be understood as an *object spectacle*, which in a narrative film occurs when the film's central character is introduced to viewers. Object spectacle emerges when spectators are prodded "to look at a particular object as a spectacle *in it-self* ... the focus ... is often the body ... [T]he effect ... is of a direct, exhibitionistic communication with the spectator ... [T]he purpose is to amplify the spectator's emotional response to the object ... " (Lewis, 2014, p. 218). In the I.S. narrative, the revealing of Caliph Ibrahim is an object spectacle that, through the spectacular display of al-Baghdadi's body, establishes connections between ruler and followers, underlying Debord's understanding of spectacle as *social* relations mediated by images. Here, al-Baghdadi breaks with Assad and Hussein: whereas their bodies were ubiquitous in public and media space, his body was visible sparingly. This is likely due to the fact that al-Bahgdadi leads a clandestine existence in a perilous environment, whereas dictators before him were in full control of their realm. But rare appearances that are extremely ritualized and tightly choreographed add to al-Baghdadi's mystique and infuse charisma into the Caliph's fear-dominated relationship with subjects, given that authoritarian cults enact a balance between charisma and fear (Sassoon, 2016).

Online propaganda preceding the announcement performed the role that cueing plays in narrative film: it "helps to reinforce the link between the spectator and the spectacle, essentially bridging the transition from voyeuristic narrative to exhibitionistic spectacle" (Lewis, 2014, p. 219). In the middle of a military blitzkrieg toward Mosul and frantic digital propaganda, al-Baghdadi's speech marked a slowing down of action in order to redirect attention from the heat of the battle to the paramount issue of the Caliphate. Dressed in black against the mosque's off-white, beige, and gray backdrop, al-Baghdadi marked a pause (and a contrast) in a narrative of military conquest dominated by vivid colors of desert, sky and fire. Depicting him from a low angle as a sacred yet human figure, the rise of the Caliph is typical of object spectacle, which "[r]epresents a temporary foregrounding of certain elements of the mise-en-scène through the use of color, camera angles, certain temporal distortions such as the brief slow motion movement, lighting and so on" (Lewis, 2014, p. 220). The Caliph's appearance was the "big reveal," the *major object event* that showcases the role of display as I.S.'s technique of rule, a moment when charisma fused with fear (Figure 2).

The Caliphate's global ambition, implicit in the universal, geographically unmarked new name "The Islamic State," was bolstered by the online release of "I.S.I.S. takeover maps," counterfactual maps showing various European, African, Asian, and even American countries as I.S. provinces (Kraidy, 2017b), underscoring the display logic of I.S.'s spectacle. I.S.'s occupation of vast territory notwithstanding, it is I.S.'s *display* of territorial control—real or suggested—that underscores the group's inflated self-representation. Suggesting that I.S.'s dominion would imminently expand worldwide was essential to the group's global dissemination of fear and anxiety (Kraidy, 2017b). Bolstered by the threat to Sykes–Picot's colonial borders, the unveiling of the Caliph and declaration of the Caliphate bound the Caliph's body to the Caliphate's realm.[2]

Figure 2. "I.S.I.S. takeover map".

The spectacle's logic of display articulates I.S.'s territorial accomplishments and fantasies, its mythical attachments to locales like the town of Dabiq—a bond redolent of what the Algerian Situationist Abdelhafid Khatib called "psychogeography" (Bonnett, 2006)—and the group's warped depiction of history. Debord grasps spectacle as a "paralysis of history and memory;" resurrecting the Caliphate revived memories of Muslim unity under a leader who combined earthly rule as sultan and divine power as caliph—an entity that ceased to exist in the 1920s. At the same time, I.S. defines the centuries between Islam's rise and today as an era of Western domination and local tyranny, all the better to erase that period of history, vindicating Debord's (1967, p. 28) claim that "[T]he first intention of spectacular domination is to make historical knowledge disappear." I.S., then, can be called a "nostalgic caliphate" (Kraidy, 2016). Nostalgia and spectacle have a natural, though fraught, mutual affinity, since spectacle includes what Bonnett (2006, p. 23) called an "unrooted" nostalgia, "a free-floating sense of loss that presents permanent marginality and 'the alienated life' as a political identity."[3] But the Situationists, like most Marxists, were hostile to nostalgia, considering it past-bound sentimentality that stood in the way of future-oriented change through revolution.

Here Debord (1967, p. 24) brings an interesting perspective on a vexing issue—the extent to which I.S. is indeed Islamic, when, after opining that "philosophy ... never succeeded by itself in exceeding theology," he argues that spectacle is "the material reconstruction of the religious illusion." Debord's (1967, p. 24) next sentence seems tailor-written for I.S.: "the spectacular technique," he writes, "did not dissipate the religious clouds where men had placed their own powers detached from themselves." Rather, "it merely linked them to a terrestrial basis ... it no longer rejects life into the heavens, but harbors its absolute denial, in the shape of a fallacious paradise." I.S. is in effect a physical base for extremist religious interpretations, a material manifestation of the religious illusion, marketed—fallaciously—as a paradise for potential recruits and denizens.

To lure sympathizers to its territory, I.S. deployed techniques honed by local concentrated spectacular regimes. In Syria, Bashar al-Assad's regime deployed "an ideology of 'the good life'—in this case, combining economic liberalization with fears of sectarian disorder and 'nonsovereignty'—operated to organize desire and quell dissent" (Wedeen, 2013, pp. 842–843). In Iraq, Hussein "believed that the people … 'have been searching over eight hundred years' for a ruler like him *who would lead them into a good life*" (Sassoon, 2016, pp. 202–203, emphasis added). In contrast, I.S.'s version of the ideology of the good life at targeted at outsiders I.S. was trying to recruit, and thrived on sectarian sentiment. Defined in terms of a socio-religious utopia, it articulated claims of a pure, authentic, and truly Islamic society unburdened by Western influence and local subversion, with images of the good life—premised on a puritanical vision of Sunni Islam—showcasing spectacular sunsets and Ferris wheels and showing contented-looking people—mostly men—shopping in markets, fishing in rivers, praying piously, conversing amicably. Indeed, a majority of official I.S. visual media releases focus on non-violent aspects of life in the Caliphate. For example, of the 9,000 official images I.S. released in 2015 and 2016, less than half (48%) have a military theme, and others depict governance, commercial, religious, lifestyle, and other themes (Milton, 2016, pp. 23–29) of daily life.

The vaunted I.S. currency, the dinar, is exemplary of *secondary* display as technique of rule, its announcement being *a minor* object event among others. I.S. rolled out the currency—on August 29, 2015 in a 55-minute online video, *The rise of Khilafah: return of the gold dinar*, advertised in early September 2015 in *Dabiq*, issue 11, with the hashtag #return_of_the_gold_dinar in Arabic and English, and then in a five minute video in early October—not only as an insignia of sovereignty but also as an instrument of economic war against the United States (*The Economist*, 2015). Inspired by a seventeenth-century Ottoman caliphal currency, I.S.'s dinar is minted from 24-karat gold and may be worth U.S.$139 apiece (Moyer, 2015). It depicts a world map with seven wheat stalks that may reference a verse from the Koran: "Those who spend their money in the name of Allah are like a seed that has yielded seven wheat stalks, in each stalk there are a hundred seeds, and Allah multiplies … for whoever He wishes" (Bulos, 2014). Much publicized online, the currency did not enter wide economic circulation. Rather, it uncannily echoes Debord's (1967, p. 45) own claim that "[t]he spectacle is money one can *only look at.*" I.S.'s currency is an archetypal spectacular image: "an 'abstract representation' of the totality of the commodity world, a world where exchange-value has increasingly come to dominate use-value;" it operates as "a general equivalent of commodities," notionally representing "a world colonized by alienated goods and roles." Indeed, "spectacular images act like money—as a general equivalent" (Eagles, 2012, pp. 183–184). I.S.'s dinar's raison d'être, then, is not its economic usefulness; it is rather what Mulvey (2004, p. 841) described, in her analysis of narrative pleasure in film, as "to-be-looked-at-ness." Minted in gold, including symbolic graphics, and unveiled in a "documentary video" as a financial weapon against the U.S. dollar, the dinar's *display* matters more than its *use* (Figure 3).

Understanding I.S.'s spectacle of state-building goes beyond re-grafting religion in Iraqi and Syrian territory or displaying a currency to explain the lure of the Caliphate. For this we have to go to the Belgian Raoul Vaneigem, whose *Traité de savoir-vivre à l'usage des jeunes générations* (1967/1994) was another influential Situationist text. Whereas Debord focused on the macro-aspects of spectacle, Vaneigem emphasized individual creativity, love, and

Figure 3. The dinar: currency of the Caliphate.

ways for individuals to achieve self-fulfillment in spectacular society, processes in which pleasure plays a central role, since "the pleasure principle is the lifeblood of every attempt to realise oneself, to communicate, to participate" (Vaneigem, 1994, p. 252).[4]

Once compelled to perform *hijra* (migration) and move to I.S. land, migrants "confirm" their entry to the spectacle by embracing the Caliph as a master spectacular image that mediates their social relationships with other subjects, unifying Muslims in the name of God.[5] After having acted on their desire for that image, these migrants confront major changes. Like participants in the spectacle, they "cannot be entirely reduced to the idiotic machine," so they are "rechanneled, dispersed and squandered in roles" (Vaneigem, 1994, p. 133). In his July 4, 2014 speech, al-Baghdadi called on engineers, medical doctors, and judges to join I.S., though roles shift. Once in I.S., a Tunisian professor may play a leadership role in I.S. communication, an Egyptian dentist may become a military commander, an Iraqi farmhand a suicide bomber. But these roles often prove unsatisfactory, because spectacle offers only an "illusory unity" (Eagles, p. 182). We can understand why, for a number of immigrants, the experience of life under I.S. disappoints. This is bound to happen, since the spectacle offers goods and roles by way of manipulating individuals; relations with contrived images that attract—or distract—attention. As King (2000, p. 4) puts it, spectacle is "the production of images at which we might wish to stop and stare." Once people go beyond stopping and staring, and go on to *living* in the concentrated spectacle, the inconsistencies between their desire for images and their lived experience make disillusionment inevitable.

The counter-spectacle

Against I.S.'s spectacle, Arab cultural producers, artists, and bloggers mounted a series of anti-I.S. performances that together can be described as a counter-spectacle. Various artist-activist collectives challenged I.S.'s imagery with posters, videos, and jokes while Aliaa al-Mahdy, the "naked blogger" of Cairo, staged a body performance of herself menstruating, and a colleague defecating, on I.S.'s banner (Kraidy, 2016). On Egyptian, Iraqi, Kurdish, Lebanese, and Palestinian television, comedians skewered I.S., circulating images debasing I.S.'s grandiosity into various types of grotesque. Here I focus on one case study, the Iraqi television satire *Dawlat al-Khurafa*, a weekly program dedicated to exposing I.S.'s holy pretenses and its obsession with the trappings of earthly power: oil, money, weapons, territory, women—longstanding spoils of men's wars.

Dawlat al-Khurafa

The title sequence (recurring opening scene) of *Dawlat al-Khurafa*, a satirical show on state-owned al-Iraqiyya TV (Kraidy & Khalil, 2009), counters the spectacle of the June 2014 declaration of the Caliphate. The show is set up like a musical, in a fictional Iraqi town taken over by I.S., recalling the Lebanese musical theater of the Rahbani brothers, where opening scenes typically show a diverse cast of characters who circulate and meet in a central square surrounded by shops and a coffeehouse. A singer in a colorful shirt and rimmed hat arrives on a motor-tricycle, gets off, and starts dancing, wielding a golf club, a cipher of the bourgeois good life, representing the "American cowboy" invader of Iraq (T. Swadi, personal communication, June 12 2017) (Figure 4).

In the coffeehouse, town-dwellers play backgammon, drink tea, smoke shisha and cigarettes; women and men walk around the central square, running errands. In its editing, the sketch evokes popular pan-Arab music videos, some of which have grappled with Iraqi politics (Kraidy, 2013). Less than one minute later (at 00:56), the devil (*ibliss*) appears in red leotard and black horns, brandishing a pitchfork and surrounded by a cast of characters straight out of Michael Jackson's *Thriller* video. The devil's entourage include Stalin, Count Dracula, and The Joker lookalikes, a "woman with the Mossad logo," and a woman resembling Shaykha Moza, Qatar's erstwhile first lady, casting I.S. as an international conspiracy (T. Swadi, personal communication, June 12 2017). We see a medieval torture chamber, with dangling chains, swords dripping with blood, then a bird's nest with an egg. The egg hatches and out comes the self-proclaimed Caliph, chick-sized and arms flung up, before morphing into an adult lifting dumbbells made out of human skulls. Sitting with advisors in the torture chamber, the Caliph contemplates cardboard panels that say "Booby Trapping," "Sectarianism," "Forced Migration." At that moment, with al-Baghdadi himself playing conductor, waving whips through the air, hirsute I.S. militants in *shalwar kameez* (connoting Afghan *mujahedeen*), others in olive fatigues (symbolizing the Baath party) clutching machine guns and sitting on a stage with purple velvet drapes,

Figure 4. *Dawlat al-Khurafa* screen grab.

intone a song proclaiming pornography prohibited, except *jihad al-nikah* (commonly translated "intercourse jihad;" *nikah* technically means "matrimony"), calling on the "head chopper" to enforce the rules: "We banned cigarette smoking, we forced all Christian to flee," the song continues (it rhymes in Arabic). Three minutes in, al-Baghdadi brandishes two handguns and shoots all his men, then—the scene's apotheosis—blows himself up—but only after the foreign characters exit the stage, underscoring that Iraqis are I.S.'s main victims (T. Swadi, personal communication, June 12 2017)—creating a huge orange flame as a backdrop to the title, *Dawlat al-Khurafa.*

The first scene in the second episode shows the Caliph sitting on a throne with over-the-top golden decorations and mauve upholstery, listening to a media advisor recommending that I.S. launch a satellite TV channel, in order to "influence the larger possible number of people" and control public opinion.

"Tell me, what should we call the channel?" the Caliph inquires

"Blood TV, sir," his advisor answers.

Then we see a group of clean-shaven men chatting in the coffeehouse, discussing what I.S. rule has banned (smoking) and what it has mandated (beards), worrying about what the new regime means to their lives. A scene inside a house between an elderly man and a cleric shows the latter trying to calm the former down, about "these [I.S.] monsters."

Five minutes later, a fake newscast featuring planetary maps shows I.S. as a global death cult. As the graphics roll, a river of red blood floods one city after another on a map of Iraq featured on the screen, and skulls proliferate. A logo composed of a skull dripping with blood appears on the globe. After this the broadcast shifts to the coffeehouse, where lights are dimmed and everybody looks at the television set hanging high, about to feature a program from I.S.'s new channel. A program called *Dam Be She* appears (*dam* is Arabic for "blood;" *be she* spoofs the English letters "B" and "C," "B" for "broadcasting," "C" for "corporation," the *sh* phonetically evoking Dae*sh*, the derogatory nickname Arabs use for I.S. (during the Arab satellite revolution, television channel names shifted from full names or French acronyms to American-style, three-letter acronyms, like L.B.C. and M.B.C.; see Kraidy, 2010).

This marks the beginning of the day's "Bulletin of Destructions," which features a female anchor covered completely by a white bedsheet. Sitting with a male anchor behind a desk and under three large white skulls and streaks of red blood on the wall behind them, she nearly suffocates as her male partner declaims the self-incriminating news that "[T]he valiant *mujahideen* of Islamic State destroyed 200 mosques, killed 300 worshippers in their successful war on idols." The satire then shifts to a "clean energy car bomb" story, reflecting "the Caliph's insistence on the preservation of the beauty of nature." The story features an I.S. "engineer," outraged that the "brother suicide bombers" were "using cars that produce carbon dioxide," a gas that is "harmful to health." He continues, "What will I say to God when he asks, 'Why are you polluting'?" he asks, deadpan. To solve the problem, the engineer produces "a booby-trapped solar energy car," which he pledges to "export to every apostate nation," then promises, "If you buy two car bombs, you get one delivered to you for free." This sketch reflects parody's typical reliance on excess and incongruity.

A commercial break features ads exhorting viewers to "blow yourself up and win," promising "a virgin with every blast," "a pile of sheets for every suicide belt," and "if

ISIS BEYOND THE SPECTACLE

you blow up a school full of children, you get one hundred virgins," and other tragic-far-cical offers. Then "breaking news" announces a press conference from the "Palace of the Caliphate." We move to the Caliph's press conference. A foreign female correspondent, wearing a black *abaya* (robe) but with her head uncovered, asks the Caliph, "Did you slaughter a sheep in my honor?"

Al-Baghdadi, sitting on his mauve and gold throne, answers, "A sheep? I slaughtered 300 men in your honor." He continues,

> I propose, dear sister, that you add to the agenda of the Heretic Nations [*al-umam al-mul-tahida*; this is Arabic wordplay on "United Nations": *multahida*, "heretic," from the verb *lahada*, or "deviate," "abandon one's faith," is phonetically close to *muttahida*, "united".] the passing of an international law allowing *jihad al-nikah*. We tried and achieved beautiful results, so it must go global!

The journalist inquires, "What is *jihad al-nikah*?"

Al-Baghdadi casually explains, as his advisors laugh out loud, "You offer your body and marry 20 Islamic State fighters, for the sake of announcing the word of Right!"

To which the correspondent retorts, "Wow, nice! I see, so you have started a porno-graphic movie production company?"

Al-Baghdadi responds, "No, all I wish for you is that you rest in our home, and then we can continue our dialogue."

The title *Dawlat al-Khurafa* undercuts the Caliphate's claims of legitimacy by under-scoring its apocryphal nature. Its title sequence establishes I.S. as a bloody, murderous, immoral death cult, blowing up mosques, killing children, enslaving women under false pretenses masquerading as religious principles, focused on keeping I.S. in power at any human, ethical, or moral cost. The recurrent use of blood and eggs as symbols of life and fertility, repeated hints at sexuality, the sheer incongruity of some sketches (a green car-bomb?!), and the systematic mockery of I.S.'s grandiose plans to rule the world are typical satirical tropes. The show follows Hariman's (2008) four-stage parodic process: (1) doubling, (2) carnivalesque spectatorship, (3) leveling, and (4) enabling a polyvocal public discourse. The title sequence, announcing the arrival of I.S. and the unveiling of the Caliph, is a tit-for-tat recreation of al-Baghdadi's July 4 speech—a *doubling*. The parody creates a copy (the show's title sequence) of the original (al-Baghdadi's speech). This creates a gap between copy and original, opening the original for *carnivalesque spec-tatorship*, which turns the serious humorous, the sacred profane, the heroic prosaic, for carnival "celebrates temporary liberation from the prevailing truth ... marks the suspen-sion of all hierarchical rank, privileges, norms and prohibitions ... [was] the true feast of time, the feast of becoming, change and renewal ... hostile to all that was immortalized and complete" (Bakhtin, 2009, p. 109).

In effect, the parody pulls the self-proclaimed Caliph down from his pedestal and, through animal symbolism (the hatching egg), turns him into something grotesque (and his monumental status into a miniature curiosity), in this case the offspring of a witch and a demon; this is *leveling*. This exposes the Caliph to public mockery, his author-itative monologue broken to pieces and open to popular ridicule, enabling a *polyvocal discourse* about the group. Every week, after the title sequence, actors in *Dawlat al-Khurafa* proceed to skewer I.S., its atrocities, and its pretensions, mounting a counter-spectacle.

Fun against fear?

In sum, *Dawlat al-Khurafa* turns *fear* of I.S. into *fun* at I.S.'s expense. As Bayat (2007, p. 434) defines it, "fun" is "an array of ad hoc, nonroutine, and joyful conducts … games, joking, dancing, … social drinking … playful art, music, sex, and sport," entailing "particular ways of speaking, laughing, appearing, or carrying oneself—where individuals break free temporarily from the disciplined constraints of everyday life, normative obligations, and organized power." In other words, fun is "a metaphor … of individuality, spontaneity, and lightness, in which joy is a central element" and entails "unpredictable expressions and practices." Fun has always and everywhere been subject to regulation. From a Situationist perspective, this is particularly true in autocratic societies dominated by concentrated spectacle. Bayat (2007) mentions the Islamic Republic of Iran, Saudi Arabia, and Afghanistan under the Taliban as polities that enact extensive controls over people's behavior and desires. I.S.'s more extreme governance illustrates how, when "moral authority is merged with a state whose legitimizing ideology is too exclusive," coercion ensues (Bayat, 2007, p. 458).

Indeed, such political regimes:

> reproduce themselves, in part, by publicizing various threats to the individual (especially via images). The feeling of fear that *these threats (whether supposed or real) generate within the individual is then soothed as each* regime also purports to offer each individual protection. (Eagles, 2012, p. 187, emphasis in original)

As I have argued elsewhere (Kraidy, 2010), religious fundamentalists see believers primarily as potential sinners, and act to preempt opportunities for the occurrence of sin. I.S. epitomizes an extreme anti-fun paradigm. Its puritanical moral code, which focuses on controlling the body through dictating styles of clothing and grooming, and banning alcohol, tobacco, and music, extends to its techniques of display. In I.S. propaganda videos, laughter is banned, and "[V]ideographers were explicitly instructed … to avoid filming people who seemed to be joking around because then the group might be seen as wasting the money of the people" (Milton, 2016, p. 2). "Fun," Bayat (2007, p. 455) writes, "presupposes a powerful paradigm, a set of presumptions about self, society, and life" that subverts the ruling ideology when its rigidity rejects fun , generating "fury among the Islamist moral–political authority." Fun entails "letting go," allowing the body to temporarily lose control over itself so one can laugh, dance, etc. Letting the body exit prevailing social norms and rules conjures up the possibility of the collapse of the socio-political order. Just as Saudi leaders glimpsed in the wave of Arab reality television programs in the 2000s socio-cultural rituals of identity and community that rivaled their own clerico-political rituals of power (Kraidy, 2010), so do I.S. leaders perceive fun to be a threat. Indeed, there is evidence that I.S. militants watched the show and responded to it, discussing it online and reshooting the "Cutter of Heads" sequence into an anti-Shii parody of *Dawlat al-Khurafa* (T. Swadi, personal communication, June 12 2017).

Dawlat al-Khurafa's parodic doubling of "Dawlat al-Khilafa" enacts a passage from what Mulkay (1988) calls the "serious mode," a solemn and one-voiced discourse asserting the Caliphate is a reality, to the "humorous mode," a polyvocal and contentious rhetoric exposing the Caliphate as a myth (see Table 1). In the serious mode, which reflects I.S. official discourse, society speaks (or pretends to speak) with one voice, reality is

Table 1. Fear versus fun, the spectacle and its double.

"Dawlat al-Khilafa" (Islamic State)	*Dawlat al-Khurafa* (television parody)
Original/serious mode	Copy/humorous mode
The Caliphate is a reality	The Caliphate is a myth
Monovocal/ceremonial	Polyvocal/contentious
Hierarchical	Flat
Monumentalization	Miniaturization
Binary black and white	Polychromatic
Ritualistic/fastidious	Orgiastic/laid-back
Puritanical/sacred/sanitary	Prurient/profane/somatic
Fear	Fun

indubitable, and contradictions are not tolerated (Mulkay, 1988). In contrast, *Dawlat al-Khurafa* is a conveyor of the humorous mode, where reality and unreality are blurred, and polyvocality and disagreements are celebrated. The satire flattens I.S.'s hierarchical structure, and, in the miniscule Caliph hatched in an egg, at once miniaturizes the monumental status of the Caliph and redefines him from sacred to animalistic. In the obsessive fastidiousness skewered in *Dawlat al-Khurafa*, one glimpses I.S.'s rigid micro-rituals of power, and in the show's orgiastic atmosphere one sees a fun antidote to I.S.'s culture of fear. Satire pits a prurient, profane, and somatic experience against I.S.'s puritanical enforcement of what it considers sacred. The first is premised on bodily license, the second on corporal coercion. The journey from "Dawlat al-Khilafa" to *Dawlat al-Khurafa* is a journey from fear to fun.

Is resistance futile? Or is it possible to have a counter-spectacle?

This article has dissected non-violent components of I.S.'s spectacle and analyzed the counter-spectacle embodied in an Iraqi television program dedicated to satirizing I.S. and its totalitarian politico-religious discourse. I.S.'s spectacle advances a vision of globalization as homogenization of the world in the image of I.S.—a wet dream of doctrinal purity and cultural uniformity. Indeed, spectacle for Debord (1967) is "the opposite of dialogue" (p. 23), the "uninterrupted discourse that the prevailing order holds about itself, its laudatory monologue ... the self-portrait of power in the era of its totalitarian administration of the conditions of existence" (p. 26). I.S. weaves a self-righteous, virulent, exclusionary narrative of itself, tolerating no dialogue, brooking no compromise. Finally, I.S.'s planetary ambitions and self-spun heroics resonate with Debord's claim that spectacle "covers the whole surface of the world and basks indefinitely in its own glory" (p. 21). In I.S.'s logic of spectacular display, viral self-depictions as a world-dominant power are more relevant than actual world domination. Resonating in an Arab social environment where political humor has deep roots (Fahmy, 2011; Kraidy, 2016), the counter-spectacle fragments the illusory unity of I.S. discourse into symbolic satirical smithereens.

There is an ironic affinity between Situationism and the world according to I.S. When Debord claimed that the Situationist International was "the most dangerous subversion there ever was," he could have been describing I.S. (Debord, 1989, p. 175). Counter-spectacle aims to disrupt I.S.'s spectacle and unsettle the group's narrative through spectacular subversion. The Situationists, after all, developed the notion of *détournement*, or diversion, to describe tactics of subversive disruption and redirection. They were "adopters of intoxication, subterranean agitators, revolutionaries, theorists of insurrection ... diverters of images" (Bourseiller & Raynal, 2017, p. 5). As a subversion of a subversion, however, the counter-spectacle risks harking back to its target—the counter-spectacle is in constant danger of cooptation by the spectacle. Debord (1967) argued compellingly that spectacle was "fundamentally tautological," "its means are its ends." If spectacle is tautological, is a counter-spectacle anything other than a new cycle of spectacle? Answering that question fully risks fueling the spectacle, but grappling with this issue sheds light on the relation between fear and fun in the I.S. spectacle and counter-spectacle.

The challenge of understanding the I.S. spectacle is that the fear it peddles is porous to fun. In the group's self-display, fear and fun engage in sporadic entanglement and inter-mittent osmosis. Hirsute I.S. militant posing on Instagram with kitten, bemoaning the dearth of candy, or enjoying poetry recitations points to a lighter side of Caliphate life. For some potential male recruits, stories of sex slaves, Captagon use, and the ability to play with guns and inflict violence are *fun* aspects of joining I.S. After all, asking potential recruits to join I.S. is akin to an invitation to what the Situationists called *dérive*, or "drift," the act of letting oneself move into a new space. Fun, then, is an ingredient of I.S.'s creation and circulation of fear. Debord (1967, p. 19) follows his definition of spectacle as "the affirmation of appearances and the affirmation of all human, meaning social, life, as mere appearance," "[B]ut critique that reaches the truth of the spectacle unveils it as a visible *negation* of life; as a negation of life, that *has become visible*." The I.S. spectacle, then, is a bizarre mix of Debord's macro-vision of spectacle and Vaneigem's focus on indi-vidual pleasure and drive. By displaying likely suicide bombers and martyrs to the cause as emblems of normalcy, caressing kitties, eating Skittles, etc., I.S. makes death—the ultimate negation of life—look fun. If fear is central to the kind of concentrated spectacle I.S. projects from Syria and Iraq, a notion of fun is at the heart of the worldwide diffuse spectacle that I.S. harnesses.

Ultimately, I.S.'s success in portraying itself as universal public enemy rests largely on its ability to exploit the global commercial media architecture (Kraidy, 2017c, 2017d), a system that thrives on what Giroux (2014) calls "the grotesque production of moral panics in their appeal to fear, insecurity and imminent danger." I.S. achieves an integrated spectacle by grafting its concentrated spectacle, its technology of rule, onto the planetary diffuse spectacle of cable news histrionics and the instant circulation of stories via social media. I.S. not only thrives on kneejerk "mainstream" media coverage of its atrocities, but deftly tailors its releases to the news cycle, diverts attention by hijacking hashtags of global events like the Olympics, or implants apps that turn sympathizers' smartphones into prolific pro-I.S. bots, in order to insert its non-violent spectacle of the good life into global media obsession over I.S. violence. In addition, the near absence of indepen-dent journalists in I.S. territory means "the media is more reliant on material produced" by I.S., leading mainstream outlets to "unwittingly … serve Islamic State's objectives" (Williams, 2016). The use of Hollywood-style special effects and a videogame aesthetic helps I.S. videos and images circulate widely, including on news media (Dauber & Robin-son, 2015; Kraidy, 2017c; Lesaca, 2015; Samir, 2016). As such, the I.S. spectacle is equally a symptom of the crisis of Arab politics or of the "Islamic world" as it is a symptom of the workings of Western neoliberal democracy (on spectacle, democracy, and war, see Giroux, 2006, 2014; Kellner, 2005). Giroux (2014) noted the irony residing in the fact that "the vocabulary of moral absolutes pitting good against evil" used by I.S. "is a binary discourse that mirrors a similar vocabulary used in the interest of the national-security surveillance state and the corporate sponsored war machines of battle-ready domestic and global forces of repression" (2014).

The I.S. spectacle is planetary, consisting of images expertly crafted for global circulation. This spectacle is not violent wholesale, and the Situationists provide us with an analytical toolkit for understanding less gory components of the I.S. spectacle, which echoes Debord's remark that, "[w]hen the spectacular was concentrated, the largest part of the society around it escaped it; when it was diffuse, a small part; today nothing. The spectacle has mixed with all reality, by irradiating it" (Debord, 1988, p. 23). The I.S. spectacle is part and parcel of a larger extravaganza undergirding neoliberal democracies, where fear and fun, violence and safety, truth and falsity, mix with abandon. In this expansion of unreality lies one of our era's most fundamental challenges, the blurring of the boundary between the real and the unreal on a global scale, which I.S. understood how to exploit long before the advent of the notion of "fake news."

Notes

1. All translations from French (Debord, 1967, 1988) are mine.
2. In addition, display as trickery was also important in the group's warfare, as in its design, construction, and deployment of decoy plywood tanks to attract Western aerial bombing, or its fastidious filming and dissemination of ostentatiously iconoclastic videos showing graphic destruction of ancient monuments.
3. This resonates with Svetlana's Boym's (2001) "reflective nostalgia," as opposed to "restorative nostalgia."
4. Vaneigem called self-realization, communication, and participation "the unitary triad" (1994, p. 236). Clearly, he was more optimistic than Debord about our ability to resist spectacle.
5. This can be understood as an invitation to what the Situationists called *dérive*, or "drift," an intentional digression into a new space.

Funding

I am grateful to the Carnegie Corporation of New York for awarding me an Andrew Carnegie Fellowship for the project from which this manuscript is drawn, and to members of my JINCS (JIhadi Networks of Culture and Communications) research group at the Center for Advanced Research in Global Communication (CARGC) at the Annenberg School for Communication at the University of Pennsylvania, particularly Revati Prasad Mohammed Salih and Marina Krikorian, for feedback.

References

Al-Ghazzi, O. (2013). Nation as neighborhood: How Bab al-Hara dramatized Syrian identity. *Media, Culture & Society, 35*(5), 586–601.

Atwan, A. B. (2015a). *Islamic state: The digital caliphate*. London: Saqi Books.

Atwan, A. B. (2015b). A portrait of caliph ibrahim. *The Cairo Review of Global Affairs, 19*, 67–75.

Bakhtin, M. (2009). *Rabelais and his world*. Trans. H. Iswolsky. Bloomington, IN: Indiana University Press.

Bayat, A. (2007). Islamism and the politics of fun. *Public Culture, 19*(3), 433–459.

Bonnett, A. (2006). The nostalgias of situationist subversion. *Theory, Culture and Society, 23*(5), 23–48.

Bourseiller, C., & Raynal, J. (2017). *Les situationnistes: La révolution de la vie quotidienne (1957–1972)*. Bruxelles: Le Lombard.

Boym, S. (2001). *The future of nostalgia*. New York, NY: Basic Books.

Bulos, N. (2014, November 13). Islamic State wants to create its own currency. *Los Angeles Times*. Retrieved from http://www.latimes.com/world/middleeast/la-fg-islamic-state-currency-2014111 3-story.html

Dauber, C. E., & Robinson, M. (2015, July 6). ISIS and the Hollywood visual style [Blogpost]. Jihadology. Retrieved from http://jihadology.net/2015/07/06/guest-post-isis-and-the-hollywood-visual-style/

Debord, G. (1967). *La société du spectacle*. Paris: Gallimard.

Debord, G. (1988). *Commentaires sur la société du spectacle*. Paris: Gallimard.

Debord, G. (1989). On wild architecture. In E. Sussmann (Ed.), T. Levin (Trans.) *On the passage of a few people through a rather brief moment of time: The situationist international 1957–1972* (pp. 174–175). Cambridge, MA: MIT Press.

Donghi, L. (2014). Replacing bodies with pictures: Al-Qaeda's visual strategies of self-configuration. *Diffractions, 3* (Fall). Retrieved from http://www.diffractions.net

Eagles, J. (2012). The spectacle and détournement: The situationists' critique of modern capitalist society. *Critique: Journal of Socialist Theory, 40*(2), 179–198.

Fahmy, Z. (2011). *Ordinary Egyptians: Creating the modern nation through popular culture*. Palo Alto, CA: Stanford University Press.

Gerges, F. (2016). *ISIS: A history*. Princeton, NJ: Princeton University Press.

Giroux, H. A. (2006). *Beyond the spectacle of terror: Global uncertainty and the challenge of the new media*. New York, NY: Routledge.

Giroux, H. A. (2014, September 30). ISIS and the spectacle of terrorism: Resisting mainstream workstations of fear. *TruthOut.org*.

Hariman, R. (2008). Political parody and public culture. *Quarterly Journal of Speech, 94*(3), 247–272.

Kellner, D. (2005). *Media spectacle and the crisis of democracy: Terrorism, war and election battles*. Boulder, CO: Paradigm Publishers.

King, G. (2000). *Spectacular narratives: Hollywood in the age of the blockbuster*. London: Tauris.

Kraidy, M. M. (2010). *Reality television and arab politics: Contention in public life*. New York, NY: Cambridge University Press.

Kraidy, M. M. (2013). Contention and circulation in the digital Middle East: Music video as catalyst. *Television and New Media, 14*(4), 271–285.

Kraidy, M. M. (2016). *The naked blogger of Cairo: Creative insurgency in the arab world*. Cambridge, MA: Harvard University Press.

Kraidy, M. M. (2017a). This is why the islamic state shocks the world with its graphically violent imagery. *The Monkey Cage*, Retrieved from https://www.washingtonpost.com/news/monkey-cage/wp/2017/02/09/this-is-why-the-islamic-state-shocks-the-world-with-its-graphically-violent-imagery/?postshare=8391486648976374&tid=ss_tw&utm_term=.28f001bb6c8d, February 9

Kraidy, M. M. (2017b). Rethinking Media events: Terror, territoriality, temporality. *Television and New Media, 18*(6), first published online March 23, 2017. doi:10.1177/1527476417697197

Kraidy, M. M. (2017c). The projectilic image: Islamic state's digital visual warfare and global net-worked affect. *Media, Culture & Society, 39*(8), 1194–1209. first published online September 4, 2017. doi:10.1177/0163443717725575

Kraidy, M. M. (2017d). Revisiting hypermedia space in the era of islamic state. *The Communication Review, 20*(3), 165–171.

Kraidy, M. M., & Khalil, J. F. (2009). *Arab television industries*. London: British Film Institute/ Palgrave Macmillan.

Lesaca, J. (2015, September 24). On social media, ISIS uses modern cultural images to spread anti-modern values [Blogpost]. *Tech Tank*. Retrieved from https://www.brookings.edu/blog/te chtank/2015/09/24/on-social-media-isis-uses-modern-cultural-images-to-spread-anti-modern-values/

Lewis, S. (2014). What is spectacle? *Journal of Popular Film and Television, 42*(2), 214–221.

Milton, D. (2016). *Communication breakdown: Unraveling the islamic state's media efforts*. New York, NY: Combating Terrorism Center.

Moyer, J. W. (2015, June 24). A first look at alleged Islamic State currency. *Washington Post*. Retrieved from https://www.washingtonpost.com/news/morning-mix/wp/2015/06/24/a-first-look-at-alleged-islamic-state-currency/?utm_term=.2aef84a5f64d

Mulkay, M. (1988). *On humor: Its nature and its place in modern society*. Oxford, UK: Basic Blackwell Inc.

Mulvey, L. (2004). Visual pleasure and narrative cinema. In L. Braudy & M. Cohen (Eds.), *Film theory and criticism: Introductory readings* (6th ed., pp. 837–848). Oxford, UK: Oxford University Press.

Naji, A. B. (2004). *Idarat at-Tawahhush* [Will McCants, Trans. *The management of savagery* (2006)].

Neale, S. (1979). Triumph of the will: Notes on documentary and spectacle. *Screen, 20*(1), 63–86.

Samir, A. (2016, January 16). Daesh propaganda campaigns inspired by Hollywood. *Assafir* [Arabic]. Retrieved from http://www.assafir.com.lb

Sassoon, J. (2016). *Anatomy of authoritarianism in the arab republics*. Cambridge, UK: Cambridge University Press.

Stern, J., & Berger, J. M. (2015). *ISIS: The state of terror*. New York, NY: Harper Collins.

Sunni rebels declare new "Islamic caliphate,". (2014, June 30). *Aljazeera*. Retrieved from http://www.aljazeera.com/news/middleeast/2014/06/isil-declares-new-islamic-caliphate-20146291732 6669749.html

Tran, M., & Weaver, M. (2014, June 30). Isis announces Islamic caliphate in area straddling Iraq and Syria. *The Guardian*. Retrieved from https://www.theguardian.com/world/2014/jun/30/ isis-announces-islamic-caliphate-iraq-syria

Vaneigem, R. (1967/1994). *Traité de savoir-vivre à l'usage des jeunes générations*. Paris: Gallimard. Trans. by D. *Nicholson-Smith as Revolution in Everyday Life*. London: Rebel Press.

Vick, K. (2014, June 29). ISIS militants declare Islamist "Caliphate." *Time*. Retrieved from http:// time.com/2938317/isis-militants-declare-islamist-caliphate/

Wedeen, L. (1999). *Ambiguities of domination: Politics, rhetoric and symbols in contemporary Syria*. Chicago, IL: University of Chicago Press.

Wedeen, L. (2013). Ideology and humor in dark times: Notes from Syria. *Critical Inquiry, 39*(4), 841–873.

Williams, L. (2016, February). *Islamic state propaganda and the mainstream media*. Sydney: Lowy Institute for International Policy.

Woods, K, M., & Lacey, J. (2007). *Iraqi perspectives project: Saddam, and terrorism, emerging insights from captured Iraqi documents* (Vol. 5). Alexandria, VA: Institute for Defense Analysis.

The viral mediation of terror: ISIS, image, implosion

Ryan E. Artrip and François Debrix

ABSTRACT

Operations involving the capture, processing, and transmission of terrorist events, campaigns, or images produce effects well beyond the representational/informational functions of media. This article examines several unspoken effects involved in the mediation of terrorism. We analyze the extent to which several mechanisms and operations of western media may be complicit in, if not fundamental to, the global production and administration of terror, particularly at the level of its image and what we call virality. We theorize the ways in which media not only "mediate" terror, but also function to regulate and/or administer it and, in particular, to exacerbate, amplify, and proliferate images and activities of Islamic State in Iraq and Syria (ISIS) across global networks of digital exchange. We argue that key to understanding the strategies and circulating effects of ISIS's media involvement is the tendency of viral media operations to overproduce, overextend, and oversaturate. The condition of oversaturation denotes a hyperactive global media circuitry that is collapsing under its own weight. This condition reflects a strategic tendency of terror, which underlies all mediatic processing of images deployed by ISIS. It also reveals a vulnerability for terrorist strategy to exacerbate and exhaust the hyperactivity of media, and thus to accelerate the implosive collapse of the globally networked system. We theorize how implicit and unintended effects or outputs of the mediatic processing of terrorist meanings, images, and discourses may work to overstimulate the global system to the point of its reversal, exhaustion, or implosion.

Introduction

On February 5, 2003, weeks after the executive decision to invade Iraq had been made, U.S. Secretary of State Colin Powell addressed the United Nations Security Council in an effort to make the international case for support of military action (Breslow, 2016; Powell, 2003). His speech has become infamous. In addition to citing non-existent weapons of mass destruction, the speech falsely claimed that Abu Musab al-Zarqawi was an Al-Qaeda operative with close ties to Saddam Hussein's regime, thus establishing a relationship between Al-Qaeda and Iraq (Mazzetti, 2006). At the time of the speech, Zarqawi was rather insignificant: a radical militant from Jordan, who had been rejected as an Al-Qaeda recruit. Yet his name was mentioned a total of 21 times throughout Powell's speech. Zarqawi would eventually be recognized as a primary architect of the organization that would become the Islamic State, or Islamic State in Iraq and Syria (ISIS) (McCants, 2015).

It is impossible to say with any degree of certainty how ISIS's development would have been different if Zarqawi's name had not been publicized by the US. It is not our purpose to build an empirical case regarding the direct or indirect causality of Zarqawi's rise to prominence. Anecdotally, however, Powell's speech (and the war that followed) allows us to problematize the relationship between mediation and terror. Particularly, it raises several concerns and questions about the hidden potentials of the discursive and media-driven production of terror, terrorism, and terrorists.

The assumed function of media is mediation. Mediation refers to some basic transmission or connectivity between two or more points. It implies the absence or unavailability of immediacy. In its ideal form, mediation means that media accurately or truthfully represent empirical, social, or political reality, the complexities of which are not immediately accessible. But what does mediation do besides mediate or represent? What are some of the unspoken or less apparent effects of mediation, and the mediation of terror and terrorism in particular? And to what extent are mechanisms and operations of western media implicated in the global production, distribution, or administration of the image of terror?

Our article addresses these questions. In seeking to address these concerns, we examine processes and operations that, we believe, are crucial to today's mediation of terror/terrorism. Some of the key processes and operations are: (1) the effects of global media outside or beyond their intended representational functions; (2) the capacities of digital and viral media to enable images of terror to be (re)produced, (re)circulated, or (re)mediated as representations of the factual, the true, or the real; (3) the constant demands to assign meaning or truth to mediated images, including those that reference, depict, or incite terror/terrorism in the context of a so-called "post-truth" era of meaning; (4) the violence and virulence of those constant and pressing demands for meaning and truth through techniques and methods that amount to what may be called media oversaturation; (5) the implosive or auto-destructive tendencies of an oversaturated global media circuitry, particularly in relation to the viral dissemination of images and messages of terror by groups such as ISIS; and (6) the vulnerabilities to the global media system that result from oversaturation and lead to a principle of reversal or reversibility of meaning with regard to media effects.

By examining ISIS's media strategies, we argue that key to understanding the effects of ISIS's images of terror is the tendency of viral and digital media to overproduce, overextend, and oversaturate. This condition of oversaturation denotes hyperactive operations of "representation" (or, rather, of what may stand for representation today) by and within a global media system or circuitry that may be in the process of collapsing under its own weight. But oversaturation also signals a significant vulnerability that enables terrorism to exacerbate media hyperactivity and to try to accelerate the global media's implosive collapse (although such a collapse is never guaranteed). Thus, throughout this article, we seek to theorize how the effects of terroristic imagery work to overstimulate the global media system to the point of what we call its saturation, exhaustion, and reversal.

Mediation and the virality of the image

A crucial feature of the contemporary media system (and its accompanying global circulation of images) is oversaturation. This oversaturation of media is characterized by so-called viral patterns of production, dissemination, and consumption of content, often achieved through globally networked digital platforms. Enabled by a seemingly exponential growth of networks and by ever-widened thresholds of social connectivity, digital technologies have ushered in an unprecedented intensity of information production. Today's global mediascape is perhaps best defined by its immeasurable volume of communicative activity, constituted by an interminable accumulation/circulation of representational images (thus, it may be more apt to call it a global media circuitry). In order to theorize the relevance of the accumulative/circulatory effects of representation taking place throughout contemporary media processes, we turn to Jean Baudrillard's theory of simulation.

According to Baudrillard's theory of simulation, images have a tendency to "exceed" their original or intended function to represent, reflect, or describe some facet of reality. Images eventually overtake, overwhelm, and erase the possibility of originality or referential certainty. For Baudrillard (1983b), this takes place over the course of four "successive phases of the image" (p. 11). The first stage corresponds to the representational function of the image in its most ideal form. It describes a moment in the development of western thought—less likely an actual historical moment than one retroactively imposed on or assumed by western thought itself—whereby any reality can be perfectly reflected by an image. A second stage emerges as a response or opposition to the notion of representational faithfulness. It introduces the possibility of representational malfunction (often deployed intentionally), and it relates to what Baudrillard (1993) refers to in *Symbolic Exchange and Death* as "the counterfeit," something that, Baudrillard claims, is "the dominant schema in the 'classical period'" (p. 50). With the counterfeit, the image does not accurately represent anymore but rather "masks or perverts a basic reality" (Baudrillard, 1983b, p. 11). Representation gives way to distortion. Or, to put it somewhat differently, representation as distortion can now mislead, hide, cheat, dissimulate, or facilitate the production (and valuation) of lies and untruths (or counter-realities).

In a third stage, Baudrillard (1983b) theorizes that the image now "masks the *absence* of a basic reality" (p. 11). The third stage marks a radical break from the first and second stages, and from representation in general. Representation becomes more or less a ruse or a lure; it can no longer be trusted (it cannot even be trusted to spread lies or falsehoods). In the third stage, the image's "true" function is neither to reflect nor to distort, but rather to mask the impossibility of representation. Baudrillard (1996) conceptualizes that a crater has been left in the wake of a reality whose referentiality/representability has been "murdered" by the image itself, by the lure of representation, and by the desire to over-signify by way of the image. This third stage is marked by an over or hyperactive global (re)production of images and meanings in a panic mode eager to restore reality/referentiality at all costs. The demands that the real always be meaningful are everywhere in excess. "There is a proliferation of myths of origin and signs of reality; of second-hand truth, objectivity and authenticity. [...] there is a panic-stricken production of the real and the referential, above and parallel to the panic of material production," writes Baudrillard (1983b, pp. 12–13). A panic-driven sense of reality's radical absence generates a crisis about the capacity of verifiable truth and representable meaning. Still, according to this (il)logic, it is not enough to say that the absence of the real creates a void of meaning and truth inside which the entirety of western thought and its belief-systems disappear. Frantically, this void also stimulates and simulates reproductive effects driven by disappointment (that the real is no more) but also by desire (that the quest for the real produce more and more reality). Thus, this stage of "representation" or of reality-production also inevitably turns toward proliferation and saturation of all the signs that can stand for the real itself. The less reality is present, the more its signs, as substitutes for the real, proliferate. As Baudrillard (2005) puts it: "We live in terror both of the excess of meaning and of total meaninglessness" (p. 134). Demands on reality to be exponentially re-enacted, displayed, and proliferated (the new modalities of representation in this third phase) further deepen the absence of the real. Demands for evermore meaning (everything must make sense, be meaningful) exacerbate a general loss of certainty. Meaning, too, is about the exponential production and display of signs, signs that stand for what is meaningful. As Baudrillard (1988) writes, "Everywhere one seeks to produce meaning, to make the world signify, to render it visible. We are not, however, in danger of lacking meaning; quite to the contrary, we are gorged with meaning and it is killing us" (p. 63).

Lastly, Baudrillard (1983b) arrives at a fourth stage of the image/simulation. Here, the image, indebted to the effects of absence-proliferation resulting from the third stage, "bears no relation to any reality whatever: it is its own pure simulacrum" (p. 11). This stage of the image relates to a phase of the "real" in which the effects of representation (or what formerly could be called representation) can now be conceptualized as a series of independent operations. Images now circulate and reproduce in more or less complete abstraction from the demands of referentiality. In effect, the "real" has been hollowed out by its own representations (as we saw in the third stage). Nothing is left of the real but its simulacra, its sign-images that circulate and are exchanged indiscriminately throughout a global mediascape. At this stage, when we point to a "real" object in the world, we actually point to a hyper-mediation of the object and of its sign-function, often to manifold images, void of originality by virtue of having been hyper-circulated. The mediation of reality has led to the disappearance of the real and representation, and we find instead a hallucinatory complex of "hyperreality" whereby things appear and in fact are "more real than the real" (Baudrillard, 1983a, p. 99).

Baudrillard's diagnosis about representation, reality, and their fateful (hyper)-mediation is reflected through many of the operations of contemporary media, particularly those that involve the proliferation and saturation of inputs and outputs in the global circuitry. The immeasurable volume of hyper-produced digital contents seems to have overwhelmed the global circuits of communication, representation, and meaning/signification. The globalized world is faced with an irreducible complexity of interdependent transmissions, exchanges, and always expanding and morphing communication channels occurring between a multitude of networked actors/actants, interests, and media across the shifting realms of speculative finance, statecraft, international intelligence, the management of political processes, journalism, news-reporting/making, publishing, academia, or "scientific" expertise, and everyday consumer practices, on and on, ad nauseam. There occurs a widespread hyper-generation, hyper-distribution, and hyper-signification of causality and connectivity that, in turn, become virtually indistinguishable categories, excreted by digitally mediated social exchange, and often emerging as a series of signs or symptoms of the boundless growth of an implosive global system. As the system grows, all meanings, certainties, and truth-claims implode.

Within this implosive global system, mediation of the true and the real may remain operative, but only according to a logic of functional contradiction. Indeed, the promise of certainty is continually (re)produced concomitantly with its disappointment or deferral. This is perhaps the fateful or fatal strategic extension of the culture industry's logic of domination and libidinal exploitation that had once been outlined by Horkheimer and Adorno (2002). As Horkheimer and Adorno put it,

> [t]he culture industry endlessly cheats its consumers out of what it endlessly promises. The promissory note of pleasure issued by plot and packaging is indefinitely prolonged: the promise, which actually comprises the entire show, disdainfully intimates that there is nothing more to come, that the diner must be satisfied with reading the menu. (p. 111)

Today, however, the operationalization of promise-disappointment functions beyond the strategic scope of consumer marketing and the culture industry. The mediatized subject is constantly hit by a barrage of direct and indirect promissory notes about various forms and versions of certainty, security, and truth emanating from multiple news media pundits, commentators, ideologues, technocrats, politicians, community activists, and fellow "digizens." Increasingly, the reality of power (social, political, economic, etc.) is being scrambled by a hyper-real overproduction of conflicting "truths" and "untruths," "reals" and "unreals," "facts" and "alternative facts," or "news" and "fake news" that exacerbate the implosion of ideologically incoherent and semantically fragmented images purporting to represent some sort of social/political/economic reality (Artrip & Debrix, 2014). Put differently, in seeking to diagnose and represent the true and the real, media today often produce a series of "undecidable symptoms, and an assortment of vague and contradictory diagnoses" (Baudrillard, 1995, p. 48).

Even mainstream news commentaries today echo a vaguely postmodern concern that we have somehow entered a dangerous "post-truth" era of mediated social and political reality (Davies, 2016; Flood, 2016). One widespread sentiment in response to this "post-truth crisis" is to fetishize "fact-checking" technologies and related epistemic media/truth policing practices. This sentiment commonly implores that countermeasures be taken in response to "fake news" proliferation. Yet, the machineries that produce and disseminate the true and the untrue are one and the same. Both involve the same conditions of reproduction, the same thirst for reality, and the same system of operationalized promise/disappointment. The imperative to "fact-check" suggests that media need to fight against a threat to their own legitimacy and against the endangerment of truth. But journalists and pundits who tout "fact-checking" as some panacean form of political/social resistance appear to do so in complete ignorance or denial of the hyper-real effects of today's global media. They fail to see that, in the words of Baudrillard (2005), "[t]he excess of information engenders undecidability of facts and confusion of minds. [...] The excess of transparency engenders terror" (p. 193). The ethos/pathos of "fact-checking" assumes that the immediacy of truth is still possible, or that media can or must remain neutral conduits for the transmission of reality. Thus, the fetishization of "fact-checking" does not care to address (or cannot make itself address) the more difficult situation, but one that is arguably at the root of the so-called post-truth condition: truth is always already mediated. Truth is always already vulnerable to the challenges of "alternative" forms of reality assessment and representation. The viral form of today's media simultaneously demands and prohibits a hegemonic instantiation of truth. Perhaps this simultaneous and contradictory demand for and prohibition of epistemological hegemony has always been a central feature of liberal democracies and their quests for truth. The devout faith in the "marketplace of ideas" in (neo)liberal democratic designs—rooted in the virtues of transparency, freedom, and competition—promises that (like the infamous invisible hand of the market, perhaps) it will eventually always be able to sort out fact from fiction. But the radical equivalency and universal fungibility of all ideas make it such that each attempt to instantiate a hegemonic truth tends only to energize an oppositional or contradictory attempt.

In the domain of news and political media, the user-subject's search for truth resembles a shell game, the plight of which is perhaps nowhere more evident than with Counselor to President Trump Kellyanne Conway's insistence on "alternative facts" in opposition to the seemingly more measured, documented, quantitative, and conventional facts reported about public attendance at Trump's presidential inauguration (Bradner, 2017). The new U.S. executive's blatant disregard for referential reality, made evident by the continual torrent of images, signs, and contradictory truth-claims disseminated from the state apparatus (or via the president's Twitter account), reflects a stage of simulation in which the lie operates as a self-sustaining simulacrum. The lie is no longer a "counterfeit" (as it was in Baudrillard's second phase of the image), but rather a free-floating signifier. The lie no longer antagonizes truth or the real. Rather, the lie makes sense only in relation to other lies that do not even care anymore to appear truthful. The lie mirrors the hyper-real condition and operations of media because it functions according to a framework of "truth" that assumes no weight about reality, assigns no inherent value to the real, and makes no referential claims. There is no certainty left when it comes to truths and lies. What is left is an unending play of symptoms emanating from the oversaturation (an oversaturation of images, signs, statements, and "realities," once again) of an undifferentiated global system. Everything becomes uncertain (Baudrillard might say that it is indifferent), reduced to the universally fungible mode of information/news. As Baudrillard (1995) intimated, "everything which is turned into information becomes the object of endless speculation" (p. 41).

The "implosivity" of this system (and its apparent chaos of meanings) has arguably been a strategic advantage for Trump and his advisors. But, interestingly enough, it has been so also for an organization like ISIS, a terror/terrorism organization at war with the U.S. presidency and what the US and the west may represent. In particular, in its efforts to unleash various videos and images of its terror campaigns, ISIS has found the "endless speculation" of today's media representation/realities useful to its enterprise. Journalists Miller and Mekhennet (2015) have offered an intriguing description of ISIS's media strategy. They write that:

> [ISIS] exerts extraordinarily tight control over the production of its videos and messages but relies on the chaos of the Internet and social media to disseminate them. Its releases cluster around seemingly incompatible themes: sometimes depicting the caliphate as a peaceful and idyllic domain, other times as a society awash in apocalyptic violence.

The dual messages are designed to influence a divided audience. The beheadings, immolations and other spectacles are employed both to menace Western adversaries and to appeal to disenfranchised Muslim males weighing a leap into the Islamist fray. (paras. 40–41)

The enigmatic or uncertain structure of ISIS's terror/terrorist organization described by many scholars and pundits (see, for example, Micallef, 2015; Stakelbeck, 2015; Stern & Berger, 2015) may well be an effect of its digital strategies. As William McCants (2015) has noted in his book *The ISIS Apocalypse*, it may be difficult to explain the apparent contradictions of ISIS—across its propaganda, military tactics, religious and ideological rhetorics, and uses of apocalyptic language—outside a commitment to "establish[ing] an ultraconservative Islamic state at all costs" (p. 154). But can the goal of ISIS really be reduced to what, for McCants, still appears to be a rather coherent strategy or objective? The multiplicity of contradictions at play in the operations of ISIS, noted by Miller and Mekhennet, among others, is a mirror of those at play within and throughout the global media system. And, as we saw above, the production of contradictory claims to truth—all equally plausible, all potentially valued as fact-worthy or even as truth-worthy—is a symptom of an oversaturation of meaning/representation offered by the global media system that can be used by a wide array of social/political actors (again, Trump advisors have had no difficulty making this "post-truth" system theirs too). Moreover, the speculative and fungible processing of global "events" (and their facts) by media systems may also serve as an opening or opportunity for terror and terror groups like ISIS that can further inject into these systems a multiplicity of images, often forming additional contradictory narratives and truth-effects, each capable of being processed variably and with possibly many different goals or outcomes in mind by a wide range of media users/subscribers.

Thus, it may not be accurate to assume that the Islamic State's media campaigns seek to render more visible a coherent ideology about the terror organization or wish to impose a clear message about ISIS's authoritarian form of governance. Unlike perhaps the operations of earlier advanced terror organizations, such as Al-Qaeda, that seemingly sought to project onto the west—through both mediatic and material means—a mostly unified and principled program of terror and terrorism, the strategies of ISIS are more frantic and fragmentary. They are somewhat more uncertain and contradictory, also. ISIS's media strategies may be more appropriate for and aligned with the speculative, fungible, and implosive operations of today's viral and often digital media whereby facts, alternative facts, and verifiable fact-checking are all equiprobable outcomes of the globally mediated event. Indeed, as McCants (2015) remarked, "[t]his is not Bin Laden's caliphate" (p. 153). Thus, ISIS challenges western life not only by means of exterior militant and brutal force (its terror attacks), frantic and speculative (and often unplanned) as these may be, but also by way of an infiltration, usage, and perfection of global (and western) techniques of mediation/information/representation and of their "post-truth" effects. ISIS takes advantage of the oversaturated and hyper-connective global condition of digital/viral media that, in a way, allows the image and meanings to spread like viruses.

Indeed, when ISIS successfully injects an image of terror into the global media circuitry, that image behaves according to the hyper-real logic of an opportunistic virus. As some pundits noted about ISIS's use of still images and recorded videos of western subjects' decapitations in 2014 and 2015 (often western journalists), (Stern & Berger, 2015), the

ISIS image/visual message of terror or even horror (Debrix, 2017) attacks a facet or sub-system, and it appropriates available weaknesses. This is a virus that, digitally as well as mediatically, thrives thanks to the complicity in global media between the lie and the truth, between reality and its simulacrum. In this way, ISIS images, even its most gruesome ones, do not stop at appropriating and recruiting the lives and actions of immediate subjects, nor at those most directly affected by the violence of globalization. The virality of ISIS images also entangles western subjectivities, not only by distributing fear, but also by recruiting support. Those who are most susceptible to this exposure may be motivated by ISIS to act as sympathizers or perpetrators. More broadly, anyone whom ISIS's viral images reach is also infected, or "recruited" into accepting the fact/truth that, at any moment, and virtually anywhere, ISIS can enlist anyone with a propensity to be/feel affected by ISIS's anti-western message.

ISIS's image-driven and fact-producing viral recruitment machine (a recruitment machine of terror and horror) is also designed to "crowdsource" supporters and combatants, even in areas that seem to be geographically and ideologically distant and perhaps "outside" the dreamed-of caliphate (Koerner, 2016). Yet, in a way, ISIS's goal is also to "crowdsource" its opponents by mobilizing a symptomology of terror acts and facts that, whether they are true or false, real or fake, ideologically consistent or incoherent, manage to keep primarily western consumers of the viral/digital image in a state of virtually constant uncertainty and always anticipated insecurity.

Despite their obvious horror, the media activities of ISIS once again tend to mirror the strategic deployment of most media proliferation techniques today (no matter their coherent or incoherent purposes). They accelerate the viral spread of representational contents, images, and signs of the "truth." Whether one likes it or not, ISIS images do not have a monopoly over the implosion/oversaturation of representation and reality. Take for example the organized presence of ISIS on Twitter. According to a report by U.S. researchers Vidino and Hughes (2015) on media and homegrown U.S. terrorism, ISIS typically extends its visibility and reach on Twitter by orchestrating activities between three types of user accounts: "nodes, amplifiers, and shout-outs" (p. 24). The "nodes," Vidino and Hughes argue, are primary users responsible for most of the content production. "Amplifiers" do not produce, but rather disseminate content by means of the "favorite" or "retweet" features of Twitter. It is uncertain whether the activities of these accounts are driven by human users or a botnet of automated tasks. Lastly, the function of a "shout-out" is to support the new accounts of nodes that were previously banned. Although suspensions of ISIS-affiliated Twitter accounts are frequent, they are largely ineffective. In fact, censorship protocols like account bans may exacerbate the digital virulence of ISIS as a user will typically wear the ban as a "badge of honor and a means by which an aspirant can bolster his or her legitimacy" (Vidino & Hughes, 2015, p. 24). Thus, the attempt to suppress ISIS activity not only fails, but also provides users with all the more voracity, reach, and virulence to further disseminate messages and images of terror and ISIS's own version of "alternative facts." Again, this is symptomatic of a general tendency of viral media to swarm programmed functions, meanings, and effects through global informational networks.

The virulence of the image deployed by ISIS is not just an outgrowth of its recruitment campaigns (it is not just about an ideology and how it may appeal to some). The virulence of ISIS's images is also not just the result of the effects that the distribution/propagation of incendiary words or images may have on a larger public (it is not just about media reception either). What is notable about ISIS's media virulence is its terrorizing capacity to infiltrate and oversaturate the global media system to the point that such a mediated exposure to images of terror and horror can trigger the reversal of allegedly intended media and representational functions (reality and representation, "truth" reporting, communication exchange, production of meaning, and the search for certainty/accuracy). In this way, ISIS, perhaps not unlike other contemporary viral media users, nodes, or amplifiers of the "post-truth" age, may accelerate the global media system's implosion or auto-destruction of meaning. The next section further addresses this question of implosion or auto-destruction by highlighting and theorizing the principle of reversal/reversibility that is crucial to the way media operators today, including ISIS, partake of the (re)production of regimes of truth and meaning.

The mediation of the (non-)event and strategies of reversal

The generalized exchange of digital/viral media, on ISIS's side or through western media networks, renders possible what we call a principle of reversal of today's media. Reversal here is an expression of the fungibility of meanings, truths, and facts. Reversal, or the principle of reversibility of today's digital/viral media, is not limited to what ISIS's own media networks and image platforms seek to unleash. It is also not just about a targeted response by the west to ISIS's viral productions of terror/horror. Again, reversal is a generalized principle of truth's operationality; it hints at the modalities of deployment—aleatory and unpredictable as they may be—that are available for the truth-effects and truth-claims that are produced to circulate, without a referential core, throughout the global media circuitry. Take, for example, the onslaught of responses to an interview of Kellyanne Conway wherein she referenced "the Bowling Green massacre"—a fabricated terrorist event/non-event—in an apparent effort to justify Trump's first executive order for a travel ban on seven predominantly Muslim countries in January and February 2017 (Schmidt & Bever, 2017). Conway misspoke about, misremembered, or misunderstood a 2011 occurrence in which two Iraqi citizens were arrested in Bowling Green, Kentucky and federally charged for material support of Al-Qaeda.

In this iteration of what several of Trump's advisors and spokespersons labeled an "alternative truth," Conway claimed that the massacre was unfamiliar because it had not been widely covered by U.S. news media. Ironically, the Bowling Green Massacre soon gained widespread coverage as the media response to this "alternative event" became a spectacular (non-)event in itself. It was not long before people went to social media to circulate memes like "Never Forget Bowling Green" or to reproduce "Kennedy moment" types of expressions such as "where were you when you heard about the Bowling Green Massacre?". One site (www.bowlinggreenmassacrefund.com) even appeared to solicit donations for a Bowling Green Massacre victims' fund, although the link was redirected to the American Civil Liberties Union's donation page (Seppala, 2017). A frenzy of reactions related to the "alternative event" swarmed the mediascape. These took the form of (social) media responses one would expect to find after an actual tragedy (supposing one could still think in terms of an "actual" tragedy). Yet, they also signified the non-eventness of the initially identified event/massacre. Moreover, the anti-immigrant and Islamophobic public relations function (intended or not) of

Conway's interview became an event in and of itself. But what might have been an "alternative" strategy to produce a media event such as this also underwent a profound and profuse reversal. At once, it became capable of shifting from fact to fake news, from non-event to viral media event, and from pro-immigrant ban strategy to a proliferation of viral/virulent media tactics aimed at deviating the possible ideological/policy intention behind Conway's statement.

This "alternative" terrorist event is more than a simple parody of the new "alternative fact" regime of U.S. power and its media strategies and effects. The mode in which this event/non-event unfolded online and offline was nearly identical to the mediated display of the aftermath of an "actual" terrorist event or tragedy, such as the unfortunately more and more frequent attacks on civilian lives by ISIS sympathizers in places like Barcelona, Berlin, Istanbul, London, Manchester, Nice, Paris, or Turku, among others. The Bowling Green Massacre took place primarily through the mediation of its likely absence. The non-event/alternative fact, through its imminent reversal—one minute it is fake, the next minute it is real; in one instant it is about an ISIS attack, in the next it is about the US needing to adopt aggressive immigration and anti-Muslim policies to fend off such an attack—became hyper-real by way of some of the above-mentioned memes and other digital/viral expressions of its presence, but also through ceaseless political commentary and truth politics accompanied by a frenzy of images inscribing it with meaning(s) and truth(s) (some of these images in western media at the time of the Bowling Green pronouncement were arbitrarily borrowed from previous ISIS scenes of terror/horror, also).

Not unlike many reactions to beheadings by ISIS in western media, the terrorist attack and its shadow are subjected to mechanisms of potentially endless re-mediation. Thus, they are capable of (re)producing the same types of outputs, effects, and affects, including a contagion/virulence of meaning and truth. Perhaps this is, as Baudrillard might suggest, because the real of the event is always already absent, or at least rendered unknowable as a result of hyperreality. Might it be that the real of the November 2015 ISIS attacks in Paris, for example, is as inaccessible as the (un)real of the Bowling Green Massacre? By posing this question, we do not mean to be insensitive about or dismissive of the sense of loss felt by many as a result of what took place in Paris (or in any other recent terrorist tragedy). Rather, we wish to bring to the fore a puzzling yet eerily uncomfortable and disturbing commonality, the result of the principle of reversal/reversibility of media events, about contemporary modalities of mediation shared by both the event and the non-event, something that may lead to their possible indistinguishability/non-differentiation.

At the moment when a terrorist attack irrupts into the western mediascape and, often, into a western cityscape too, its immediacy has already virtually disappeared. The instantaneous global mediation of such an event—driven, perhaps, by some impossible will to articulate its irreducible horror—provokes a mass desire/need to capture the atrocity. Yet it also helps to render such a capture virtually impossible. The phenomenon is caught in/by real time (media time), virulently disseminated across the global informational circulatory system, all the while exponentially amassing a collection of content in the form of news and social media commentary, visual media documenting the terror/horror, and various other hyper-reactive inputs and outputs of networked sharing (all of this often before the violence has even ceased). Again, as we intimated in the previous section of this article, this is something that ISIS's own images of terror/horror count on.

Diffusion and, indeed, profusion, and their likely pathway onto reversal/reversibility of meanings and truths, are more urgent than precision or accuracy about ideological claims and messages. ISIS's work gets done by taking advantage of the virality/virulence offered by the prevalent global media circuitry and by what, within and through it, the principle of reversal/reversibility (with its truth-effects, fact-checks, and meaning-claims) does to the event.

Thus, suffocated by the weight of its own image reflected back, the event becomes engorged with meanings. Its reality becomes indeterminable. And, in this fourth order simulacrum (going back to Baudrillard's theory of simulation), the media system's own response to the image of terror is to (re)circulate it in infinite exchange, that is to say, to subject it to the constant gauntlet of semiotic profusion. The sum of effects from the (re)mediation of the violent terrorist (non-)event enables an almost cinematic prolifer-ation of images of terror/horror also. This may explain, in part, the well-documented sen-timent that the 9/11 attacks somehow appeared to be staged. Indeed, the 9/11 terrorist event itself seemed too unreal, too much "like a movie," as the attacks took place in (tele)-visual real time (Debrix, 2008; Rickli, 2009). Thus, what characterized the hyper-mediation of 9/11, as Baudrillard (2005) once remarked, was "the feeling that seizes us when faced with the occurrence of *something that happens without having been possible*" (p. 130). One might suggest that the choreographed or stylized (as some have argued; see Stern & Berger, 2015) effects of ISIS's videotaped beheadings of westerners in Syria or Iraq around 2014 and 2015 may also be one of those "somethings" (perhaps "something" is a better term than event today) that "happen[ed] without having been possible."

The media operations involved in the capture, processing, and transmission of meaning via the terrorist event or image produce effects well beyond their representational func-tions. Thus, like terrorist attacks perhaps, they explode the event's meaning/truth into image-fragments scattered throughout a global mediascape of interminable and indeter-minable exchange, throughout the global media circuitry. Image fragments, the "some-thing" of a terrorist event as we suggested above, are "upvoted," "retweeted," and "status updated" on the same networked interfaces as cat memes, online TV series and films, YouTube videos, or corporate advertising. Images of mediated terror and horror, radically abstracted from what little originality or immediacy of the event might have been possible in the first place, become globally fungible, fused and confused with all other types of digitally and virally mediated images. The irruption of the terrorist attack/act/fact is reduced to a series of infinitely reversible yet still exchangeable/distribu-table meanings and images that are folded into the very functions and processes of the west's globally mediatized (and mediatically globalized) meaning and value systems. This is perhaps what the principle of reversibility of the "event" (and its truth-effects) is meant to achieve: an effort to flood the system to the point of the collapse of meaning/truth. Reversibility and oversaturation feed each other's energies.

Conclusion: reversibility and hegemony

Spectacular images of horror/terror that infiltrate western media, including images circu-lated by ISIS, may challenge the west's ideological domination and power. But they do not fundamentally stifle its globalizing spectacular manifold (Debord, 2000). No oppositional force can repress, reform, or reconstitute "the Global," as Baudrillard once put it

(Baudrillard, 2003). Still, some can take advantage of it. Thus, the biggest danger to the system today is the system itself, that is to say, a universalized modality of communicative and informational (global) governance that has been increasingly saturated by its own media processes, techniques, and technologies, that has been overwhelmed by its own production and circulation of images/contents/facts/truths/meanings, and that, perversely perhaps, cultivates its terroristic non-western (but sometimes western too) outgrowths, whether it does so purposefully or not. Thus, the principle of reversibility is part and parcel of the global system itself. What guarantees its exponential expansion today through a boundless dissemination of images, signs, and meaning-effects is also what can amount to its implosion (and vice versa). In one of his last interviews, Baudrillard referred to this characteristic of the global system as a matter of hegemony, in opposition to the old concept of domination. Baudrillard states:

> [D]omination has made way for hegemony ... There is no longer a dual relationship. Everyone is an accomplice ... There are no longer dominants and dominated, but a kind of total annexation (nexus=networks). Everyone is caught up in the network and submits to this hegemony. Who benefits? We can no longer calculate in terms of benefits for one power or another. We can no longer go back in history to find out who is responsible for the domination. We are both victims and accomplices, guilty and not responsible. Hegemony is within us ... [H]egemony brings domination, and therefore alienation, to an end ... We have fallen into an irreversible vertigo; we are drawn to the black hole ... [This is] what I call integral reality. And this integral reality, the signature of this new hegemony, is frightening because we cannot resist it. If we want to resist hegemony and escape it using the means we once used against domination (revolt, critical thought, negative thought, etc.), there is no hope. (Baudrillard, 2010, p. 117)

Recent strategies of terror may have understood the passage from domination to hegemony (via the global system) and the annexing force of what Baudrillard calls the system's "integral reality" much better than western military strategists, western foreign policy experts, western political leaders, western journalists, pundits, and even academics. For example, there is an eerie resemblance between Baudrillard's diagnosis about the reversibility of the global system giving way to total hegemony (and, in particular, Baudrillard's claim about the inability to offer resistance from within the system itself) and *The Management of Savagery*, a text originally published on the Internet in 2004 by Abu Bakr Naji, who purportedly was once the head of media operations for Al-Qaeda. To conclude this article, we briefly examine this text, if only because it has been taken to be influential on Islamist/extremist terroristic strategies, including on some of the strategies deployed by ISIS's media users and image mobilizers (Jackson & Loidolt, 2013).

Naji's (2006) text initially describes several "elements of cultural/civilizational annihilation" in the west, most of which address the assumed inevitable decadence of western/secular/bourgeois values (p. 7). Naji outlines the significance of these elements in the following passage:

> Whenever a large mixture of these elements are combined within the superpower and those elements mix in such a way that they energize each other, that superpower's speed of collapse increases. Whether these elements are actively present or latent, they need an assisting element to activate them and cause the downfall of that superpower and its centralization (of power), no matter how much military power it possesses. As we have said, this is because the power of its centralization, embodied by the overwhelming military power and the deceptive media halo, can only be in a cohesive society. (p. 7)

The strategy recommended by Naji is not one of direct military opposition to the west (or, more specifically, to the U.S. superpower). Domination and resistance/opposition are no longer feasible or useful at a time of global hegemony and when integral reality/reversibility can always reappropriate all acts and facts and their meanings. Rather, Naji's text takes for granted that the target, western civilization/U.S. power, is already in a process of self-collapse as a result of its oversaturation, particularly given the presence of certain visible "elements" of its demise (for example, signs of social and cultural dysfunction in and about western societies circulating throughout the global media system). Because a "superpower" supposedly loses its force without cohesion, not so much antagonizing these elements but rather encouraging their expansion/propagation to the point of their collapse becomes strategically central to ensuring the downfall of the west (but perhaps not of the global hegemonic system). Thus, *Management of Savagery* reflects an effort to identify, target, and somehow affect those elements deemed more vulnerable to what we have called oversaturation and reversibility in order to accelerate a hoped-for (but perhaps vain) total systemic collapse. Again, the key point here is not so much to create or cause the defeat of the "superpower," but rather to speed up its fateful demise, its auto-destruction. Naji (2006) continues:

> What if this assisting element is the decree of God which He ordained in order to act upon these three axes? It would not only work to activate the latent elements of cultural annihilation but confront the military power with exhaustion. This confrontation and exhaustion directly affects the third axis, which is the deceptive media halo. It removes the aura of invincibility which this power projects, that nothing at all stands in front of it. (p. 8)

What Naji calls the "deceptive media halo" of western superpower is described here as an apparatus of projected appearance for omnipotence, power, and domination. But this, itself, and as Baudrillard might add, is an illusion of power/domination in an age of hegemonic reversibility. This "deceptive media halo" can only give way to what Baudrillard termed an "irreversible vertigo" of meaning, truth, fact, value, and power. Moreover, Naji implies, without the superpower's reliance on media structures and effects, it is impotent. Its power/domination is exposed, and thus, riding along with the global media circuits, the west has no choice but to surrender to the global hegemony of the system. Military force may still be there, but, in a way, it remains a quaint and often obsolete representational façade (at least when faced with the "halo" of terrorist visual strategies), perhaps a remnant of earlier stages of the visual/representation (and thus of power), going back to Baudrillard's phases of simulation.

According to Naji, the west's power is upheld mostly by way of an illusory aura. The media-driven reproduction/enforcement of the west's image of/as superpower or dominant force—its main simulacrum, perhaps—is a crucial vulnerability. Of course, in stating this, Naji remains (ideologically) blind to the fact that the terrorist networks (Al-Qaeda and ISIS) he hopes to empower are also sustained through modes of media illusion by way of the same "deceptive media halo" that partakes of the same integral reality, of a single hegemony. Still, Naji's emphasis on media illusions and their effects in terms of projections of "real" power or force may have been an incentive for several of the media/image campaigns deployed by ISIS. In particular, the emphasis on the fact that strategies of exhaustion may be effective when dealing with self-proclaimed military superpowers is an insight gathered from previous combat strategies in wars of attrition, many of which have characterized colonial/post-colonial struggles. But it is also a point derived from a recognition of the contemporary operations of a globally hegemonic media circuitry within which principles of oversaturation and reversibility of meanings, facts, and truths are always engaged. Here, once again, a terrorist media strategy, a strategy adapted to the global viral mediation of terror, is on display. This strategy wants to suggest (or, better yet, wants to believe) that, in order to defeat the west, ISIS and other terrorist groups like it need to take advantage of the global media circuitry, or need to make use of the vulnerabilities that western media have created for themselves by leaving power, domination, and representation behind and by placing the fate of the west (but is it only the west?) in the invisible and deceptive hands of integral reality and its hegemony.

We suggested at the beginning of this article that, following Baudrillard's diagnosis about the fate of the image and representation, oversaturation and, to some extent, reversibility left western media systems open to vulnerabilities, and, in particular, to the kind of vulnerabilities that terrorist networks such as ISIS could exploit. Yet, those vulnerabilities are about the west, its values, and the quest for truth that the west trusted (its) media systems to take charge of. Those media vulnerabilities, identified and targeted by a terror strategist like Naji, and theorized more generally (not just with regard to terror/terrorism) by Baudrillard, are there, but very little seems to be able to be done about them since, as Baudrillard once again argues, we are all complicit in this process of hegemonic annexation of everything (starting with the real). As Baudrillard concludes, and we tend to agree with him, what hope can there be for meaning, the real, or even the image, not just when we are faced with ISIS's viral media strategies, but when all claims to meaning and truth can only make sense and take place within the overwhelming context of the global media circuitry, its hegemony, and its continually frantic (re)production of integral reality? Contemporary strategies of mediation of terror (and counter-terror) may have no choice but to cope with this "reality." But can they? And to what end?

References

Artrip, R. E., & Debrix, F. (2014). The digital fog of war: Baudrillard and the violence of representation. *International Journal of Baudrillard Studies, 11*(2). Retrieved from http://www2.ubishops.ca/baudrillardstudies/vol-11_2/v11-2-tofc.html

Baudrillard, J. (1983a). *In the shadow of the silent majorities, or, the end of the social, and other essays.* New York: Semiotext(e).

Baudrillard, J. (1983b). *Simulations.* New York: Semiotext(e).

Baudrillard, J. (1988). *The ecstasy of communication.* New York: Semiotext(e).

Baudrillard, J. (1993). *Symbolic exchange and death.* Thousand Oaks, CA: Sage.

Baudrillard, J. (1995). *The Gulf War did not take place.* Bloomington: Indiana University Press.

Baudrillard, J. (1996). *The perfect crime.* New York: Verso.

Baudrillard, J. (2003). The violence of the global. *CTheory.* Retrieved from http://www.ctheory.net/articles.aspx?id=385

Baudrillard, J. (2005). *The intelligence of evil or the lucidity pact*. New York: Berg.

Baudrillard, J. (2010). *The agony of power*. Los Angeles: Semiotext(e).

Bradner, E. (2017, January 23). Conway: Trump White House offered "alternative facts" on crowd size. *CNN*. Retrieved from http://www.cnn.com/2017/01/22/politics/kellyanne-conway-alternative-facts/

Breslow, J. M. (2016, May 17). Colin Powell: U.N. speech "was a great intelligence failure." *PBS; Frontline*. Retrieved from http://www.pbs.org/wgbh/frontline/article/colin-powell-u-n-speech-was-a-great-intelligence-failure/

Davies, W. (2016, August 24). The age of post-truth politics. *The New York Times*. Retrieved from https://www.nytimes.com/2016/08/24/opinion/campaign-stops/the-age-of-post-truth-politics.html?_r=0

Debord, G. (2000). *Society of the spectacle*. Detroit: Black & Red.

Debrix, F. (2008). *Tabloid terror: War, culture, and geopolitics*. New York: Routledge.

Debrix, F. (2017). *Global powers of horror: Security, politics, and the body in pieces*. London: Routledge.

Flood, A. (2016, November 15). "Post-truth" named word of the year by Oxford Dictionaries. *The Guardian*. Retrieved from https://www.theguardian.com/books/2016/nov/15/post-truth-named-word-of-the-year-by-oxford-dictionaries

Horkheimer, M., & Adorno, T. W. (2002). *Dialectic of enlightenment: Philosophical fragments*. Stanford, CA: Stanford University Press.

Jackson, B. A., & Loidolt, B. (2013). Considering al-Qa'ida's innovation doctrine: From strategic texts to "innovation in practice". *Terrorism and Political Violence, 25*(2), 284–310.

Koerner, B. I. (2016, April). Why ISIS is winning the social media war. *Wired*. Retrieved from https://www.wired.com/2016/03/isis-winning-social-media-war-heres-beat/

Mazzetti, M. (2006, September 9). C.I.A. said to find no Hussein link to terror chief. *The New York Times*. Retrieved from http://www.nytimes.com/2006/09/09/world/middleeast/09intel.html

McCants, W. F. (2015). *The ISIS apocalypse: The history, strategy, and doomsday vision of the Islamic State*. New York: St. Martin's Press.

Micallef, J. (2015). *Islamic State: Its history, ideology, and challenge*. Vancouver, Canada: Antioch Downs.

Miller, G., & Mekhennet, S. (2015, November 20). Inside the surreal world of the Islamic State's propaganda machine. *The Washington Post*. Retrieved from https://www.washingtonpost.com/world/national-security/inside-the-islamic-states-propaganda-machine/2015/11/20/051e997a-8ce6-11e5-acff-673ae92ddd2b_story.html?utm_term=.832284eb00cb

Naji, A. B. (2006). *The management of savagery: The most critical stage through which the Umma will pass*. Cambridge: The John M. Olin Institute for Strategic Studies, Harvard University.

Powell, C. L. (2003, February). *Remarks to the United Nations Security Council*. Washington, D.C.: U.S. Department of State. Retrieved from https://2001–2009.state.gov/secretary/former/powell/remarks/2003/17300.htm#

Rickli, C. (2009). An event "like a movie"? Hollywood and 9/11. *Current Objectives of Postgraduate American Studies, 10*. Retrieved from http://copas.uni-regensburg.de/article/viewArticle/114/138#_ftn1

Schmidt, S., & Bever, L. (2017, February 3). Kellyanne Conway cites "Bowling Green massacre" that never happened to defend travel ban. *The Washington Post*. Retrieved from https://www.washingtonpost.com/news/morning-mix/wp/2017/02/03/kellyanne-conway-cites-bowling-green-massacre-that-never-happened-to-defend-travel-ban/?utm_term=.f502d4bcb001

Seppala, T. J. (2017, February 3). Facebook users pretend the "Bowling Green Massacre" is real. *Engadget*. Retrieved from https://www.engadget.com/2017/02/03/facebook-users-pretend-the-bowling-green-massacre-is-real/

Stakelbeck, E. (2015). *ISIS exposed: Beheadings, slavery, and the hellish reality of radical Islam*. Washington, DC: Regnery.

Stern, J., & Berger, J. M. (2015). *ISIS: The state of terror*. New York: Harper Collins.

Vidino, L., & Hughes, S. (2015). *ISIS in America: From Retweets to Raqqa*. Washington, DC: The George Washington University.

Cold War redux and the news: Islamic State and the US through each other's eyes

Barbie Zelizer

ABSTRACT
This article considers the ways in which the media apparatuses of Islamic State and the United States have adopted a Cold War frame for covering each other. In so doing, it demonstrates not only the degree to which U.S. news provides a template for news crafted elsewhere, but also how the past undergirds the present in unknowing and often unpredictable ways.

The rise of Islamic State and its crystallization into a public entity associated with terror has been seen by most observers as spectacular, meteoric and unexpected, and western media have by and large covered it as such. This article argues that the mediated representation of and by Islamic State is more predictable than assumed because it draws from long-standing conventions crystallized during the Cold War. Focusing on US and Islamic State's mediated coverage of each other during a time of ongoing conflict, the article shows how both sides to the conflict invoke sentiments and conventions central to the Cold War and its strategic contouring of journalism. Though the Cold War is not the only circumstance that motivates coverage associated with Islamic State, its manifestation in coverage by both the US *and* Islamic State illustrates its widespread invocation.

Cold war mindedness evolved in the late 1940s, went underground when the Cold War ended in 1989 and surfaces periodically when difficult events in need of explanation occur (Zelizer, n.d.). This article shows how its mindset drives the coverage that Islamic State and US media produce about each other today. Examining the relays that ensued from both media environments between 2014 and 2017—in the US case, those from both conventional media outlets and the so-called "news upstarts" of Vox, Mashable, BuzzFeed, International Business Times, Vocativ and Vice; in the case of Islamic State, primarily English-language relays with some analysis of relays in the 28 other languages in which Islamic State media operate—it demonstrates that coverage of the current US–Islamic State conflict mimics what unfolded in US news media toward the USSR during the Cold War. In this light, the Cold War can be said to offer a set of interpretive tenets for making sense of the complex and ambiguous violence of contemporary public life. With so much of global media flows drawing from and/or mimicking US media, these interpretive tenets are of substantial relevance worldwide.

The setting for Cold War redux

The importation of a Cold War mindset into coverage of and by Islamic State is in many ways predictable. The Cold War was a war more of ideas than of battles or physical conflict, making its representation crucial across nearly five decades of prosecution. Though invoking the label requires underlining the exclusion from discussion of then-current proxy wars in Korea, Vietnam, Guatemala, Nicaragua and elsewhere—an exclusion that many Cold War scholars hold responsible for generating a "chronically underanalyzed" gap across most existing scholarship (Mumford, 2013, p. 1)—the idea of the Cold War helped sharpen ideological conflict between the US and the USSR Institutions of all kinds, journalism included, were required to stay on board with its aims.

Being a journalist during the Cold War involved repairing to the dissonant aims of practicing journalism independently while accommodating the Cold War mindset. Central to that mindset was a stance toward newsmaking that rode on acts of compliance, deception, simplification and demonization. With journalism as its driver, Cold War mindedness generated strategic cues that focused on the combination of three elements: a clear binary positioning of enemy formation as an uncrossable divide between "us" and "them", a counterintuitive notion that one does not have to see war to act as if it exists, and a largely uncritical reliance on the media to realize the war's aims across the territory of the other side (Zelizer, n.d.). Playing to these notions situated US journalists in a default setting that minimized the chance that they would counter its aims. Invoked in a widespread, often frenetic fashion, the Cold War mindset helps explain how, in Dallas Smythe and Hugh Wilson's (1968, p. 67) words, a "system designed for the free expression of opinion accepted a Cold War propaganda rhetoric out of touch with the free world."

This is critical, for after the Cold War ended, Cold War mindedness did not disappear. Instead, it went underground, lurking as a rich mnemonic scheme that waited to pounce into relevance, whose traits would be creatively employed in lending shape to conflicts' representation across time. It is thus no surprise that US journalism regularly adapts coverage of complex conflicts—like that associated with Islamic State—to better cohere with deep-seated Cold War conventions and sentiments. Due to US centrality in the global flow of news, some of those conventions and sentiments have emerged as relevant interpretive tenets for conflicts occurring in surprising and unexpected quarters around the globe, many—like those of Islamic State—dissonant with US aims. Although the war between the US and Islamic State is real and incurs casualties and damages, its information component remains central, and it is in large part sustained by the Cold War mindset.

Islamic State and the US cover each other via two complex and sophisticated mediated environments, each of which comprises multiple organizations and platforms, large numbers of people, high degrees of coordinated activity and variable skill sets. Though clearly different in tone, independence and authority—the US media are largely commercially driven but relatively politically independent, while Islamic State's media apparatus is commercially free but politically constrained by authoritarian rule—they similarly reflect deep-seated antagonism. Each combines old and new media, involving a complex mix of voices in giving shape to the conflict as it unfolds.

Each media environment has distinct characteristics. US relays about Islamic State reflect the independent efforts of separate news outlets, most commercially driven, which strive for some degree of independent newsmaking—however affected they may be by common, often unvoiced ideological orientations—alongside slower and one-sided government relays and invested social media activity. Deprived of access to the territories under Islamic State control, US media outlets do not operate by one uniform strategy but instead intermittently entertain different kinds of newsmaking tactics—full-out coverage, media blackouts, self-censoring, outsourcing, withholding information and developing alternative news sources. In most cases, these efforts have stopped short of articulating a full embrace of official propaganda. When counterpropaganda efforts were announced by US officials in early 2016, the unenthusiastic response was more like "shuffling the deck chairs rather than introducing new, proven strategies," with the move fervently opposed by executives of new media outlets such as YouTube, LinkedIn, Twitter, Facebook, Apple and Microsoft (Miller & DeYoung, 2016). Coverage of areas affected by Islamic State is left more to precarious labor than full-time staffers, fostering coverage that often takes the form of discrete and simplistic relays, offered in response to dramatic events and unconnected to larger trends (Seib, 2017). Nonetheless, an eclectic mix of those reporting on Islamic State still exists: conventional news organizations and social media outlets, bloggers, stringers, freelancers and special websites with devoted coverage using open source tools.

While similarly complex, Islamic State's media apparatus fares better. Boasting a "bureaucracy and organization that rivals that of a multinational corporation or government agency, not a group of backwoods fighters" (Milton, 2016, p. 10), it relies on tight production and loose dissemination (Miller & Mekhennet, 2015), where it strategically tailors the messages, tones and themes of its relays while distributing them through decentralized hubs. Though Islamic State's media apparatus appears to be contracting (Milton, 2016; Winter & Clarke, 2017), it bypasses conventional media outlets and skillfully engages in its own information distribution: "ISIS fighters," said one news executive, "do not give interviews. They speak directly into the camera" (quoted in Simon & Libby, 2015). Using a changing repertoire of social media that is generally user-curated, dependent on peer-to-peer sharing (Klausen, 2015) and organized across a set of interconnected media hubs—the news agency A'maq, coordinated provincial media offices and social media outlets—Islamic State boasts a complex media network described as a "swarmcast" for its display of resilience, speed and agility (Fisher, 2015; Ronfeldt & Arquila, 2001, para. 2). In both cases, the mediated environment is buttressed by extensive offline activity that helps to fashion strategic understandings of the conflict.

Against these circumstances, Cold War cues drive relays of the US–Islamic State conflict. With the media deeply schooled in how to think about hostility and enmity, in what is required to know and see of the wars such enmity fosters and in what could be the media's role therein, the Cold War mindset has been easily reproduced in US and Islamic State coverage of each other. Such a Cold War redux, and its direct borrowing from conventions established during the Cold War, raises questions, however, about memory's role in forcing long-held interpretive prisms on current events, regardless of their relevance.

Binary notions of enmity

The most essential prism of the Cold War mindset involves accepting the notion of an enemy—he or she who is not us and who threatens us. Muting both dissident and neutral voices, enmity offers a way to represent conflicting factions with simplicity, uniformity and internal consistency: "we" are virtuous, compassionate, tolerant, fair; "they" are extremist, brutal, primitive, despotic. It remains key to sharpening, articulating and keeping notions of collective identity alive (Spillmann & Spillmann, 1997), an endeavor that intensifies in times of conflict.

Central to enemy formation are dichotomies, which successfully reduce the complex, unmanageable and often indecipherable realities of war into binaries (Finlay, Holsti, & Fagen, 1967). Offering mirror images that position perceived enemies as diametrically opposed to each other, enmity divides sides into "good" and "bad," where "exactly the same behavior is moral if WE do it but immoral if THEY do it" (capitals in original) (Osgood, 1961, p. 13). A range of antithetical values helps clarify what "us" and "them" mean—good/bad, right/wrong, moral/immoral—and it maintains the divide between the two as uncrossable. Particularly resonant in times of uncertainty and turmoil, enmity's expressions of distrust, polarization, zero-sum thinking, negative stereotypy, guilt projection, deindividualization and rejection of empathy "turn established values upside down" with "the otherwise forbidden" newly encouraged (Beck, 1997, p. 66). In this way, enemy images turn into incubators for all sorts of projections, such as ethnic prejudice, political intolerance or religious fundamentalism.

Enmity drives the relationship between Islamic State and the US, widely reflected in each entity's coverage of the other. From the US side, enmity toward Islamic State draws upon the Cold War application of a centuries-old dichotomy between "East" and "West." Though that dichotomy dates to the very beginning of American identity formation, where the fledgling US encountered a deep-seated opposition "between the Occident and Orient, civilization and barbarism" (Malia, 1999, p. 6), it was easily mapped onto Cold War notions of the "USSR" and "US" and then reapplied over time to countless subsequent conflicts. As US enemy formation replaced the threat of communism with ill-defined threats on multiple continents, Islamic fundamentalism became a favored target. Since 2015, Islamic State has ranked among the most widely perceived US enemies and is the only non-nation entity among them (Norman, 2016), and some US officials regard Islamic State as the US's "main enemy" in the Middle East (Stewart & Landay, 2017, para. 12). No surprise, then, that by early 2017 the US was leading a 68-member alliance against the group (Dorsey, 2017).

Islamic State similarly supports enmity toward the US Proclaiming its war on western values as necessary for the caliphate's resurgence, the group sees the US obstructing its plans for apocalyptic confrontation, though it rejects the idea that the US is its chief enemy. Rather, the US is one among many infidel countries, all of which require uprooting (Islamic State, 2016). In *Foreign Affairs'* view, Islamic State distinguishes between

> the lands governed by the caliphate, which it calls *dar al-Islam* ("the domain of Islam"), and the lands of its enemies, known as *dar al-harb* ("the domain of war"). In this black-and-white world, ISIS seeks to eliminate what it calls the "gray zone"—multicultural societies, especially in the West, where Muslims and non-Muslims coexist peacefully. (Revkin, 2016, para. 2)

The media apparatuses of both sides reflect the clear contours of this enmity. Islamic State relays hold the US as an emblem of the evils of western civilization, while US media regard Islamic State as representative of pro-terror Islamist forces (Zelizer, 2017). Such enmity easily transforms into what looks like an "existential clash of civilizations" (Revkin, 2016, para. 3).

Enmity underscores the necessity of aligning with one side or the other. For instance, when Trump functionary Steve Bannon characterized US efforts against Islamic State as a "global war against Islamic fascism" (Feder, 2016, para. 19), the Al-Qaeda-backed newspaper *Al-Masra* saw his comment as proof that "the West is locked in a civilizational war with Islam" (cited in Guilford, 2017, para. 1). By generalizing a specific enemy into an emblem of some greater vice, clear statements of enmity allow the ferocity of imagined danger—Islam's war against the infidels or the West's so-called war on terror—to mobilize the media in a way that helps foment and sustain enmity across an evolving roster of antagonists.

Dichotomous thinking thus puts the US and Islamic State on opposite sides, where, true to notions of Cold War enemy formation (Bronfenbrenner, 1961), they adopt mirrored versions of each other: each side's media portray the other as immoral, the other's government as corrupt, the other's people as duped, ill-served and badly represented by the government. Though the particular values ascribed to the us/them binary may differ—Islamic State derides the US as apostates, while the US targets Islamic State's barbarism—the enmity cemented is formulaic and wholly predictable.

Examples abound. Islamic State regularly targets the US and other western nations as heretics and fools: *Dabiq* magazine, over its two-year run, featured a regular section titled "In the Words of the Enemy" which ridiculed US political and military action, while its successor—*Rumiyah*—offers ongoing tips on whom to attack and how, classifying Macy's Thanksgiving Day Parade in New York City as "an excellent target" (Just Terror Tactics, 2016, p. 12). Once Trump assumed power, antagonism intensified, as Islamic State supporters saw his rhetoric as making clear that US enmity was directed against Islam and not just terrorism (Amarasingam, 2017, paras. 7–9).

A similar sense of enmity drives US coverage, where deep-seated cues, such as those offered by the Cold War mindset, offer guidelines for covering Islamic State: *The Atlantic* called the group "a key agent of the coming apocalypse" (Wood, 2015), while *USA Today* characterized its 2015 Paris attacks as part of a "war of modernity against medievalism, of civilization against barbarity" (Editorial Board, 2015, para. 12). Fox News described Islamic State's 2016 attack on Brussels as "terrorists that are coming for us and our way of life" (Schoen, 2016, para. 10).

At the same time, enmity requires a clarity of purpose on the part of those fostering it, with aspirational aims presented in structurally similar ways even if they differ in content: the US orients to freedom and democracy above all else, while Islamic State aims to entrench absolute religious certitude, positioning itself as "the true believers and defenders of Sunni being, rights, and property" (Zelin, 2015). Thus, Islamic State's media celebrate the provision of health care, education and restored infrastructure, promoting a "utopian image of early, conquering and united Islam that it cultivates meticulously (and which works all the better the less versed in Islamic culture the audience actually is)" (Harling & Birke, 2015). US media project the image of a fearless and ongoing struggle to sustain democracy, liberty, equality and human rights, arguing, as in the *New York Post*, that "if we don't fight ISIS over there, we'll soon be fighting here" (Chavez, 2015).

Dichotomies of enmity are also fueled metaphorically. US media have likened Islamic State's actions to the genocide in Rwanda or the siege of Sarajevo: a *New York Times* editorial called out the parallels between Islamic State and the Holocaust (Editorial, 2016), while CBS News' *60 Minutes* likened Islamic State's mass killings to those engineered by Hitler (Logan, 2016). Among Muslims, the conflict has been seen in the context of the Iran/Iraq War of the 1980s (Amin, 2017) or, with much debate, the slaughter of Islam's first radicals, "the Khawarij" (Arnold, 2017). In one observer's words, Islamic State wants "to be seen as the group that's returning to the very earliest iteration of Islam" (Charlie Winter quoted in Engel, 2016). Islamic State's media apparatus thus frames its conflict with the US in the context of generations of infidels violating Islamic sanctity: in its drive for what *The Atlantic* (Wood, 2015, last para.) called the "imminent fulfillment of prophecy as a matter of dogma," Islamic State remains confident that "it will receive divine succor."

Long-standing binary notions of enemy formation thereby wait for the opportunity to become relevant. Not only does enmity offer a clear-cut understanding of whose side one needs to be on, but it links simultaneously to the decades-old aim of saving Islam on the one hand, or saving the free world on the other. Lost from consideration is where such dichotomies begin and end and for whose ends they prevail.

Recognition of invisible war

Piggybacking on enmity in the Cold War mindset is the idea of invisible war—the notion that war does not have to be seen in order to elicit response. Fostering the impression that unseen war is real if enough people with power will it so, it was relevant to the Cold War because no battles, corpses or skirmishes between the US and the USSR offset what was primarily a mediated information campaign, and the aim of the logic of deterrence remained one of non-engagement. Though the war between Islamic State and the US differs because it involves carnage and destruction, the coverage of Islamic State nonetheless rides upon the invisible dimensions of many aspects of the war's prosecution. With few familiar attributes of traditional war—recognized governments or symmetrical rules of military conduct—and with new aspects of unseen war provided by smart bombs, drone attacks, digital monitoring and virtual war, only partial moments in the war's prosecution are visualized from both sides (Zelizer, 2016).

Thus, in much the same way that enmity offers mirrored versions of the moral uprightness of one's own side and moral turpitude of the other's side, the orientation to unseen war involves depicting only those aspects of warfare that each side wants shown. This involves a predilection for self-censorship that generates explicit and implicit parallels, with each side showing itself as victor and the other as defeated. Though war's depiction and description are always smaller than its events, the conflict between Islamic State and the US takes on singular attributes in each side's mediated coverage of the other.

Islamic State's coverage of the US is run by a strong investment in "the phantasmagorical" that orients to unseen war as "the best way to compensate for real-world limits" (Harling & Birke, 2015, para. 1). With the war "not only in the field but also in the media" (quoted in Lynch & Weiss, 2016), the group is organized via two axes: one military, the other mediated and "confronting the Satanic" media of the West (Al-Muhajir, 2017, p. 23). Dedicated to animating the "battlefield of Twitter and Facebook" (Shiloach, 2016), Islamic State allows real battlefields to eclipse representation. This aim, typical of information wars, makes their invisibility, styled after that of the Cold War, particularly valuable:

> Jihadist groups were never naive enough to think that they could defeat the US militarily on the battlefield. Rather, the point was to draw Americans into a war of attrition, let them punch themselves out, make American Muslims aware of their insecure place in the country, and make American citizens afraid of each other. (Amarasingam, 2017, para. 17)

In such a context, the media often call the shots, as noted by a former cameraman who remembered an execution he had filmed that "wasn't run by the executioner. It's the media guy who says when they are ready" (quoted in Miller & Mekhennet, 2015). In addition to censoring information, controlling the internet, banning satellite dishes and cutting off competing media outlets, Islamic State uses multiple tactics to strategically leave many aspects of its activity invisible.

The slippages of unseen war allow the group to represent the war as it deems relevant. Islamic State relays rarely show the group's fighters fully, but instead obscure them with masks or faces pixilated from the images (Hall, 2014). The names of its two glossy magazines dance around a tenuous link with reality: *Dabiq* was named for the northern Syrian town whose occupation features in prophecies about the coming apocalypse, while its successor, *Rumiyah*, orients even more to the imaginary, signaling an imagined Islamic occupation of the Roman Empire. First *Dabiq* then *Rumiyah* depict sweeping battlefield victories that are often more aspired to than real: *Dabiq* (Remaining and Expanding, 2014) detailed the group's plans for expansion across the Arabian Peninsula, while *Rumiyah* (Untitled, 2017, p. 10) imagined an attack against a Baptist church in Dallas that it proclaimed "a popular Crusader gathering place waiting to be burned down." Islamic State's first full-length documentary—*Flames of War* (2014)—spliced together real images with fantastical ones and imagined victorious scenes alongside depictions of real battles. In this way, Islamic State's media act as a "force multiplier to make [Islamic State] appear active in many locations even though most of its activities are in Iraq and Syria" (Zelin, 2015).

Islamic State frames itself through what Stern and Berger (2015, 110) called a "unified narrative"—one that does not need to show war to instill belief and support for its prosecution. For that reason, only a portion of its relays are violent in nature, with the remainder focused on religion, education, governance, commerce/business and social services. This means both that Islamic State provides extensive information not focused on the war and that its war-related information is not a complete representation of what ensues. Though Islamic State "projects an image of always being on the march [where] there is always progress, with enemies being killed, defeated or territory taken over" (Zelin, 2015), a greater Islamic State universe remains largely unseen; because war is invisible, it can be given an aspired trajectory regardless of how much its events cohere. Thus, *Rumiyah* magazine promised that "even if America came with all of its forces—rather with all of its men and women—to wage war against us, then indeed we shall be victorious" (Untitled, 2016, p. 20), a sentiment articulated as it celebrated "the attack in Minnesota [that] terrorized the Crusaders" (Untitled, 2016, p. 34).

At the opposite side of unseen war is the graphic violence associated with Islamic State. It comprises much of what the world sees and discusses even though it constitutes an extremely small universe: estimates of depicted violence vary from 2% (Coker & Flynn, 2015; Winter, 2015) to less than 9% (Milton, 2016, p. 300) of all mediated Islamic State relays. The disproportionate focus on violence, however, has left accompanying depictions of "markets, service provision and agriculture ... wholly ignored" by western media

(Winter, 2015, p. 32), hiding the fact that the use of spectacle, strategically reserved for particular audiences, "fatally derail[s] mainstream understanding of the organization and its appeal" (Winter, 2015, p. 7). As one analyst noted, "life goes on even while the war is continuing" (Zelin, 2015), and keeping this impression intact is a key part of Islamic State's media apparatus, where it sidesteps war and shows "normalcy within the territory it controls" (Zelin, 2015; see also Winter, 2015). Both *Dabiq* and *Rumiyah*, for instance, regularly treat their audience to images of individuals receiving health care, nurturing children, building infrastructures and engaging in a productive commercial life— offering what one observer labeled a "perfectly functioning society where Muslims live happily in accordance with their Islamic principles" (Williams, 2016, para. 14).

Moreover, online activity is surpassed by offline media activity, where the role of radio, the press and media kiosks has been "almost totally obscured by the world's fixation on its online equivalent" (Winter, 2016, para. 5). Such offline activity has helped Islamic State "extend its reach, infiltrate its message into remote regions with no online infrastructure, and sustain a constant information presence in population centers" (Winter, 2016, para. 7).

US coverage similarly repairs to unseen war. In large part this is facilitated by the dependence of US information efforts—like those of other western nations, stopgap measures that "maintain a foothold … until there can be greater military involvement" (Cobain et al., 2016)—on "deploying mostly symbolic tools" (Harling & Birke, 2015). Such a dependence renders the war with Islamic State similar to the Cold War, whose analogy remains intact: John Kerry pronounced the Cold War a simple version of the fight against Islamic State (Taylor, 2015), while the *Huffington Post* labeled Orlando "today's Cold War Moscow" after an attack on a local nightclub (Orlando Shows, 2016). In a piece critical of then-presidential candidate Donald Trump's attempt to create a strongman image, CNN ran a headline mocking his equation of the Cold War and Islamic State (Collinson, 2016).

Realistic relays have not necessarily been part of the picture of US coverage. Instead, as evident during the Cold War, "the worse things get, the more we seem willing to describe things as we wish they might be rather than as they are" (Harling & Birke, 2015). The speculation and imagination associated with unseen war thus prevail.

Examples are numerous: CNN featured a close-up of a Muslim woman in a video about Islamic State recruitment in Michigan, though she was unconnected to the group (Rodriguez, 2016). The appellation of the "Iraqi army" referenced what was in effect "a worndown collection of abused and often corrupt men who fled as the Islamic State advanced" (Harling & Birke, 2015). A column in the *Washington Post* suggested that Halloween costumes be employed to fight Islamic State (Moyer, 2014). Notions of collateral damage, virtual war, sphere of influence, power vacuum, infiltration—many of which first surfaced during the Cold War—regularly appear in US coverage (Youssef, 2016). Relevant here has been the focus on drones and other computerized equipment that facilitate the reliance on unseen war, many such devices newly improvised and homemade (Joscelyn, 2017).

Thus, as might be predicted, US media focus on defeat in the same battlefields that Islamic State pronounces itself victorious. Nowhere was this as clear as in the early feature-length films that each side produced on the war where similar battles were hailed by the two sides as polarized examples of victory or loss (Zelizer, 2016). The insistence on imagining what cannot be seen emblematizes its value: "Even as [Islamic State] faces setbacks on the battlefield, it has made forays into our collective psyche" (Harling & Birke, 2015).

Equalization of media reach with impact

Alongside proclamations of clear enmity and a belief in invisible war is a celebratory embrace of media influence—the idea that media reach is equivalent to media impact. Central to the Cold War notion that winning the war meant simply making contact with those under the grip of the other side, the "struggle for the hearts and minds of men" was presumed to end in victory. Cold war support for information outreach took place through not only the activities of Voice of America or Radio Free Europe but also journalists across the media who consolidated the belief that everyone would inevitably "sense the inherent truthfulness of US news" (Cooley, 1952, pp. 44–45). This notion of media impact, built into journalism's notions of itself and its presumed inevitable influence, drives much of the global media environment. It is no surprise, then, that it emerges as relevant to both Islamic State and US media relays.

Islamic State coheres to the idea of media impact with great diligence, for the influential entrenchment of symbolic targets in the ideological war between the West and Islam was relevant from the earliest days of the group's emergence. Though Syrian intellectual Sadik al-Azm had noted before the rise of Islamic State that the events of 9/11 were "proof that the West has won the war of ideas between the two sides [because] no one who can convince others of the virtues of their political views flies airplanes into buildings" (quoted in Gray, 2015), by and large fighting an information war brought with it its own symbolic currency.

Islamic State's belief in media influence is not incidental, for it is clearly laid out in the group's central monograph—Abu Bakr Naji's (2004/2006) *The Management of Savagery: The Most Critical Stage Through Which the Umma Will Pass*. Called the second most important book for Islamic State after the Koran, the monograph offers a "communications theory of global religious revolution," whose main thesis stipulates that the: military power of the West and the "subservience" of Islamic believers to the ideals of secular democracy and nationalism is maintained through … an illusory "media halo" that must be countered (Raschke, 2014). Positioning global jihad as a tool to "destroy a large part of the respect for America and spread confidence in the souls of Muslims," Abu Bakr Naji located its disruptive nature in its ability to "reveal the deceptive media to be a power without force" (Raschke, 2014). Thus, central to Islamic State's efforts is the staging of symbolic acts and relays that are thought to diminish the western media halo.

This helps explain why Islamic State's media apparatus is both extensive and complex and why it is heavily influenced by Western tropes, chosen to enhance the impact of its relays. Entrenched in cultural references that resound in the West, Islamic State relays call to mind video games like *Call of Duty* as easily as they mimic films like *Natural Born Killers* (Dettmer, 2014; Kang, 2014). In *The Guardian*'s view:

> Virtually every frame has been treated. The colour is so saturated, the combatants appear to glow with light. Explosions are lingered over in super slow motion. There are effects giving the feel of TV footage or old photographs. Transitions between clips are sheets of flame and

blinding flashes. Graphics fly across the screen. Sonorous, auto-tuned chanting and cacophonous gunfire reverberate on the soundtrack. (Rose, 2014, para. 8)

The promise of media impact permeates the core of Islamic State's relays, with the group's operatives considering information one of their key assets. As one noted in May of 2016, "Just like bullets have an impact on the enemies, your tweets have an impact on them ... The war is not only in the field but also in the media" (quoted in Lynch & Weiss, 2016).

On the US side, coverage of Islamic State is driven by a similarly deep belief in media influence, which in *Foreign Policy*'s words is activated to "win the hearts and minds in the Muslim world" (Helmus & Kaye, 2009, para. 1). From its earliest sightings in the US media, Islamic State has been characterized as skillfully waging a media war. In April of 2016, then-commander of the US Cyber Command Admiral Michael Rogers told the Senate Armed Services Committee that the group was trying to "harness the power of the information arena" so as to propagate its ideology. Ironically, CNN's report of Rogers' statement ran a heading that proclaimed such efforts "a real-life cyberattack imitat[ing] the movies" (Brown, 2016).

Arguing the need for a counterattack, in 2016 US Deputy Secretary of Defense Robert Work announced a US cyber campaign against Islamic State "just like we have an air campaign ... I want to use all the space capabilities I have" (Frenkel, 2016). Widely read as a coded reference to the malware being dropped onto social media forums frequented by Islamic State supporters, the belief in equating reach with impact was clear. And because a war for cold-war-inspired "hearts and minds of men" implied that targets of persuasion would present not only along the way but also at campaign's end, US media outlets energetically produced a wide span of articles, videos, photos, radio broadcasts and social media posts in the effort, underscoring, as *The Guardian* noted more broadly, that "information is a vital element of modern conflict" (Cobain et al., 2016).

However, in large part, US media have not inhabited the media landscape as deftly as has the media apparatus of Islamic State. Already in 2016, the *Huffington Post* pointed to "11 rules for journalists in covering ISIS [as] issued by ISIS" (Taibi, 2014). When videos and photographs of beheadings began to widely circulate, US media were awash with possible responses, none of them particularly effective. Faced with the challenge, in the Associated Press' Santiago Lyon's view, of "how to show reality without succumbing to propaganda" (quoted in Simon & Libby, 2015), US journalists displayed the images alongside mitigating discourse that attested to their inhumanity, cruelty and immorality. Some news outlets replaced the about-to-die photos, taken for their shock value at the moment before death (Zelizer, 2010), with images from happier times. In covering the death of US hostage Kayla Mueller, for instance, the *New York Times* depicted its story with multiple pictures of her smiling at home and hugging her dog (Callimachi & Schmitt, 2015, p. A12). Some media outlets blocked graphic images altogether, with *The Atlantic* even querying whether an Islamic State documentary produced by Vice had broken the law (March, 2014).

Offsetting Islamic State coverage, then, has been the key response by US media, rather than more fully and proactively anticipating what ensues from Islamic State relays. Thus, Islamic State's 2015 attack on the Paris club Bataclan received widespread media attention —what *Variety* characterized as "wall-to-wall coverage" (Lang, 2015). *The Nation* offered its view of why such coverage mattered:

> Countries are moved to protect individuals (within and beyond their borders) by pressure from citizens. Citizens can only pressure their government to act if they are aware of the hardships facing those who are imperiled. And citizens (and policy-makers) rely on media to keep them informed. (Darling-Hammond, 2016, para. 7)

Despite discourse equating reach and impact—underscored too by a lawsuit against Facebook, Twitter and Google on the grounds that their "material support" assisted those plotting the attack (Johnson & Reyes, 2016)—left relatively unaddressed was a terror attack in Beirut one day earlier, raising the question of which events were most relevant to upholding belief in impact.

US media thus appeared cobbled in their attempts to reconcile a belief in media impact with the fact that reach was emanating from hostile quarters, and that dissonance distilled the impact of their own media relays. As Al Jazeera noted, "by hyping the threat [of Islamic State], the US is falling into the group's trap" (Al-Gharbi, 2014). With conventional US media primarily engaged in blocking, nullifying and countering Islamic State relays, fuller coverage of the group was often left to the so-called "news upstarts," who "expanded their mandate to fill the void" (Moses, 2014, para. 1). All of this prompted the *Columbia Journalism Review* already in 2014 to reflect critically on how inadequate—and familiar—Islamic State coverage seemed (Colhoun, 2014).

With both sides embracing the notion that reach equaled impact but with Islamic State acting upon that notion more forcefully than the US, the aim of winning the minds and hearts of the other side ended up serving one side to the conflict more than the other. For the US, it rested more fully in the Cold War past from which it was taken than in coverage of the current conflict.

Conclusion

The relevance of the Cold War mindset in coverage of and by Islamic State suggests that mnemonic structures carry on and disseminate in peculiar ways over time and often in dissonant and unpredictable locations. More important, it suggests that even in a so-called new entity like Islamic State, an old media logic—specifically, one established in the United States over half a century ago—nonetheless runs much of its media apparatus, adding an odd permutation to understandings of the well-trodden effects of the global flow of news.

The default setting for explaining global conflict from the perspectives of both the US and Islamic State reveals formulaic elements in its display: an orientation toward binary separations of us versus them, an emphasis on winning versus losing, an absence of structural explanation, a focus on exaggerated black-and-white descriptions of enemy character, an underlying judgment call of right versus wrong, an elision of war's signification and a dependence on the media to set things in motion.

Each of these strategies should be very familiar to those familiar with US journalism, for they are part of the way that the past drives US news writ large. But what is peculiar here is the Cold War mindset's perseverance as the deep memory that inspires Islamic State's own media activity. Though Cold War mindedness is not the only deep structure undergirding its media apparatus, Islamic State mimics the cues by which the global flow of news, largely led by US media, tends to unfold. This suggests that the minds behind Islamic State's media apparatus are not as far from the long-standing platforms of the US media landscape as assumed.

In 2015, the *Washington Post* proclaimed that "in its propaganda war against ISIS, the US tried to play by the enemy's rules" (Miller & Higham, 2015). This analysis suggests the opposite: Islamic State plays by US media rules, following a mnemonic pattern that the US media set in place long ago.

All of this underscores the degree to which the media apparatuses of the US and Islamic State borrow liberally from a media precedent set by the US during the earliest years of the Cold War. That shared foundation makes binaries less distinct, renders invisible war into an objective that profits both sides and dilutes the projection of impact because it already exists. If nothing else, this should at least give pause about what is being accomplished—and lost—by incorporating Cold War conventions and sentiments into the coverage of contemporary news events.

Acknowlegement

This article was written while the author was the Helsingin Sanomat Foundation Fellow at the Collegium for Advanced Studies at the University of Helsinki.

References

Al-Gharbi, M. (2014, September 30). By hyping ISIL threat, US is falling into group's trap. *Al Jazeera*. Retrieved from http://america.aljazeera.com/opinions/2014/9/islamic-state-united statessyriairaqmilitaryintervention.html

Al-Muhajir, A. H. (2017, January 6). Paths to victory (Part 3). *Rumiyah*, 22–24.

Amarasingam, A. (2017, March). What ISIS fighters think of Trump. *Politico*. Retrieved from http://www.politico.com/magazine/story/2017/03/what-isis-fighters-think-of-trump-214843

Amin, S. (2017, March 14). Bloodshed in the Middle East. *Pakistan Observer*. Retrieved from http://pakobserver.net/bloodshed-in-the-middle-east/

Arnold, M. (2017, March 16). ISIS: Intellectual roots and the question of religious authenticity. *The Islamic Monthly*. Retrieved from http://theislamicmonthly.com/isis-intellectual-roots-question-religious-authenticity/

Beck, U. (1997). The sociological anatomy of enemy images. In R. Fiebig-von Hase & U. Lehmkuhl (Eds.), *Enemy images in American history* (pp. 65–87). Providence, RI: Bergahn Books.

Bronfenbrenner, U. (1961). The mirror image in Soviet-American relations: A social psychologist's view. *Journal of Social Issues*, *17*(3), 45–56

Brown, R. (2016, April 5). Top military official warns of ISIS attacks. *CNN*. Retrieved from http://edition.cnn.com/2016/04/05/politics/isis-cyberattacks-michael-rogers/

Callimachi, R., & Schmitt, E. (2015, February 10). With proof from ISIS of her death, family honors Kayla Mueller. *New York Times*, A12.

Chavez, L. (2015, November 20). If we don't fight ISIS over there, we'll soon be fighting here. *New York Post*. Retrieved from http://nypost.com/2015/11/20/if-we-dont-fight-isis-over-there-well-soon-be-fighting-here/

Cobain, I., et al. (2016, May 31). How Britain funds the "propaganda war" against ISIS in Syria. *The Guardian*. Retrieved from https://www.theguardian.com/world/2016/may/03/how-britain-funds-the-propaganda-war-against-isis-in-syria

Coker, M., & Flynn, A. (2015, October 13). Islamic State tries to show it can govern in Iraq and Syria. *Wall Street Journal*. Retrieved from http://www.wsj.com/articles/in-a-shift-islamic-state-tries-to-show-it-can-govern-1444779561

Colhoun, D. (2014, November 14). Why ISIS coverage sounds familiar. *Columbia Journalism Review*. Retrieved from http://archives.cjr.org/behind_the_news/why_isis_coverage_sounds_famil.php

Collinson, S. (2016, August 15). For Trump, Cold War = ISIS, *CNN*. Retrieved from http://www.cnn.com/2016/08/15/politics/donald-trump-isis-campaign-revival/

Cooley, H. (1952). *Vision in television*. New York: Channel Press.

Darling-Hammond, S. (2016, January 13). Lives fit for print: Exposing media bias in coverage of terrorism. *The Nation*. Retrieved from https://www.thenation.com/article/lives-fit-for-print-exposing-media-bias-in-coverage-of-terrorism/

Dettmer, J. (2014, September 23). How ISIS ripped off natural born killers. *The Daily Beast*. Retrieved from http://www.thedailybeast.com/articles/2014/09/23/how-isis-ripped-off-natural-born-killers.html

Dorsey, J. (2017, March 25). Defeating the Islamic State: A war mired in contradictions. *Huffington Post*. Retrieved from http://www.huffingtonpost.com/entry/defeating-the-islamic-state-a-war-mired-in-contradictions_us_58d732ece4b06c3d3d3e6e93

Editorial. (2016, March 18). Genocide and the Islamic State. *New York Times*, A26.

Editorial Board. (2015, November 16). The nature of this war: Our view. *USA Today*. Retrieved from http://www.usatoday.com/story/opinion/2015/11/14/paris-attacks-islamic-state-terrorism-editorials-debates/75788436/

Engel, P. (2016, September 26). This is the name ISIS hates being called more than "Daesh." *BusinessInsider.com*. Retrieved from http://www.businessinsider.com/isis-khawarij-2016-9?r=US&IR=T&IR=T

Feder, L. (2016, November 15). This is how Steve Bannon sees the entire world. *Buzzfeed*. Retrieved from https://www.buzzfeed.com/lesterfeder/this-is-how-steve-bannon-sees-the-entire-world?utm_term=.uqqvEPB6m#.rsJopB0NM

Finlay, D., Holsti, O., & Fagen, R. (1967). *Enemies in politics*. Chicago: Rand McNally.

Fisher, A. (2015, June). Swarmcast: How jihadist networks maintain a persistent online presence. *Perspectives on Terrorism*, 9(3). Retrieved from http://terrorismanalysts.com/pt/index.php/pot/article/view/426/html

Flames of War. (2014, September). [Film] Al Hayyat media center. Trailer retrieved from https://www.youtube.com/watch?v=PYDchUAG1y0

Frenkel, S. (2016, May 12). Everything you ever wanted to know about how ISIS uses the internet. *Buzzfeed*. Retrieved from https://www.buzzfeed.com/sheerafrenkel/everything-you-ever-wanted-to-know-about-how-isis-uses-the-i?utm_term=.ilO7GM3907#.lcy7JR1Br7

Gray, M. (2015). Beyond the spectacle of violence. *Insidestory.org*, September 17. Retrieved from http://insidestory.org.au/beyond-the-spectacle-of-violence

Guilford, G. (2017, March 2). A pro-Al Qaeda newspaper put Steve Bannon on the front page because they think he's right. *Quartz.com*. Retrieved from https://qz.com/923057/steve-bannons-on-the-cover-of-a-pro-al-qaeda-newspaper-because-they-think-hes-right/

Hall, M. (2014, November 1). "This is our call of duty": How ISIS is using video games. *Salon.com*. Retrieved from http://www.salon.com/2014/11/01/this_is_our_call_of_duty_how_isis_is_using_video_games/

Harling, P., & Birke, S. (2015, March 3). The Islamic State through the looking-glass. *The Arabist*. Retrieved from http://arabist.met/blog/2015/3/3/the-islamic-state-through-the-looking-glass

Helmus, T., & Kaye, D. (2009, October 14). Fighting terror the Cold War way. *Foreign Policy*. Retrieved from foreignpolicy.com/2009/10/14/fighting-terror-the-cold-war-way/

Islamic State: Although it leads global unbelief, the US is an enemy like all other enemies. (2016, April 10). *MEMRI* (Special Dispatch No. 6381). Translation from *Al-Naba* 23 (2016, March 22). Retrieved from https://www.memri.org/reports/islamic-state-although-it-leads-global-unbelief-us-enemy-all-other-enemies#_edn1

Johnson, A., & Reyes, P. (2016, June 16). Father of American killed in Paris attacks sues Facebook, Twitter, Google. *NBC News*. Retrieved from http://www.nbcnews.com/storyline/paristerror-attacks/family-american-killed-paris-attacks-sues-twitter-facebook-googlen593351

Joscelyn, T. (2017, March 18). Islamic State uses improvised weapons of war in Mosul, Iraq. *LongWarJournal.org*. Retrieved from http://www.longwarjournal.org/archives/2017/03/islamic-state-uses-improvised-weapons-of-war-in-mosul-iraq.php

Just terror tactics. (2016, November). *Rumiyah* 3, Safar 1438, 10–12.

Kang, J. (2014, September 18). ISIS's call of duty. *The New Yorker*. Retrieved from http://www.newyorker.com/tech/elements/isis-video-game

Klausen, J. (2015). Tweeting the *jihad*: Social media networks of western foreign fighters in Syria and iraq. *Studies in Conflict and Terrorism, 38*(1), 1–22.

Lang, B. (2015, November 14). US media goes wall-to-wall with Paris terrorist coverage attack. *Variety*. Retrieved from http://variety.com/c2015/tv/news/paris-attacks-media-1201640615/

Logan, L. (2016, May 8). The killing machine. *60 Minutes*. CBS News. Retrieved from http://www.cbsnews.com/videos/the-killing-machine/

Lynch, S., & Weiss, A. (2016, May 22). ISIS hashtag goes viral. *Vocativ.com*. Retrieved from http://www.vocativ.com/321161/isis-hashtag-goes-viral-thanks-to-trolls-insulting-the-terror-group/

Malia, M. (1999). *Russia under western eyes*. Cambridge, MA: Belknap Press of Harvard University Press.

March, A. (2014, October 1). Is Vice documentary on ISIS Illegal? *Atlantic Monthly*. Retrieved from https://www.theatlantic.com/international/archive/2014/10/is-vice-documentary-on-ISIS-illegal/380991/

Miller, G., & DeYoung, K. (2016, January 8). Obama administration plans shake-up in propaganda war against ISIS. *Washington Post*. Retrieved from https://www.washingtonpost.com/world/national-security/obama-administration-plans-shake-up-in-propaganda-war-against-the-islamic-state/2016/01/08/d482255c-b585-11e5-a842-0feb51d1d124_story.html?utm_term=.6e22d2dede8e

Miller, G., & Higham, S. (2015, May 8). In a propaganda war against ISIS, the US tried to play by the enemy's rules. *Washington Post*. Retrieved from https://www.washingtonpost.com/world/national-security/in-a-propaganda-war-us-tried-to-play-by-the-enemys-rules/2015/05/08/6eb6b732-e52f-11e4-81ea-0649268f729e_story.html?utm_term=.bd62b07bc429

Miller, G., & Mekhennet, S. (2015, November 20). Inside the surreal world of the Islamic State's propaganda machine. *Washington Post*. Retrieved from https://www.washingtonpost.com/world/national-security/inside-the-islamic-states-propaganda-machine/2015/11/20/051e997a-8ce6-11e5-acff-673ae92ddd2b_story.html?utm_term=.f9b42b399de4

Milton, D. (2016, October). *Communication breakdown: Unraveling the Islamic State's media efforts*. West Pt, NY: United States Military Academy, Combating Terrorism Center at West Point.

Moses, L. (2014, August 27). How the news upstarts covered ISIS. *Digiday.com*. Retrieved from http://digiday.com/publishers/upstarts-covered-isis/

Moyer, J. (2014, October 23). ISIS Halloween costumes are what we need to fight the Islamic State. *Washington Post*. Retrieved from https://www.washingtonpost.com/posteverything/wp/2014/10/23/isis-halloween-costumes-are-what-we-need-to-fight-the-islamic-state/?utm_term=.929d084d0206

Mumford, A. (2013). *Proxy warfare*. Cambridge: Polity.

Naji, A. B. (2006 [2004]). *The management of savagery: The most critical stage through which the umma will pass*. Translated by William McCants, with funding from John M. Olin Institute for Strategic Studies. Cambridge, MA: Harvard University Press.

Norman, J. (2016, February 22). Four nations top US's greatest enemy list. *Gallup*. Retrieved from http://www.gallup.com/poll/189503/four-nations-top-greatest-enemy-list.aspx?version=print

Orlando shows that ISIS is today's Cold War Moscow. (2016, June 14). *Huffington Post*. Retrieved from http://www.huffingtonpost.com/entry/orlando-shows-that-isis-is-todays-cold-war-moscow_us_575ee250e4b079c7cee5ff89

Osgood, C. (1961). An analysis of the Cold War mentality. *Journal of Social Issues, 17*(3), 12–19.

Raschke, C. (2014, August 14). The (global) society of the (grisly) spectacle. *Political Theology Today*. August 14, 2014. http://www.politicaltheology.com/blog/the-global-society-of-the-grisly-spectacle-isis-and-the-media-smart-islamist-internationale/

Remaining and expanding. (2014, October). *Dabiq* 5, Muharram 1436.

Revkin, M. (2016, November 14). ISIS' perfect enemy. *Foreign Affairs*. Retrieved from https://www.foreignaffairs.com/articles/middle-east/2016-11-14/isis-perfect-enemy

Rodriguez, M. (2016, August 13). CNN used Michigan Muslim woman's face in video about ISIS recruitment—she's not in ISIS," *Mic.com*. Retrieved from https://mic.com/articles/151478/cnn-used-michigan-muslim-woman-s-face-in-video-about-isis-recruitment-she-s-not-in-isis#.Re8RB79VI

Ronfeldt, D., & Arquila, J. (2001, October). Networks, netwars and the fight for the future. *First Monday*, 6(10). Retrieved from http://ojs-prod-lib.cc.uic.edu/ojs/index.php/fm/article/view/889/798

Rose, S. (2014, October 7). The ISIS propaganda war: A high tech media jihad. *The Guardian*. Retrieved from https://www.theguardian.com/world/2014/oct/07/isis-media-machine-propaganda-war

Schoen, D. (2016, March 28). "ISIS is the enemy, America – not Obama, Hillary or Bush." *Fox News*. Retrieved from http://www.foxnews.com/opinion/2016/03/28/will-terrorism-finally-make-america-whole-again.html

Seib, P. (2017, June 3). Mainstream media fails in terrorism coverage. *Newsweek*. Retrieved from http://www.newsweek.com/mainstream-media-fails-terrorism-coverage-619883

Shiloach, G. (2016, July 27). Pro-ISIS group angry supporters left Twitter, *Vocativ.com*. Retrieved from http://www.vocativ.com/345472/pro-isis-group-berates-supporters-for-leaving-the-twitter-battlefield/

Simon, J., & Libby, S. (2015, April 27). *Broadcasting murder—militants use media for deadly purpose*. New York, NY: Committee to Protect Journalists.

Smythe, D., & Wilson, H. (1968). Cold War mindedness in the mass media. In N. Houghton (Ed.), *Struggle against history* (pp. 59–78). New York, NY: Clarion.

Spillmann, K. R., & Spillmann, K. (1997). Some sociobiological and psychological aspects of "images of the enemy". In R. Fiebig-von Hase & U. Lehmkuhl (Eds.), *Enemy images in American history* (pp. 44–63). Providence, RI: Bergahn Books.

Stern, J., & Berger, J. M. (2015). *ISIS: The state of terror*. New York, NY: HarperCollins.

Stewart, P., & Landay, J. (2017, June 19). By keeping US focus on Islamic State, US risks wider Syria war. *Reuters*. Retrieved from http://www.reuters.com/article/us-mideast-crisis-usa-analysis-idUSKBN19A319

Taibi, C. (2014, October 7). 11 rules for reporters covering ISIS, issued by ISIS. *Huffington Post*. Retrieved from http://www.huffingtonpost.com/2014/10/07/rules-journalists-syria-11-territory-media_n_5945012.html

Taylor, G. (2015, February 25). John Kerry's shock claim: Cold War was simple compared with Islamic State fight. *Washington Times*.

Untitled. (2016, October). *Rumiyah* 2, Muharram 1438.

Untitled. (2017, January). *Rumiyah* 5, Rabi' al-Akhir 1438.

Williams, L. (2016, June 5). *Islamic State propaganda and the mainstream media*. Sydney, Australia: Lowy Institute for International Policy. Retrieved from http://www.lowyinstitute.org/publications/islamic-state-propaganda-and-mainstream-media

Winter, C. (2015, July). *The virtual "caliphate": Understanding Islamic State's propaganda strategy*. London: Quilliam.

Winter, C. (2016, March 27). Totalitarianism 101: the Islamic State's offline propaganda strategy. *Lawfare.com*. Retrieved from https://www.lawfareblog.com/totalitarianism-101-islamic-states-offline-propaganda-strategy

Winter, C., & Clarke, C. (2017, January 31). Is ISIS breaking apart? *Foreign Affairs*. Retrieved from https://www.foreignaffairs.com/articles/2017-01-31/isis-breaking-apart

Wood, G. (2015, March). What ISIS really wants. *The Atlantic*. Retrieved from https://www.theatlantic.com/magazine/archive/2015/03/what-isis-really-wants/384980/

Youssef, N. (2016, January 21). US admits to bombing 29 civilians in ISIS war. *The Daily Beast*. Retrieved from http://www.thedailybeast.com/articles/2016/01/21/exclusive-u-s-admits-to-bombing-29-civilians-in-isis-war.html

Zelin, A. (2015, August). Picture or it didn't happen: A snapshot of the Islamic State's official media output. *Perspectives on Terrorism, 9*(4). Retrieved from http://www.terrorismanalysts.com/pt/index.php/pot/article/view/445/html

Zelizer, B. (2010). *"About to die": How news images move the public*. New York, NY: Oxford University Press.

Zelizer, B. (2016, November). Journalism and deep memory: Cold War mindedness and coverage of Islamic State. *International Journal of Communication, 10*, 6060–6089.

Zelizer, B. (2017). Seeing the present, remembering the past: Terror's representation as an exercise in collective memory. *Television and New Media*. doi:10.1177/1527476417695592

Zelizer, B. (nd). *How the Cold War drives the news*. Unpublished draft manuscript.

Deflating the iconoclash: shifting the focus from Islamic State's iconoclasm to its realpolitik*

Ben O'Loughlin

ABSTRACT
This article explores the tension between religious and political motivations in the strategy of Islamic State. It develops the Arendtian model of politics as a space of appearance through the work of Silverstone, Devji and Cavarero to consider how Islamic State exhibits itself in this space using religious modalities. This space is conceptualized as a global media ecology. Whilst no political actor can control how it is recognized within that ecology, religious and even ethical modalities grant Islamic State a compelling attention-grabbing and persuasive capacity. However, greater exposure of its pragmatic, realpolitik behavior might deflate that identity. The second half of the article sets out several examples of such behavior. The article concludes by suggesting that icons are something all societies live with but the news media that constitute the global space of appearance remain transfixed by iconic acts or icon-smashing. This leaves publics-cum-audiences adrift, uncertain and anxious about the nature, actions and threat of Islamic State.

Introduction

From 9/11 to the most treasured temple in Palmyra, Islamist destruction reminded us that we (not Islamist extremists) have objects and values we hold as untouchable and inviolable. A narrative has emerged anchored around the idea of an iconoclash (EUNIC, 2015) as images cascade across global audiences: bizarre images that anger, transfixing images of horror, and terrifying images that repel. These take the form of what are already the templates or stereotypes of, respectively, the angry pointing cleric clip and the antiquities vandalism montage, the beheading video and the burning man in a cage gif, interspersed with live footage of the latest terrorist attacks. This narrative about the circulation of images expresses a visual economy akin to the economic exchange of valued goods: a clash through the tit-for-tat of icons and images that signify something of worth (Bourdieu, 1991; Gursel, 2016; Mitchell, 2011). Each "side" in the war on terror has shown trophies of valuable people, objects, targets destroyed or being destroyed,

*This article arises from a public debate with Courtney Beale, Senior Director for Global Engagement at the National Security Council, United States, on 21 April 2016. The event was held at New York University, Washington DC, as part of the Iconoclash series convened by the European Union National Institutes for Culture (EUNIC), and organized by Wilfried Eckstein of the Goethe Institute.

the exchange of shock then horror and awe at audacity. This visual economy was exemplified by the orange Guantanamo jumpsuit prompting the production of the orange hostage jumpsuit. In all of this, the public-cum-audience is positioned as passive, left with no choice but to gaze at mass-mediated atrocities and feel that the very media used in everyday life—the web, smartphones—are themselves sources of the dangers that enable these atrocities.

In this article I argue that if we are to properly respond to this iconoclash, we must understand why it is happening. It is happening in part because of Islamists' drive to restore pride and dignity and avenge historical humiliation by creating a game of equals. However, this iconoclash is ultimately driven by geopolitical strategy and must be responded to in those terms. Yet it is that very tension that provides resources to undermine the spectacular and appealing religious and ethical claims Islamic State projects through global media. Whilst accounting for the additional capacity that a religious dimension affords political violence, greater attention to the geopolitical, secular motives and actions of Islamic State could help deflate its presence and reduce its appeal.

This article first sets out a conception of the global space of appearance through which Islamic State performs its violent gestures and others react. The first section of analysis introduces Hannah Arendt's understanding of politics as the exchange of claims within a space of appearance. Since McLuhan's (1962) notion of a global village and the widespread adoption of transnational broadcasting in the 1990s and digital media in the 2000s, it has become possible to speak of a global space of appearance (cf. Silverstone, 2007). Internet access is not universal and problems of firewalls and translation remain. However, it is conceivable not only that individuals on any part of the planet can explore live and recorded footage from most other parts of the world, but that they can interact with and share digital content themselves, and also produce their own content (Merrin, 2014). They can present themselves and their political claims to the world. Anyone can enter the space of appearance. These conditions allowed Al-Qaeda to construct themselves as a global political entity in the twenty-first century's first decade and allow Islamic State to follow a similar strategy in the 2010s. The logics driving behavior in this global media space are set out in the first, largely theoretical section of this paper. It is also necessary to unpack the lines of communication between Islamic State and its recruits and news media portrayals of Islamic State and its recruits that make Islamic State a presence to wider publics. In this context, it becomes possible to make sense of Islamic State constructing their identity and presence in the world as a game of equals in a single space of appearance rather than something external to our cosmos.

The second section of this article compares Islamic State's actual behavior with the way it has been constructed—by itself and by journalists around the world—as waging an image war against icons dear to its opponents. This analysis concludes that any image war *can be presented as* secondary to political strategy: that Islamic State's constructed identity as a fearsomely puritan actor motivated by transcendent ideals is at odds with the realpolitik driving its observable actions. This is not to reduce the religiosity of Islamic State to captivating disguise or ephemeral status, nor to argue that religiosity is just another driver of motive alongside ethnicity that is ultimately secondary to political interests. Rather, the aim is to show how the religious dimension of the movement provides unique materials that can be harnessed for tactical and strategic aims, not least by producing what Brubaker (2016) calls different "modalities" of media content that are compelling to audiences they seek to recruit or seek to intimidate. Non-religious modalities would not prove so compelling.

Such an analysis develops the trajectory of work on media and politics as a space of appearance running through the writings of Arendt, Silverstone, Devji and Cavarero, four scholars who have previously not been explicitly linked but who have all considered how politics involves the display of violence within a shared, visible space. All are useful for bridging the concerns of media and communications scholars with the logics that underpin how groups and individuals use media technologies in everyday politics and domestic protest (e.g. Aslan, 2015) with the concerns of political science scholars about how strategy is formulated and enacted in these media spaces, and how these media spaces allow the sedimentation of particular political and religious discourses that groups like Islamic State can utilize to legitimize their goals and behavior.

Alongside the development of this theoretical trajectory, the analysis is also concerned with the practical problem of reducing the attractiveness of Islamic State to potential recruits. The article points to contradictions in the presentation and actuality of Islamic State that could be exploited by political leaders, journalists and those in the "radicalization industry" (Hellyer, 2008) charged with de-legitimizing Islamic State.

A global space of appearances?

Hannah Arendt provides a framework for thinking about how Islamic State uses media. She argues that the "political" is a horizontal series of human interactions that continually re-establishes the basis for a community through the voicing of a full diversity of claims and perspectives (Arendt, 1963). Cavarero summarizes this theatrical model of politics as a "plural and interactive space of exhibition" (Cavarero, 2000, p. 57). Since it is a shared space, one can only exhibit one's identity and claims *in relation to* others. While any actor tries to control and project its narrative, its narrative is also being told by others—it is a joint venture. For this reason, Al-Qaeda operated a media-monitoring unit to observe how its identity was presented and discussed in Western as well as Arabic news media (Awan, Hoskins, & O'Loughlin, 2017). Did the identity of the Al-Qaeda narrated by journalists coincide with the identity Al-Qaeda wished to be seen as? The affordances of global digital media made it possible for Al-Qaeda to know this and adjust strategy if it felt mis-recognized, for instance for a short period it produced videos with Al-Qaeda figures dressed in Western suits to appear more credible to European audiences (Hoskins & O'Loughlin, 2011). Indeed, for Arendt, it is in *acting* that one is seen. Action is what makes a difference: "It is the function ... of all action, as distinguished from mere behavior, to interrupt what otherwise would have proceeded automatically and therefore predictably" (Arendt, 1970, pp. 30–31). However, the legitimation of one's actions—one's words and deeds—remains the gift of the other: consent is relational, bestowed by one's audience or constituency, not innate and decided by oneself (Hoskins & O'Loughlin, 2010).

This leaves all political actors vulnerable: Arendt's notion of politics as a space of appearance seems to elevate exhibitionism, even narcissism, but all actors are exposed to criticism, misrepresentation or simply being ignored. Islamic State acts, others witness those acts, and turn their reflections into a narrative about Islamic State. What do Islamic State's acts signify? In what context is it understood? As audiences reflect, drawing on information from the journalists, politicians and others who act as intermediaries and interpreters of global news, Islamic State's identity forms: who they are and what they are. As for what they stand for, in an Arendtian space of appearance, debate and action are not driven by the rational exchange of reasoned claims, as per the Habermasian public sphere (Habermas, 1989). Rather, persuasion demands rhetoric, gesture and performance.

The task for Islamic State is to control to the best of their abilities what aspects of their words and deeds are witnessed, and by whom—and what aspects are not. It has to project its uniqueness if it is to retain its identity: claiming attacks in Dhaka or Nice might give Islamic State a sense of momentum or presence, but does it become "just another Al-Qaeda," following the template of a scattered network of self-radicalizing individuals who happen to claim their flag? They face the difficulty of becoming known to a global audience. Writing in the Arendtian tradition, Silverstone notes that, since the proliferation of satellite television, "the mediated images of strangers increasingly define what constitutes the world" (Silverstone, 2007, p. 4). What kind of strangers do Islamic State present themselves as? This question pertains insofar as they present themselves to potential recruits or actual supporters. Since wider publics come to know Islamic State via news media, we must also ask: what kind of strangers are Islamic State presented to us as?

At first glance the ongoing iconoclash illustrates Islamists' efforts to show *our* (Western) cultural interpenetration and equivalence with *them*. Arendt posited a single space of appearance; the fundamental problem of politics was how we all get along together in that space. Islamic State seek to be counted, to be recognized, alongside others (of course in a violently antagonistic way that betrays the spirit of Arendt's space). It is about showing we share the same visual regime and thus the same space, now. It is not a clash of spaces but a clash within a single global media ecology (Fuller, 2007; Hoskins & O'Loughlin, 2010; cf. McLuhan, 1962; Postman, 1970; Volkmer, 2014). It is about changing how we think of the terrain within which the clash plays out. Global news media become conduits for this, as Al-Qaeda and now Islamic State learn what will bring them attention and a place on that terrain.

A decade ago Devji observed how Al-Qaeda appeared to be using global media to ensure a universal focus on Islam. He wrote:

> It is no exaggeration to say that only in this globally mediated landscape does Islam become universal, uniting Muslims and non-Muslims alike in a common visual practice, even in a fundamental agreement over the Islamic nature of the spectacle ... We might say that a religious universality expressed in the vision of converting the world has been displaced here by the conversion of vision itself, to make of Islam a global spectacle built out of the convergence and complicity of innumerable lines of sight? (Devji, 2005, p. 93)

Islamic State extend this process, constructing a global specter of Islam upon which lines of sight are trained from across the world. That other Muslims wish to contest this specter, labeling Islamic State as Daesh instead, is recognition of Islamic State's strategy.

As they try to establish that sense of co-existence and universal presence, Islamic State employ tactics involving the production and destruction of imagery, proceeding through an ever-escalating tit-for-tat. This signals a visual economy in which certain images have greater value as they go into circulation and others sink and go un-sold or un-seen (Gursel, 2016; Poole, 1997). The use of the now iconic orange Guantanamo jumpsuit by those opposed to the US and its allies to clothe their hostages indicates the *convertability* of one life for another, but also the convertibility of Guantanamo and its jumpsuits for Western injustice per se—a doubling up from like-for-like to particular-for-general, or from direct exchange to metonymy (Burke, 1941). Islamists use their knowledge of what we say we find valuable in order to lure us into feeling, lure us into acting and even lure us into believing: believing in their belief, their steadfast belief that gives them apparent eternal fortitude and indefatigable resolve. In other words, their efforts to manage their own identity double back onto how we in the West manage ours. Silverstone, again, writes: "Since it is in the relationship we have with others which defines the nature of our own being, then such links as we might have with these mediated individuals are increasingly becoming the crucial ones for us too" (Silverstone, 2007, p. 4).

Our relations with Islamic State force us to reconsider what we value. On the one hand, Islamic State remind us we are entangled with them: their objects are our objects, their media circulations are enmeshed with ours and we are chained together, in struggle, as equals. By producing spectacles about objects that were settled for us, in place and not disturbed, Al-Qaeda and Islamic State perform an act of *breaching* (Appadurai, 1986); our frameworks are shown to be vulnerable and dependent on actors who may be opposed to us. Al-Qaeda and Islamic State have forced us to restore our faith in our own faith in visual totems: we value the Twin Towers and the Temple of Bel in Palmyra because they signify what we hold dear, in this case, respectively, global trade, nationalism or the freedom to shop, and global culture and heritage. As these totems are attacked, we must suture the breach to repair ontological security and in doing so, affirm our values within a cosmos that is suddenly, for us, shared with them. On the other hand, however, Islamic State thereby tell us exactly what we already know, believe and value: that they are barbarians and we are civilized. Islamic State deliberately modulate this constructed binary via strategic acts of breaching. As the analysis below will show, this communication strategy can be challenged.

Islamic State project a cycle of still and moving images that engender different affective states. Some images may terrify; that is, produce a feeling of disorder, panic, the urge to flee from the scene, even if mediated. The helplessness of the victims may be intended to signify the helplessness of the global audience. It signals the sheer indeterminacy of who is radicalized and who happens to be caught in an attack: the lorry in Nice in July 2016 only became part of an intelligible strategy afterwards, reminding global audiences that not even Islamic State control who commits terrorism in their name. Other images may be designed to horrify; that is, produce a sense of paralysis, of being frozen, alone, as one gazes on the image, feeling repugnance at the destruction of human bodies. Bodies are put before audiences in the global space of appearance only to be burnt or beheaded: the beheading video as the dismemberment of the body's ontological wholeness, the burning to the point it is impossible to name the body and affirm a human identity. Cavarero (2011) argues for this distinction between terror and horror, but notes that neither are new. As warrior, Achilles created fear and trembling, while Medusa's disfigurement engendered horrified paralysis. What *is* new is the global space of appearance in which the production, circulation and political effects of any such image are radically undetermined. Which person around the world happens to commit a crime in the name of Islamic State cannot be known in advance, nor which images will become iconic. It is enough simply to guarantee enough such images are produced; some will stick.

Why do this? I have argued that Islamic State use images to speak to us in a way that modulates how we think of ourselves and them—to make ourselves presences in each other's lives such that we must find a way to accommodate one another on new terms. They are reaching out to people in the region—people who may feel Islamic State is about to conquer their territory or people who may wish to join and support them. They may be showing fellow Sunnis that only they, Islamic State, are the true Muslims: showing Shia that they have backed the wrong interpretation and should recant or die. But whether the audience is near or far, they are establishing that *they* are what is happening to *us*.

News media enable this. Mainstream journalism has a history of amplifying cycles of insecurity that makes narratives like "war on terror for generations" seem common sense: dramatizing, sensationalizing and focusing on conflict while ignoring how productive multicultural relations continue in most places for most people. This is a major part of the "space" that officials in Western governments and others are trying to contest (e.g. Fernandez, 2014). It is often a space biased against peace because conflict is more newsworthy. If our connection to, and understanding of, groups like Islamic State is derived primarily from our experience with news media, then this puts a responsibility upon news media workers. Turning back to the Arendtian tradition of media analysis, editors, journalists and photographers "make the globe possible as a lived-in place, managed, travelled across, and crucially, relatable to the contingencies and uncertainties of everyday life" (Silverstone, 2007, p. 10). News media are responsible for how we imagine and process the likelihood of a person traveling from your neighborhood to Syria to join Islamic State, the likelihood of your child seeing a beheading video online, the likelihood of your nephew in the military being sent on a mission to bomb Islamic State, the likelihood of an Islamic State attack on your neighborhood.

For just as news media connect us to Islamic State when a terrorist attack happens, they also disconnect audiences from forming an understanding of who joins Islamic State and why. Mainstream news media have censored Islamic State videos in recent years, or shown only stills, or ban the use of the names of Islamic State members who carry out terrorist attacks (Borger, 2016). Social media site Twitter has made substantial progress in removing Islamic State accounts from its service (Isaac, 2016). However, whether news media have informed audiences about what Islamic State is, what it wants and how it works and why individuals join it or act in its name—this is doubtful. The consequence is a public concerned about something it does not fully comprehend, which compounds uncertainty and anxiety. Journalism left publics frustrated at their own ignorance of Al-Qaeda a decade ago at a time they wished to be informed (Awan et al., 2017). Let us return to the question—what kind of strangers are Islamic State presented to us as? In the global space of appearance, Islamic State may be a universal upon which innumerable lines of sight are trained, but as a constant yet *blurred* figure on the horizon.

When they do lurch into view, they also appear religious. How does this shape the understandings of potential recruits or wider publics? As Brubaker (2016) argues, it is not that religious violence is *sui generis*, with its own logics distinct from political or ethnic violence. However, religion has particular modalities: methods of communication that create expectations of possibility, contingency or necessity. Through these modalities the religious dimension of such groups can reinforce drives to violence in particular ways. First, religion can generate hyper-committed individuals, particularly those who convert, in this case to an Islamic State-approved Islam. That sense of commitment necessarily makes those individuals feel distinct from those they deem uncommitted and, therefore, less worthy. This feeds into both a cognitive and affective construction of extreme otherhood: that non-believers are radically separate and must be acted upon. Religion then offers specific rewards and obligations that can be used to justify that action, even violent action. While all of these mechanisms exist to an extent in other forms of violence, this religious dimension offers qualitatively different meaning, linking to transcendence. These religious modalities can all be exhibited in the space of appearance. We see them in Islamic State publicity materials: the antagonism with the uncommitted who must be punished in a way so violent that the gesture of their murder demonstrates the Islamic State member's commitment. This enters the global space of appearance to be witnessed.

Devji argues these gestures are as much ethical as religious. If we think of self-radicalizing individuals who commit acts which Islamic State later claim, such individuals may be making choices without reference to an external authority. Devji invokes Kierkegaard (1985), whose analysis of Abraham's decision to kill his son Isaac with no guarantee or even hope that God would spare Isaac suggests that the most ethical decision is one in which the person takes full responsibility for his or her actions. Abraham did not expect God to repair the situation; all fault lay with Abraham. In this sense, many acts of Islamic State and other jihadist groups affirm a person's ethical commitment independently of any religious affirmation or doctrine. The individual cannot be accused of hypocrisy when acting so completely. Their affirmation of the necessity of their violent acts is supported (or even produced by) the religious modality of Islamic State media productions that they consume—though the place of these productions within these individuals' media consumption diets is a matter for further research.

However, we have seen these religious and ethical gestures before from Al-Qaeda. What new terms are Islamic State offering through the iconoclash they stage? They seek to replace the state system and imperialism with a caliphate. Anyone outside the caliphate is welcome to join and live on those terms, or live on their own terms and die violently. It is not about whose projected afterlife is more attractive or real. It is about using imagery to change feelings and behavior in the present. It is about a new political arrangement now. The truth of any image is secondary to this strategy. The performance of religious and ethical commitment through iconic acts is a means to make and win the clash.

Portraying the primacy of political strategy

This clash of icons is a means to winning the strategic endgame. Islamic State play on our belief that they *really* believe that certain statues really come from the divine. We are all too ready to credit a naive religiosity to them, and many of their recruits join for these religious and ethical motives (Atran & Hamid, 2015). Islamic State rhetoric plays up to this. Western leaders must make clear that while Islamic State wish to create and maintain a certain religious community—a caliphate—they can use non-religious means to get there. Islamic State's strategic documents draw on non-Islamic thinkers like Sun Tsu, Clausewitz and Paul Kennedy (McCants, 2015, p. 81). This is because their strategy is a means to an end.

That the truth of any image is secondary to strategy, for Islamic State, can be seen in their pragmatic approach to both politics and iconography (see also Rogers, 2016). The exemplary case of iconoclasm would appear to be Islamic State's destruction by explosives of the palace of Nimrud in Iraq sometime in March-April 2015. In a video released on April 11 explaining the destruction, an Islamic State member says: "Whenever we take control of a piece of land, we remove the symbols of polytheism and spread monotheism in it" (Romey, 2015). However, the timing of the video's release coincided with Islamic State's defeat in battle at Tikrit. The religious violence had the aim of political distraction.

In the domain of politics, their selective destruction of idols shows they don't truly believe. In February 2015 Islamic State allowed Turkish troops to come and pick up an Ottoman shrine, the tomb of Suleyman Shah, from an area Islamic State had taken (Graham, 2015). Why did they not destroy this idolatrous object? Were the monotheists succumbing to polytheism, jihadists asked[1]? The reason was realpolitik: at the time, it suited the leaders of Turkey and Islamic State to ensure the two sides avoided any violent conflict. Thus, Islamic State can swap the chains of obligation to a deity to chains of obligation to a nation-state like Turkey as it suits. In oscillating between rhetorics of modernity and barbarism Islamic State exasperate Sunni extremist rivals who find it hypocritical to do deals with devilish state system leaders. They also confound their modern enemies who expect Islamic State to stay true to their divine chains. How can Islamic State talk of the eternal and transcendent, of the caliphate as the realization of prophecy, and then muddy themselves in the profanity of statecraft?

In the space of appearance they show themselves as true believers and they show themselves destroying things to prove it. Seeing is believing: we see them believing and we believe they believe. When President Hollande promised a "merciless" fight against Islamic State "barbarians" after the November 2015 Paris attacks, this fed into the characterization Islamic State seek insofar as it signals to their followers and prospective recruits Islamic State's commitment to purification through personal sacrifice alongside destruction of the profane (Atran & Hamid, 2015, no page). However, when Islamic State captured the Syrian city of Palmyra in May 2015, rather than destroy the iconic temple and artifacts, they used them as a stage setting for beheading videos. The temple became a globally witnessed backdrop for us to see them perform their belief. But if these icons were so idolatrous, why not destroy them? Why give them further attention by putting them in digital clips with an infinite afterlife? Here we see Islamic State put religiosity beneath political interests. Recruit, intimidate, now. As we hear the journalist's solemn voiceover as the murders are reported, including the murder of the 82-year-old archaeologist managing the site, the implication is that authorities were powerless to prevent this, that Islamic State have total control. It was only at the end of August that demolition began. The UK's Channel 4 News (2015) reported that when Islamic State obtained artifacts from the Palmyra site, they sold them to fund the war. This appears part of a systematic revenue-raising program (Roberts, 2015).

Another example concerns Islamic State's August 2016 loss of its stronghold of Manbij in northern Syria (Dewan & Alkhshali, 2016). To minimize the significance of the group's defeat in Manbij, its supporters online highlighted how Islamic State militants safely exited the town along with their families in a 500-vehicle convoy. Evidently, Islamic State surrendered Manbij to Kurdish-led US-backed forces because it realized it could not win the military battle there. Instead it chose to leave quietly, a pragmatic decision rather than the embrace of a divine warrior clash to the death. Islamic State's jihadist critics, most of whom are Al-Qaeda supporters, strongly condemned the group for leaving the Sunnis of Manbij to fend for themselves against Kurds. As with the Ottoman tomb example, Islamic State remained silent about its actions in Manbij.

The priority of political strategy is also evident in Islamic State's approach to iconography. It is reasonable to ask—why do those opposed to icons seem so eager to make them? Islamic extremists make images to circulate in multiple formats and domains. They are crafted to produce an inner feeling of the soul for the individual in front of their private screen, an awakening of piety and anger that triggers an outward debate about justice and belonging for the family around the TV screen. These images don't "send a message" to anyone except those looking for messages—the UFOologists of our foreign ministries and security think tanks who fret about Islamic State's powerful brand. The images produce a feeling, a rhythm, a ritual of attraction or repulsion, of social affirmation or consternation that ripple through our social networks. No single image has effects here. No icon changes the meaning of everything. Rather, the tactic is to build chains of amplification and immersion that make us feel that we are in this crisis together and only they have the strength to win out. This harnessing of old and new media logics to build waves of affect is not unique to Islamic State—studies show similar processes occurring among audiences during the Arab Awakening in 2011 and around the Black Lives Matter movement in the US (Freelon, McIlwain, & Clark, 2016; Gerbaudo, 2016; Papacharissi, 2015). However, polls indicate Islamic State's communications are losing this affective engagement. Between 2015 and 2016 strong opposition to Islamic State among 18–24 year-olds in 16 Arab nations increased from 40 to 60% and only 18% believed individuals joined Islamic State for religious reasons (ASDA'A Burson-Marsteller, 2016). Islamic State was viewed as what a person joins if they have no job or prospects. However, even among young men with little education or employment support is low, and support falls even further if those men are exposed to news about Islamic State violence against Muslims (Tessler, Robbins, & Jamal, 2016).

And yet still: how dare they produce images? The answer is pragmatism, interests and strategy. These images are tokens in a global exchange economy; in no way sacred, their value is immediate and imminent, in the action they can provoke now. Islamic State show other Muslims, visually, just how Islamic they are, chopping off hands and heads as they enact Shari'a law more strictly than anyone else dare. When they suffer a military defeat, a quick, shocking video of an atrocity elsewhere can distract attention. They remind audiences of terror and horror committed by Western political actors, so as to present a universal moral threshold lowest level: that terror and horror are a problem of both them and us (Cavarero, 2011). This must be challenged.

In fact, in the final analysis, images are not even needed. Audiences can react to the *very idea* that Islamic State might be destroying something, just as some Muslims have rioted after hearing stories of US soldiers flushing a Koran down a toilet (O'Loughlin, 2011). Mediation is affective and experiential, but not strictly visual (Grusin, 2015). Hence we can experience a distant event and ourselves in relation to that event without seeing a picture of it. All Islamic State has needed to do is get the notion out there that they are doing this, or might do it, or once did it, and it becomes part of our experience. Further research is needed to explain this. We know from the study of myth that an originary image is not necessary or relevant to a subsequent mythology (Barthes, 2000); what matters is how political actors narrate unfolding events in a way that directs attention to and sustains the myth. Now that each "side" has expectations and even mythologies of the other and is ready to hear the worst, this cycle of hostility can operate as an iconoclash without icons. Indeed, the very fact that Islamic State have produced new images becomes a story in itself, even if the images are not broadcast. Journalists find Islamic State's very act of communication newsworthy (Gursel, 2016). This can also be challenged and changed.

We also need research to understand how attention on the secular realpolitik of Islamic State is perceived by potential recruits as well as wider publics. This analysis has shown how Islamic State communications link statecraft to religiosity in a selective way. We do not at present understand whether a news media focus on Islamic State's realpolitik would affect Islamic State's reputation such that this would weaken the resolve of a recruit drawn in by the religious modalities, for instance, or radicalize them further because news media appear to such an individual to be misrepresenting Islamic State, no doubt for nefarious reasons.

In short, while the religious and ethical dimensions of Islamic State's actions make for compelling footage and persuasive claims to potential recruits who encounter these exhibitions in the global space of appearance, those seeking to delegitimize Islamic State would not lack material to demonstrate the banal, mundane and pragmatic aspects of its political strategy.

Conclusion: we all struggle with icons

Bruno Latour stages a conversation between a politician and a mob of critics of political iconography. The mob ask:

"Are you constructing a national representation?"
"Yes, of course," they answer, "and from the whole cloth."
"So you are inventing, through manipulation, propaganda, and trickery, what the representatives should say?"
"No, we are faithful to our constituents, because we are constructing the artificial voice that they would not have without us."
"Blasphemy!" cry the critics. "We don't need to hear any more! Lost in their illusions, they can't even recognize their own lies!" (Latour, 2010, p. 23)

Flags, crowns, "the wisdom of public opinion": human societies construct idols which are then taken to be independent objects to be venerated and even worshiped. And yet, as the critics cry, these idols are not magical. These are things made by human techniques. For Latour it is pointless denouncing either naïve souls who workshop objects or iconoclasts who smash the objects as if to liberate the naïve souls. All social practices involve mediations through which we "see" what is otherwise invisible. Microscopes let us see tiny objects. A flag lets us see a nation. Statistics let us see poverty. The art, for Latour, is recognizing these mediations for what they are and what they do; it is perfectly possible to realize I made this sculpture but feel it represents something transcendent and thus feel a sense of religiosity near it. This, we could say, is living *with* icons not looking *up* to them or *down* on them.

Islamic State appear to oscillate between looking up to or down on icons. As their leaders and recruits seek to project their identities and ambitions into the global space of appearance, icons are either smashed in religious fervor or sold on the nearest market. This oscillation exposes a tension—contradiction perhaps—between a theological organization driven by religious motives and a bureaucratic organization seeking to construct a state. Balancing analysis of the political and religious dimensions of Islamic State affords tactical possibilities to play these off against one another in ways that may diminish Islamic State's appeal.

Certainly Islamic State go with the grain of the global media ecology, and the Arendtian tradition of media analysis that conceptualizes politics as the robust exchange of claims in a space of appearance highlights why they might have been successful. However, we need to stop believing that while they believe we are more enlightened, distanced and reasonable. They don't all believe, particularly those at the top of their bureaucratic structure, hence they don't destroy idols and idolators immediately or consistently, nor do they fight to the death when under attack, but only when it suits, when the odds are in their favor. Their rhetoric can be deflated. Despite their pre-modern rituals and post-modern embrace of simulation, their immediate political objective is that of most if not all modern political movements, authority within territory: an Islamic *state*. To win the iconoclash we must show they are as grounded in the politics of interests as anyone else. The second half of this article has provided several examples.

This may present difficulties for mainstream news organizations. It would involve portraying Islamic State as a rational actor, and thereby risk legitimizing them. Here, Islamic State's effort to portray itself as so zealous as to be barbaric makes it difficult to redescribe it as an actor involved in negotiations with other states—even though this analysis has shown this to often be the case. It becomes a challenge for "us" to treat the ultimate other as rational whilst not ignoring the violence and the importance of religious modalities. Indeed, it is the twin task of journalism to both explain the realpolitik and explain the role of religious modalities in radicalization processes.

As this deflation occurs, more urgent actions are needed to dampen the effects of Islamic State communications on Western societies. News media presents to us an appearance of Islamic State and our incentives to engage with them, for instance through social media. If, as Devji argues, Al-Qaeda first and now, I would argue, Islamic State have made Islam into a global spectacle, this feeds into how anyone and everyone Islamic is understood. Devji suggested that this process creates a "generic Muslim," a martyr who loses all cultural and historical specificity (Devji, 2005, p. 94). Since Islamic State began attacks in the West or, rather, individuals started carrying out attacks in the name of Islamic State, attitudes towards Muslims have hardened, evident in several European countries' responses to the migration crisis since 2014. News media need to find ways to report Islam and Islamic State such that any conflation of religion, radicalization and migration is minimized and scrutinized.

For just as news media connect us to Islamic State when a terrorist attack happens, they also disconnect audiences from forming an understanding of who joins Islamic State and why. Mainstream news media censorship and social media restrictions lessen Islamic State's reach and presence. However, whether news media have informed audiences about what Islamic State is, what it wants and how it works, and why individuals join it or act in its name—this is doubtful. Whether news media have expressed consistently the tension in Islamic State between religious and secular goals is doubtful. The consequence is a public concerned about something it does not fully comprehend, which compounds uncertainty and anxiety. Uncertainty itself becomes a threat because one lacks the information upon which to act. Instead, one acts with Islamic State a constant yet blurred figure on the horizon.

Note

1. Personal correspondence, anonymous source.

References

Appadurai, A. (1986). Introduction: Commodities and the politics of value. In A. Appadurai (Ed.), *The social life of things: Commodities in cultural perspective* (pp. 3–63). Cambridge: Cambridge University Press.

Arendt, H. (1963). *On revolution*. New York: The Viking Press.

Arendt, H. (1970). *On violence*. New York and London: Harcourt, Inc.

ASDA'A Burson-Marsteller. (2016). *ASDA'A Burson-Marsteller Arab Youth Survey 2016*. Retrieved from http://www.arabyouthsurvey.com/en/whitepaper

Aslan, B. (2015). The mobilization process of Syria's activists: The symbiotic relationship between the use of information and communication technologies and the political culture. *International Journal of Communication*, 9(19), 2507–2525.

Atran, S., & Hamid, N. (2015, November 16). Paris: The War ISIS Wants. *New York Review of Books*. Retrieved from http://www.nybooks.com/daily/2015/11/16/paris-attacks-isis-strategy-chaos/

Awan, A., Hoskins, A., & O'Loughlin, B. (2017). *Radicalisation and media: connectivity and terrorism in the new media ecology*. London: Routledge.

Barthes, R. (2000 [1957]). *Mythologies*. (Annette Lavers, Trans.). London: Vintage Books.

Borger, J. (2016, July 27). French media to stop publishing photos and names of terrorists. *The Guardian*,. Retrieved from https://www.theguardian.com/media/2016/jul/27/french-media-to-stop-publishing-photos-and-names-of-terrorists

Bourdieu, P. (1991). Language and symbolic power. (Gino Raymond & Matthew Adamson, Trans.). In Adam Jaworski & Nikolas Coupland (Eds.), *The discourse reader* (pp. 480–490). London and New York: Routledge.

Brubaker, R. (2016). Religious Dimensions of Political Conflict and Violence. Plenary Lecture. European Consortium For Political Research (ECPR) General Conference. Charles University, Prague, 8 September.

Burke, K. (1941). Four master tropes. *The Kenyon Review*, 3(4), 421–438.

Cavarero, A. (2011). *Horrorism: Naming contemporary violence*. New York: Columbia University Press.

Cavarero, A. (2000). *Relating narratives: Storytelling and selfhood*. London and New York: Routledge.

Channel 4 News. (2015, August 19). Palmyra Archaeologist Beheaded by ISIS. Retrieved from https://www.youtube.com/watch?v=CncFUCt892M

Devji, F. (2005). *Landscapes of the jihad: Military, morality, modernity*. London: Hurst.

Dewan, A., & Alkhshali, H. (2016, August 14). Jubilation in Syria's Manbij as ISIS loses control of key city. *CNN*. Retrieved from http://edition.cnn.com/2016/08/13/middleeast/syria-isis-manbij/

EUNIC [European Union National Institutes for Culture]. (2015). Iconoclash. Retrieved from http://washington-dc.eunic-online.eu/?q=iconoclash

Freelon, D. G., McIlwain, C. D., & Clark, M. D. (2016). Beyond the hashtags:# Ferguson,# Blacklivesmatter, and the online struggle for offline justice. Retrieved from http://cmsimpact.org/resource/beyond-hashtags-ferguson-blacklivesmatter-online-struggle-offline-justice/

Fernandez, A. M. (2014, February 25). Confronting the Changing Face of Al-Qaeda Propaganda. *The Washington Institute*. Retrieved from http://www.washingtoninstitute.org/policy-analysis/view/confronting-the-changing-face-of-al-qaeda-propaganda

Fuller, M. (2007). *Media ecologies: Materialist energies in Art and technoculture*. London and Cambridge, MA: The MIT Press.

Gerbaudo, P. (2016). Rousing the facebook crowd: Digital enthusiasm and emotional contagion in the 2011 protests in Egypt and Spain. *International Journal of Communication, 10*, 254–273.

Graham, D. A. (2015). The Surreal Saga of Suleyman Shah, *The Atlantic*, 24 February. Retrieved from http://www.theatlantic.com/international/archive/2015/02/suleyman-shah-turkish-troops-raid-syria-isis-tomb/385864/

Grusin, R. (2015). Radical mediation. *Critical Inquiry, 42*(1), 124–148.

Gursel, Z. D. (2016). *Image brokers: Visualizing world news in the Age of digital circulation*. Oakland, CA: University of California Press.

Habermas, J. (1989). *The structural transformation of the public sphere*. (Thomas Burger, Trans.). Cambridge, MA: MIT Press.

Hellyer, H. A. (2008). Engaging British Muslim communities in counter-terrorism strategies. *The RUSI Journal, 153*(2), 8–13.

Hoskins, A., & O'Loughlin, B. (2010). *War and Media: The emergence of diffused War*. Cambridge: Polity.

Hoskins, A., & O'Loughlin, B. (2011). Remediating jihad for western news audiences: The renewal of gatekeeping? *Journalism: Theory, Practice & Criticism, 12*(2), 199–216.

Isaac, M. (2016, February 5). Twitter steps up effort to thwart terrorists' tweets. *New York Times*. Retrieved from http://www.nytimes.com/2016/02/06/technology/twitter-account-suspensions-terrorism.html?_r=0

Kierkegaard, S. (1985). *Fear and trembling: Dialectical lyric by Johannes de silentio*. London: Penguin.

Latour, B. (2010). *On the modern cult of the factish gods*. Durham, NC and London: Duke University Press.

McCants, W. (2015). *The ISIS apocalypse: The history, strategy, and doomsday vision of the islamic state*. New York: St. Martin's Press.

McLuhan, M. (1962). *The Gutenberg galaxy: The making of topographic man*. Toronto: University of Toronto Press.

Merrin, W. (2014). *Media studies 2.0*. London: Routledge.

Mitchell, W. J. T. (2011). *Cloning terror: The war of images, 9/11 to the present*. Chicago: University of Chicago Press.

O'Loughlin, B. (2011). Images as weapons of war: Representation, mediation and interpretation. *Review of International Studies, 37*(1), 71–91.

Papacharissi, Z. (2015). *Affective publics: Sentiment, technology, and politics*. New York and Oxford: Oxford University Press.

Poole, D. (1997). *Vision, race and modernity: A visual economy of the Andean image world*. Princeton: Princeton University Press.

Postman, N. (1970). The reformed English curriculum. In A. C. Eurich (Ed.), *High school 1980: The shape of the future in American secondary education* (pp. 160–168). New York: Pitman.

Roberts, D. (2015, September 1). Why IS militants destroy ancient sites. *BBC News*. Retrieved from http://www.bbc.com/news/world-middle-east-34112593

Rogers, P. (2016). *Irregular War: ISIS and the new threat from the margins*. London: I.B. Taurus.

Romey, K. (2015, April 14). Why ISIS Hates Archaeology and Blew Up Ancient Iraqi Palace. *National Geographic*. Retrieved from http://news.nationalgeographic.com/2015/04/150414-why-islamic-state-destroyed-assyrian-palace-nimrud-iraq-video-isis-isil-archaeology/

Silverstone, R. (2007). *Morality and media*. Cambridge: Polity.

Tessler, M., Robbins, M., & Jamal, A. (2016, July 27). What do ordinary citizens in the Arab world really think about the Islamic State? *The Washington Post*. Retrieved from https://www.washingtonpost.com/news/monkey-cage/wp/2016/07/27/what-do-ordinary-citizens-in-the-arab-world-really-think-about-the-islamic-state/?postshare=6651469624807379&tid=ss_tw

Volkmer, I. (2014). *The global public sphere*. Cambridge: Polity.

Arguing with ISIS: web 2.0, open source journalism, and narrative disruption

Matt Sienkiewicz

ABSTRACT
This paper considers American strategies for countering ISIS social media, focusing on notions of narrative and rational debate in the Web 2.0 era. In addition to chronicling an evolution in American governmental ideas about the online public sphere, the paper looks specifically at the work of Al-Tamimi, an open source journalist who verifies and catalogues original ISIS documentation. Using both textual analyses and long-form interviews with Al-Tamimi as evidence, the paper argues that Al-Tamimi's archival work serves to disrupt emotionally driven, logically questionable narratives about ISIS, whether they emerge from the group itself or its Western opponents.

Introduction: a troll army of our own

Addressing the New America Foundation in 2008, James K. Glassman, the U.S. Underse-cretary for Public Diplomacy and Public Affairs, was rather optimistic. Yes, the War on Terror was yielding uneven results, with Al-Qaeda proving a stubborn enemy both online and off. Salvation, however, was now only a keyboard away. Up to that point, Al-Qaeda had been "eating our lunch" on the internet, according to Glassman (2008). The early web, he argued, inherently advantaged those who wished to "exhort and instruct," thus giving an advantage to totalitarian voices over those of democracy. Web 2.0, however, was going to change everything. The new internet, infused with an unpre-cedented level of social and discursive interactivity, would transform into a "marketplace of ideas" in which rationality, and American values, would quickly emerge victorious.

Less than a decade later, Glassman's analysis looks something short of prescient. In 2015, Alberto Fernandez, the Coordinator for Strategic Counterterrorism Communi-cations at the Department of State, determined that rationality was a poor tool for defeat-ing extremism. To combat the emergent Islamic State (ISIS), Fernandez (2015) declared, the United States needed to create a "troll army" of its own (p. 19), mimicking the Russian practice of paying social media users to reproduce favorable messages on a massive, decep-tive scale. As has been argued elsewhere (Sienkiewicz, 2015; Sindelar, 2014), this strategy is one in which basic truth telling, let alone a commitment to rational debate, is of minor importance. As ISIS developed an increasingly emotional, narrative-driven, and bullying approach to new media, America would have to do the same. Forsaking the Habermasian public sphere, Fernandez offered a web 2.0 update of Jean Baudrillard's (2003) notion of "terroristic situational transfer" in which the tools of terrorism and the system that fights it become essentially indistinguishable (p. 9).

This paper aims to review the theoretical and scholarly perspectives on ISIS media that underpin this American strategic evolution and, most centrally, to consider what a contemporary, rational, Web 2.0 engagement with ISIS can consist of. To achieve the latter, I offer a theorization of the career of Al-Tamimi, an Iraqi-British new media journalist who devotes his life and work to the scrupulous collating, verifying, analyzing, and disseminating of primary ISIS documentation. Drawing upon textual analysis of Al-Tamimi's work and longform, qualitative interviews with Al-Tamimi himself, I argue that, through the use of open source Web 2.0 tools and strategies, he consistently disrupts emotive, inaccurate narratives surrounding ISIS.

However, despite achieving this element of Glassman's ambition for U.S. Web 2.0 strategy, Al-Tamimi's efforts do not necessarily represent a simple pathway to more effective American propaganda. Although Al-Tamimi is an explicit foe of ISIS whose family in Mosul suffers directly from their rule, his evidenced-based approach to mediating the terrorist group is one that disrupts all varieties of oversimplifying narratives, regardless of their origins. Yes, his documents serve to complicate ISIS's auto-narrativization by providing concrete evidence of the banal, conflictual, and embarrassing aspects of the organization. At the same time, his documentary evidence also disrupts Western news narratives of ISIS and, occasionally, serves to directly contradict official American stories about its war against the terrorist group. Al-Tamimi's document archive thus illustrates the ways in which open source new media journalism can become a useful check against the communication strategies of authorities from across the political spectrum. At the same time, however, I note that the realities of media economics ensure that Al-Tamimi's database also provides a set of potential narrative building blocks to be used by the right-wing institutions that fund much of his work. I begin this analysis by drawing upon communication scholarship that establishes the increasingly emotional, narrativized orientation of media messaging from and about ISIS.

From Al-Qaeda to ISIS, from argument to narrative

The strategic shift from Glassman's marketplace of ideas to Fernandez's troll army is mirrored by the development of American public discourses of terrorism, Al-Qaeda, and ISIS. Of course, it is crucial to note that neither is ISIS wholly devoid of reason nor is Al-Qaeda opposed to more emotive appeals. Retrospect has, however, repositioned Al-Qaeda as a coherent, rational, relatively predictable entity standing in contradistinction from the erratic, emotional nature of ISIS. Al-Qaeda may be still positioned as extremist, but is also increasingly understood as an institution committed to intellectual persuasion and internal consistency. They are, in other words, the types of extremists one might fruitfully argue against, if not necessarily with.

Robin Wright (2016), writing in *The New Yorker* about the ISIS-Al-Qaeda rivalry, describes Al-Qaeda as being committed firstly to "educating Sunnis to its message," thereby reinforcing the idea that rational discourse might be a plausible means of combatting the group. She understands Al-Qaeda as the "vanguard of global jihadism," employing what has become a common descriptor for the group, particularly as a means of drawing a contrast to ISIS. Jessica Stern and J. M. Berger (2015), writing for a general audience in *ISIS: The State of Terror*, invoke just this language as a means of establishing the rational nature of Al-Qaeda. Al-Qaeda, according to Stern and Berger (2015), is a "vanguard movement" comprised of "elite intellectual leaders" aiming to spark an ideological revolution. In contrast, Stern and Berger describe ISIS as a "mob," albeit a "smart" one, which uses all means available, including emotional appeal and logical contradiction, to advance its agenda. ISIS is thus understood as a group of guerilla fighters, perhaps able to engage in revolutionary rhetoric when convenient, but willing to forsake rationality for more visceral appeals whenever advantageous.

This discursive distinction is, of course, somewhat facile, as it emphasizes the disparate intellectual underpinnings of Al-Qaeda and ISIS while decentering the commonality of terrorism. It does, however, resonate with the communication and media strategies employed by Al-Qaeda and ISIS, respectively. As Stern and Berger (2015) note, Al-Qaeda, "despite its distorted worldview," aims "to appear 'reasonable'" in its messaging both online and off (p. 343). Jarrett M. Brachman (2006) identifies Al-Qaeda's web presence as largely informational, emphasizing the array of how-to guides and philosophical books available online via affiliated websites. The web, according to Brachman, served as a virtual "library" through which supporters may be educated (p. 153). Devin D. Jessee (2006), reviewing Al-Qaeda's early use of online messaging, emphasizes the creation of hierarchical information structures in which message boards served as virtual replacements for physical training grounds (p. 380).

Much as Glassman predicted, Al-Qaeda's top down form of online communication quickly became outmoded in the Web 2.0 era. Discursive rationality, however, did not emerge as the primary alternative to Al-Qaeda's hierarchical approach. Instead, ISIS took to volatile open source social media sites such as Twitter, Instagram, and Facebook in order craft primarily emotional and narrative appeals that have proven hard to rebut through dispassionate logic. What emerged was a highly interactive, but far from deliberative, form of online communication. Stripped of the top-down power held by Al-Qaeda a decade earlier, ISIS embraced its lack of administrative oversight, largely ceding control over the specific ways in which its words, images, and videos would circulate across the web. Unable to funnel communications through authoritative sources, ISIS relied on "crowdsourcing, in-house designed apps and bots, and hashtag hacking" in order to spread their message (Melki & Jabado, 2016, p. 97). Of course, as Haroro J. Ingram (2015) notes, ISIS media displays a considerable amount of forethought and, in fact, reason. It is well produced and offers a clear, intentional thematic orientation, alternating between "pragmatic" aspects of ISIS governance and "perceptual factors" such as group identity (p. 736). However, these elements are packaged so as to intersect with the emotions and consumer tendencies of social media users. Their goal, according to Melki and Jabado (2016) is to induce "Twitter storm[s]" in which ISIS material collides, often cacophonously, with popular aspects of online life (p. 97).

ISIS's messaging relies on what Zizi Papacharissi (2015) describes as the "logic of hashtags," a form of social understanding that "foster[s] tropes of belonging that evolve beyond the conventional mode of rational thought and deliberation" (p. 117). Such "logic" is one in which strength is conferred both by the accumulation of attention, as certified by "trending alerts," and other forms of social media scorekeeping, as well as the development of narratives through which diverse and dispersed users can feel united. As Henry A. Giroux (2014) argues, ISIS's visual vocabulary is one drawn from Western modes of violent, commercialized storytelling. ISIS videos display production techniques pioneered by Hollywood filmmakers, a fact excitedly reported in the Western press. Vox.com, for example, compares an ISIS video to the work of Michael Bay, a filmmaker known for brash, violent spectacles that entertain, but fall somewhat short in terms of rational messaging (Beauchamp, 2014). As Marwan Kraidy (2017) notes, ISIS mixes shocking images of atrocities with established narrative and visual tropes, making comprehensible that which would otherwise defy reason and shock the senses. Emotion and narrative thus serve to short circuit a more rational engagement with the reality of ISIS.

For Giroux (2014), this cycle of violent stimuli, originating in the West and returning in a horrific mutated form, stands in direct opposition to the properly functioning "democratic, global public sphere." The proper response, he declares, is a pedagogical strategy, at least in the West, whereby moral reasoning is applied across cultural activities, allowing consumers to better understand the ramifications both of violent Western storytelling and the emotional narrative of terror put forth by ISIS. Though more abstract, Giroux's idea strays only a little from the call for open debate and discussion of Glassman's public sphere approach to counter-extremism. For contemporary policy analysts such as Alberto Fernandez, however, such a strategy is neither concrete nor timely enough to put into action. ISIS, according to Fernandez, can only be countered by a widespread, high volume campaign that, while "grounded in facts," emphasizes power and emotion in its messaging (p. 21). On a practical level, there may well be merit in Fernandez's strategy, troll army and all. However, there are alternative means by which to adapt the promise of Web 2.0 to the realm of ISIS propaganda. In the following section I argue that Al-Tamimi employs open source new media tools not to debate with ISIS in a strict sense, but instead to offer rational impediments to ISIS narratives. In doing so, however, he not only disrupts the hashtag logics and narratives of ISIS, but also those of other institutions wishing to put forth a simplified version of reality.

Interpreting ISIS

Al-Tamimi is an unlikely ISIS fighter. Quiet, with a voice inflected by a subtle Welsh-British accent, he steadfastly denies that his work is political at all. "My goal," he says, is to "simply make material about the Islamic State available, now and for posterity." He is cautious and hyper-factual in his analysis, offering no concrete policy prescriptions and claiming that his reports are never intended to make a case for or against ISIS. His *magnum opus*, an online archive featuring thousands of verified, mostly mundane, official ISIS documents, includes no summary or narrativization. The archive page seemingly scrolls forever, serving as an ISIS-specific "digital *Wunderkammer*," to employ Robert Gehl's (2009) term for online archives such as YouTube that offer infinite paths through to which to engage vast, loosely collated visual attractions.

Al-Tamimi's approach is, in many ways, the polar opposite of the "troll" strategy to web 2.0 media that Fernandez suggests ought to form the heart of anti-ISIS media tactics. As Claire Hardaker (2010) argues, "trolling" can be conceptualized as online communication based in "aggression," "deception," "disruption," and "success" (p. 216). As I argue below, Al-Tamimi's collection and dissemination of ISIS materials does, in a rather unconventional sense, serve to disrupt narratives surrounding ISIS. They are, however, anything but aggressive or deceptive. A devotee to open source analysis, Al-Tamimi leaves every document he deems authentic freely available to other analysts because, he says, he "may be wrong" about it.

Al-Tamimi's work thus fits rather uneasily within contemporary discussions of digital anti-terrorism, falling somewhere between the rationalistic, if bygone, notions of Glassman and the more pragmatically nihilistic orientation of Fernandez. Perhaps as a result, his efforts are supported by an unusual coalition of institutions, some of which contrast sharply with his moderate political style. Born in Cardiff and a graduate of Oxford University, Al-Tamimi began his career by writing short, largely opinion-based essays on ISIS's emergence in his ancestral home of Mosul. A complete novice in the world of journalism in 2014, his first articles appeared in *The American Thinker*, a far right-wing online magazine from which Al-Tamimi would eventually demand his work be removed due to its publication of others' "fringe" ideas and theories. Nonetheless, this early, essentially arbitrary publication decision would shape his institutional future. He has subsequently received funding from both The International Institute for Counter Terrorism, an academic center based in Israel, and The Middle East Forum, a right-wing American think tank run by the controversial neoconservative Daniel Pipes.

Early in his think tank career, Al-Tamimi found himself struggling to find enough marketable opinions to meet his writing quota. In January of 2015, however, he realized that a trove of stories lay a few clicks, and much interpretive analysis, away. Starting with ISIS's breakaway from Al-Qaeda in February of 2014, the internet became flush with images of documents claiming to be the official administrative materials of the Islamic State. The purported documents were, in fact, too plentiful, making it difficult to locate "newsworthy" specimens and leaving ample opportunity for forgers to disseminate fakes. They were also, of course, written in a difficult, idiosyncratic form of Arabic. Few journalists would have the time, patience, skills, and motivation to work through the material. Al-Tamimi, with his unusual professional position and deep knowledge of Iraqi language and culture, proved the exception. Trained as a classicist at Oxford, he began to conceptualize his online work as a contemporary equivalent of the Greek inscription books he studied in school. Featuring only sparse commentary, these classic works serve to collate, organize, and present verified information that can eventually serve as the raw material for historical analysis. They are, by nature, dispassionate texts intended to foster the crafting of careful, rational argumentation.

Al-Tamimi's first foray into this document-focused approach came in a three-part series entitled "Aspects of Islamic State (IS) Administration in Ninawa Province." Much as the title suggests, the series is rather straightforward and informational, consisting almost entirely of procedural ISIS documentation and punctuated only by sparse, generally neutral commentary. For example, Al-Tamimi cites and translates the ISIS-imposed school examination schedule for the Ninawa region, including such fine-grained details as the exam questions and the rubric on which they must be graded. The materials are not particularly surprising, avoiding extremist language and focusing largely on Qur'anic exegesis while including periods for the study of biology, history, and math. In his concluding analysis, Al-Tamimi asserts, briefly, that the "extensive IS interference in Ninawa" serves to establish the extent to which the organization has achieved control over the province (Al-Tamimi, 2015a).

This series would become the template for Al-Tamimi's career in journalism. Still working with the same politically-inflected think tanks, Al-Tamimi turned his personal website into a vast archive of ISIS documentation, a small fraction of which he uses in order to write evidence-based reports for his funding partners and a variety of other institutions. In doing so, Al-Tamimi has come to embody what Matt Sienkiewicz (2014) describes as the "interpreter tier" of online citizen journalism. In a social media environment that encourages the production of countless terabytes of citizen-produced and uploaded materials, interpreter tier journalists play the crucial role of sorting, cataloguing, and vetting materials that can then be adopted and analyzed with confidence by either individuals or mainstream media sources. As Sienkiewicz (2015) notes, this process is particularly important in the context of conflict spaces such as Ukraine, Iraq, and Syria, as the materials emerging from such regions are particularly prone to misinterpretation and partisan exploitation. Steeped in the long-term observation of a particular geographic space and culture, interpreters serve their purpose by using new media tools in order to cross-reference individual pieces of user-provided media evidence, combining a variety of individually inconclusive data points in order to discern a canon of trustworthy material.

Such cross-referencing is at the heart of Al-Tamimi's work, which now consists largely of collecting, verifying, and translating both thousands of "open access" ISIS documents as well as new "original" material he receives from sources in Syria and Iraq. In both cases, Al-Tamimi relies on a combination of negative and positive markers in order to determine whether or not a document is valid and thus deserving of inclusion in his archive. For example, in early 2016 a document regarding displeasure among Yemeni ISIS members began circulating widely online. Suggesting a brewing rebellion against the local ISIS leadership, the document was particularly popular in pro-Al-Qaeda social media spaces where users were inclined to believe any plausible bad news about their rival faction. There was thus good reason to question the authenticity of the documents.

Al-Tamimi began by reviewing the format and language of the material, using his existing, verified archive as a point of departure. Most fakes, he attests, can be deduced by the presence of inconsistencies in vocabulary and nomenclature that often go unnoticed by journalists or analysts with more generalist orientations. For example, as IS continues to change its name over time (from the "Islamic State in Iraq" to the "Islamic State in Iraq and Al-Shams," for example), forgers often fail to reflect the cascade of adjustments in documentation that should appear accordingly in authentic material. In the case of the Yemen document, Al-Tamimi found only one suspicious element—a reference to a heretofore unheard of ISIS "Administration of the Distant Provinces" that was said to be overseeing the situation in Yemen. Given the scope of his archive, such novelty often represents a forger's erroneous attempt to accurately reproduce existing ISIS language. Al-Tamimi, as result, withheld judgment. Shortly thereafter, however, he stumbled on an important piece of corroborating evidence. The Al Hayat Media Center, an official ISIS outlet, released a video entitled "The Structure of the Islamic State" that, for the first time, publicly referred to the efforts of the "Administration of the Distant Provinces." With this point of cross-verification, the Yemen documents evolved from potential forgeries to trustworthy material, as only an ISIS insider would have known to use this terminology weeks before the video's release. Al-Tamimi (2016b) wrote a brief report on the documents, verifying the claims of internal ISIS strife that they suggested. He then entered them into his archive for the use of contemporary journalists and future historians.

Al-Tamimi uses a similar process in acquiring new ISIS materials from local "citizens" of the Islamic State. Regularly, Al-Tamimi receives messages from individuals in Iraq, Syria, and Turkey claiming to have official ISIS documents not yet in public circulation. In addition to the ample administrative and propaganda materials that ISIS provides to those under its rule, the shifting borders of the conflict often leave ISIS offices abandoned and replete with potentially useful information. There is, of course, a lucrative market for such documentation, forcing Al-Tamimi not only to bid for material, but also to contend with large forgers wishing to turn false but plausible items into money. This problem has grown so great in Turkey that Al-Tamimi no longer considers material emerging from that country. However, he often reviews batches of documents sent from contacts in Iraq and Syria. For example, in October of 2015 he received an email from Al-Bab, Syria featuring a variety of materials collected by a local ISIS subject. Many of these were clear forgeries, some of which Al-Tamimi had already publicly debunked. However, upon closer inspection, Al-Tamimi determined his contact to be the victim, not the perpetrator, of this deception. Mixed into the false documents were others that offered unique opportunities for verification. One, for instance, featured a list of emergency contact phone numbers for ISIS fighters. To check their veracity, Al-Tamimi simply picked up the phone and dialed, speaking directly to the people referenced in the material. Ultimately, he purchased the documents for $100. He would go on to publish a report based on this material illustrating ISIS's inconsistent use of calendars, as they oscillated between Islamic and secular dating systems.

Such revelations will not, of course, go viral. They offer little hope to strategists such as Fernandez, who envision broad-based, popular social media messaging as the only hope for countering ISIS. They do, however, serve a number of important functions. For one, they provide materials upon which responsible journalists can draw in order to provide accurate information about ISIS. Al-Tamimi has proven extremely successful in garnering mass media attention, having been sourced at least 10 times each since 2014 by *The Washington Post*, *The New York Times*, *The International Business Times*, and *The Wall Street Journal*. Al-Jazeera and the British Broadcasting Corporation have each cited him over 25 times. In most cases, Al-Tamimi appears only via a snippet of his analysis in the form of quote. Sometimes, however, his archive is linked in online stories, providing his cache of vetted information to a new group of potential readers.

Secondly, and somewhat more abstractly, Al-Tamimi's attention to detail and dedication to accuracy plays the role of disrupting the smooth flow of narratives that emerge from ISIS's Web 2.0 social media strategy. As Giroux (2014) argues, both Western commercial storytelling and ISIS propaganda succeed insofar as they discourage viewers from critically considering the visceral, emotional, narratives into which media invites them. Al-Tamimi's work offers an important, if not often heeded, reminder that the stories told by trending lists and hashtags are often complicated by a close analysis of the facts. However, just as Giroux's critique cuts in multiple directions, so does Al-Tamimi's. As I argue below, his archival, evidence-based approach to analysis is not anti-ISIS, but anti-simplification, with real implications for mass media narratives. Operating as a new media interpreter, Al-Tamimi is devoted to imposing rationality, even when it muddies narratives, into the media battle between ISIS and its opponents. Often this serves to underscore the hypocrisy, immorality, and barbarity of ISIS. However, unlike in Glassman's Public Diplomacy 2.0 utopia, transparency and reason are by no means always on the side of the U.S.

Al-Tamimi and the three disruptions

Disruption 1: the banality of ISIS

If the strategy of ISIS's social media is to offer stories, memes, and hashtag storms that simplify and commodify the group's activities, Al-Tamimi's Web 2.0 activity works to reassert the contradictions and omissions embedded in this effort. According to Charlie Winter (2015), ISIS social media is organized around six organizing narratives—mercy, belonging, victimhood, brutality, war, and utopia (p. 6). Although these stories are inconsistent with one another, they are presented as internally coherent narratives meant to appeal to different potential audiences. Al-Tamimi, through a focus on procedure and banality, makes available a surfeit material unassimilable into such simplified stories and thus potentially disruptive to them.

The story of dissent among Yemeni ISIS members described above serves just this function. By detailing internal ISIS tensions via objective, open source material, Al-Tamimi's use of the Yemen documents casts significant doubt on the unified nature of ISIS's supposed Islamic utopia. Featuring authenticated letters from lower-level Yemeni ISIS officers and soldiers, the documents verified by Al-Tamimi painstakingly outline the failures of the local ISIS leadership structure in the words of those most affected by them. Yemeni ISIS leaders, according to the documents, provide a "lack of provision of the most basic means and foundational components for the battle," including a failure to account for basic strategic, medical, and intelligence needs of their soldiers. The names of 70 fighters appear below the complaint. In a response also found in Al-Tamimi's archive, ISIS's Administration for the Distant Provinces expels the highest-ranking signees, making clear the severity of the internal conflict (Al-Tamimi, 2016b). Throughout the documents, it is clear that ISIS, for all of its high production value rhetoric, struggles with the mundane activities of operating an army, an idea absent from the narratives of ISIS online video and Twitter campaigns.

The document regarding ISIS's use of calendars that Al-Tamimi bought from his source in Al-Bab provides a different sort of narrative disruption. A religious treatise issued by ISIS's Research and Fatwa-Issuing Department, the document, via Al-Tamimi's translation, allows readers worldwide to understand a rather simple aspect of ISIS's administrative activities: the labeling of dates. Replete with Qur'anic citations, the treatise reaches the simple and clear conclusion that the *Miladi* (Gregorian) calendar "must be forgotten and not even cited alongside" the proper *Hijri* (Islamic) dating system (Al-Tamimi, 2015b). Standing alone, the document suggests a step in the process of building the sort of pure Islamic caliphate that ISIS claims to be spreading through its military conquests. However, via links to other documents in his archive, Al-Tamimi shows that even this simple directive is, in practice, impossible. Different elements of ISIS use a variety of dating styles, some of which remain unapologetically based on the Gregorian calendar. In his analysis of the calendar documentation, Al-Tamimi (2015b) suggests that the "tribal organization of society" with which ISIS must contend necessarily introduces a "clash between reality and theory." Although ISIS tells its story in the form of a linear, teleologically-oriented movement towards Sunni unity, the mundane aspects of daily life belie the ease with which such a narrative may be completed. Although this specific clerical inconsistency is not particularly damaging or sensational, it suggests the myriad ways in which Web 2.0 technology can be used to disrupt narratives that simplify the complexity of ISIS.

Disruption 2: media rabbit holes and road blocks

Al-Tamimi's archiving and close analysis does not merely serve to complicate ISIS auto-narrativization. It also, in a variety of ways, disrupts the individual stories produced by mainstream Western media sources covering the ISIS phenomenon. The documents that Al-Tamimi collates and verifies, broadly understood, represent citizen journalism, a still-emerging phenomenon much discussed and often lauded by contemporary media scholars (Goode, 2009; Kaufhold, Valenzuela, & Gil de Zúñiga, 2010; Murthy, 2011; Norris, 2017; Wall, 2015). However, as Mehdi Semati and Robert Alan Brookey (2014) argue, the power of citizen journalism remains constrained by the mainstream media structures that frame and then reproduce the raw material made available from citizen sources. In his interpreter tier analysis, Al-Tamimi is both subject to this framing mechanism and serves to disrupt legacy media efforts to simplify and narrativize ISIS.

The media-disrupting nature of Al-Tamimi's work comes in two forms: rabbit-holes and roadblocks. The former occurs when mainstream media sources choose to embrace the breadth of Al-Tamimi's archive, citing it directly in the midst of an otherwise conventional story. In June of 2015, for example, Al-Tamimi is cited in a relatively straightforward *New York Times* report on the growth of ISIS infrastructure in northern Syria (Hubbard, 2015). However, in addition to a summary of Al-Tamimi's relevant findings, the piece offers a link to his entire archive in the middle of a sentence within the story. Whereas most *New York Times* links direct the reader to specific, related stories or information, this one sends a reader to a 65,000-word document without offering any instruction as to how to find information pertinent to the main text. Once clicked, the archive becomes a nearly bottomless rabbit hole that, through its vastness and complexity, may counteract the necessarily simplified narrative offered in pages of *The New York Times*. It thus represents both an opportunity for readers to achieve a far greater breadth of knowledge about ISIS as well as a chance to question the reductiveness through which newspaper writing inevitably simplifies complex fields of information.

Al-Tamimi's research also provides roadblocks for mainstream media sources, forcing them to adjust reporting and storytelling strategies in manners that disrupt simplified, politically attractive narratives about ISIS. For example, in March of 2016, Russia's RT news service reported an "exclusive" story entitled "ISIS, oil & Turkey." The story argued in its first line that newly discovered ISIS documents revealed "stunning insight into ISIS-Turkey oil trade links" (RT, 2016a). In addition to providing a dramatic, enticing lede, this narrative also offered a tangible manifestation of the "festering rift" between Ankara and Moscow (Skinner, 2016). Turkish association with ISIS thus nicely fit an ongoing Russian narrative. Al-Tamimi, already aware of the documents being cited by RT, reviewed their contents and determined them to be authentic. He also, however, showed via close analysis that they in no apparent fashion pointed to Turkish involvement with ISIS. They merely featured general information on ISIS oil trading. Al-Tamimi tweeted his analysis and contacted RT. Within hours, the piece was edited, with the opening line now referring only to "a stunning insight into IS oil trade" and moving the speculation regarding Turkey into the latter portions of the report (RT, 2016b).

Sky News, approaching the ISIS narrative from a very different ideological perspective, ran into a similar roadblock via Al-Tamimi. Whereas RT aimed to associate ISIS with Turkey, an opponent of Bashir Al-Assad's Syrian regime, Sky News, used captured documentation to forward a narrative in which Assad and ISIS were working in tandem. This alliance, of course, fits Western narratives that position Assad as the primary villain of the Syrian Civil War and serve to justify ongoing military actions against his regime. In May of 2016, Sky ran a video detailing an ISIS agreement to withdraw from the city of Palmyra, a decision that would allow Assad's army to fill the power void left in the city (Ramsay, 2016). The story suggested that ISIS was intentionally ceding territory to Assad, thus merging two Western enemies into one. Upon hearing about the report, Al-Tamimi searched for the documents with no success. However, they were, for only a moment, used as a visual illustration in the Sky video report. Al-Tamimi was then able to extract a single legible screenshot from the video, finding enough resolution to read the material and post it to his archive. Upon close analysis he found that while the document did call for the evacuation of Palmyra, it also instructed that these troops be repositioned so as to fight Assad in Qalamoun (Al-Tamimi, 2016a). The information presented in the original report was more or less accurate, but the narrative created around it appeared oversimplified and likely false. Al-Tamimi posted his translation, which was then reposted by a number of mainstream journalists (Lister, 2016).

Disruption 3: American tales

On December 22, 2015, Colonel Steve Warren, official spokesperson for the U.S. Military's Operation Inherent Resolve, took to Twitter to provide evidence for a long desired American ISIS narrative. Posting an Arabic document with an English translation, Warren declared in his tweet "ISIL fighters ordered to dress as ISF [Iraqi Security Forces] and commit atrocities before fleeing Fallujah." ISIS (or ISIL, in U.S. military parlance) was not only losing the war, but they were committing systematic war crimes in the process. The translated document served as compelling evidence, offering a nine-point plan of retreat authored by ISIS's "Security and Military Director". The tweet was a relative blockbuster for Warren, receiving the most retweets in his account's history (Warren, 2015). By Fernandez's (2015) measure, the tweet had succeeded by offering a clear anti-ISIS perspective and inducing sufficient volume to bolster its credibility and impact. According to Al-Tamimi, however, the tweet's popularity ought to have been irrelevant. The documents were fake.

According to Al-Tamimi, the document both featured clear factual errors and failed to reflect the standards found in the myriad of previously vetted materials in his archive. Although Warren's leaflet was said to be discussing Fallujah Province, it was stamped "Ninawa Province," and it called for a withdrawal from the city of Baiji, located in the province of Salah ad-Din. The document called for soldiers to send videos to Al-Jazeera TV, an unprecedented tactic at odds with both the politics and media strategies of ISIS. Perhaps most compellingly, never before had an ISIS figured been described as a "Security and Military Director." Having seen thousands of similar ISIS materials, Al-Tamimi was disinclined to believe that such a position popped into existence just before this document was produced. Time has reinforced this stance, as the position has yet to be heard from since (Al-Tamimi, 2015c).

Immediately, Al-Tamimi offered his objections on social media, finding some success in disrupting the clean transfer of narrative from Warren to the mainstream media. In its early edition on December 23, *The New York Times* reported on the documents without any suspicion (Al-Jawoshy, Chan & Fahim, 2015a). Hours later, after being alerted to Al-Tamimi's concerns, the paper inserted a brief disclaimer, noting that "experts on the Islamic State were debating" the authenticity of the document (Al-Jawoshy, Chan, & Fahim, 2015b). Within days, Al-Tamimi (2015c) released a report entitled "Guide to Islamic State Hoaxes," outlining the suspect aspects of Warren's documentation.

Warren has stood by his tweet and the document, defending its authenticity without responding to the specific, publicly declared objections offered by Al-Tamimi (McLeary, 2015). Regardless of the veracity of the document, Al-Tamimi's interpretation of the documents offered a significant, perhaps fatal disruption to the U.S. narrative surrounding ISIS in Fallujah. Mainstream American media sources quickly moved away from discussing the content of the documents to hosting a debate over their questionable authenticity (ibid). *The Washington Post* went as far as to interview Al-Tamimi, giving him the opportunity to outline his perspective and providing links to Al-Tamimi's website. Employing publicly available evidence to support his claims, the interview compellingly suggests that Warren's belief in the document is rooted in the desire to save face and preserve the American narrative that Al-Tamimi's analysis so powerfully disrupted.

Conclusion: theorizing and critiquing Al-Tamimi

A trained classicist, Al-Tamimi's self-understanding is very much rooted in archival traditions stretching back to ancient Rome. However, in practice, his archive resonates deeply with Lev Manovich's (2001) conceptualization of the digital database as the "enemy" of narrative in the new media era. As Manovich notes, the digital database serves to challenge the cultural hegemony of the novelistic narrative, refusing to guide users down predetermined paths while eschewing the comforts, and limitations, of simple cause and effect understandings of the world (p. 225). In his "On the Concept of History," Walter Benjamin (2005) both theorizes and dramatizes this conflict through an analysis of Klee's painting *Angelus Novus*. According to Benjamin, the painting's subject, the *Angel of History*, sees the past as an ever growing "rubble-heap" that human beings constantly, perhaps foolishly, attempt to bring order to in the midst of an unceasing storm. Al-Tamimi's archive is a digital visualization of such a rubble-heap, always growing and, taken on its own, emphasizing the futility of producing stable narratives out of the protean, contradictory, and numerically overwhelming array of artifacts that emerge from the world of ISIS. The database is, in a real sense, proof that no linear story is sufficient for understanding ISIS or its enemies. The narrative disruptions analyzed above thus represent the toppling of precariously stacked structures.

However, Manovich (2001) also notes that, despite its challenge to cause-and-effect storytelling, the database nonetheless provides raw materials for many of today's digital narratives. Video games, for example, are built upon "data structures" that encourage users to experience a linear, far-ranging narrative shaped by the confines of a hidden but ever-present database (p. 223). Thus, even as Al-Tamimi's archive attempts to disrupt a variety of narratives about ISIS, it also provides a stock of images and ideas that can be later employed in the service of those wishing to construct their own stories. As Jacques Derrida (1996) notes, political power derives in large part from "control of the archive" (p. 12). As time moves on, the inclusions and exclusions of a database such as Al-Tamimi's will have considerable impact on the sorts of structures various people and institutions will be able to put together out of history's rubble.

Each element of Al-Tamimi's research thus represents what Benjamin (2005) described as a "moment of danger." As Stuart Hall (2001) explicates, archives are constantly being "re-read," under new conditions of cultural dominance. Benjamin's "danger" thus emerges from the perpetual threat that regressive institutions may seize upon a piece of the archive and employ it in order to reshape historical narratives to serve their interests. The best solution to this challenge, according to Hall, is a steadfast commitment to "inclusiveness" and "heterodoxy," the idea being that the archive must include within it sufficient materials to rebut those who wish to abuse it (p. 92).

Al-Tamimi, as I have shown throughout this paper, attempts to do just this. He is, however, simply one man working within a rather specific context. Namely, Al-Tamimi has developed his archive largely while working for the Middle East Forum, an extreme right-wing institution that, no doubt, will come to use Al-Tamimi's documents insofar as they fit the narratives they wish to reproduce. Indeed, scholars such as Mustafa Abu Sway (2006) have accused the Forum's President, Daniel Pipes, of offering inaccurate historical narratives that serve to perpetuate Islamophobia. Pipes would not support Al-Tamimi were his materials not to provide authority to his endeavors and, ultimately, his narratives. Al-Tamimi's "access" to his own archive has thus been dependent on his remaining employed by an institution that very often recreates Western representational domination over the Middle East. Moving forward, his materials are at least as likely to be used in the service of specific narrative agendas as they are to disrupt them.

Al-Tamimi's archive thus can never truly escape the juncture of economics and narrativization that shape the preponderance of contemporary online communication. Nonetheless, his work remains dedicated to the notion that the Web 2.0 archive can serve to highlight the illogics embedded in partisan, emotional narratives. In doing so, he establishes a middle approach between Glassman's idealization of online debate and Fernandez's embrace of full-on narrative warfare. Ideally, of course, Al-Tamimi's disruptions would emanate from institutions less overtly committed to their own particular narratives of the Middle East. However, as shown by the disruptive power of his interpretive, archival work, he nonetheless puts in evidence the potential power of open source approaches to contending with extremism online.

References

Abu Sway, M. (2006). Islamophobia: Meaning, manifestation, causes. In H. Schenker & Z. Abu-Zayyad (Eds.), *Islamophobia and anti-semitism* (pp. 13–23). Princeton, NJ: Mark.

Al-Jawaoshy, O., Chan, S., & Fahim, K. (2015a, December 22). *Iraqi forces fighting ISIS for Ramadi push toward city center*. Retrieved from https://web.archive.org/web/20151222182920/http://www.nytimes.com/2015/12/23/world/middleeast/iraqi-army-isis-ramadi.html

Al-Jawaoshy, O., Chan, S., & Fahim K. (2015b, December 22). *Iraqi forces fighting ISIS for Ramadi push toward city center.* Retrieved from https://www.nytimes.com/2015/12/23/world/middleeast/iraqi-army-isis-ramadi.html

Al-Tamimi, A. J. (2015a, January 17). Aspects of Islamic State (IS) administration in Ninawa Province: Part I. Retrieved from http://www.aymennjawad.org/15946/aspects-of-islamic-state-is-administration-in

Al-Tamimi, A. J. (2015b, October 17). Unseen Islamic State treatise on calendars: Full text, translation & analysis. Retrieved from http://www.aymennjawad.org/2015/10/unseen-islamic-state-treatise-on-calendars-full

Al-Tamimi, A. J. (2015c, December 24). Guide to Islamic State document hoaxes. Retrieved from http://www.aymennjawad.org/2015/12/guide-to-islamic-state-document-hoaxes

Al-Tamimi, A. J. (2016a, February 5). Sky News document Qalamoun. Retrieved from https://justpaste.it/skynewsdocumentqalamoun

Al-Tamimi, A. J. (2016b, February 29). Dissent in the Islamic State's Yemen affiliates: documents, translation & analysis. Retrieved from http://www.aymennjawad.org/2016/02/dissent-in-the-islamic-state-yemen-affiliates

Baudrillard, J. (2003). *The spirit of terrorism* (New revised ed.). Brooklyn, NY: Verso.

Benjamin, W. (2005). On the concept of history. Retrieved from http://folk.uib.no/hlils/TBLR-B/Benjamin-History.pdf

Beauchamp, Z. (2014, July 1). ISIS mocks Obama in Michael Bay-style propaganda video. *Vox.* Retrieved from http://www.vox.com/2014/7/1/5858638/isis-propaganda-video

Brachman, J. M. (2006). High-tech terror: Al-Qaeda's use of new technology. *The Fletcher Forum of World Affairs, 30*(2), 149–164. Retrieved from http://fletcher.tufts.edu/forum/archives/pdfs/30-2pdfs/brachman.pdf

Derrida, J. (1996). *Archive fever: a Freudian impression.* Chicago, IL: University of Chicago Press.

Fernandez, A. (2015). *Here to stay and growing: Combating ISIS propaganda networks.* Washington, DC: The Brookings Institution.

Gehl, R. (2009). YouTube as archive: Who will curate this digital Wunderkammer? *International Journal of Cultural Studies, 12*(1), 43–60.

Giroux, H. A. (2014). *ISIS and the spectacle of terrorism: Resisting mainstream workstations of fear.* Retrieved from https://philosophersforchange.org/2014/10/07/isis-and-the-spectacle-of-terrorism-resisting-mainstream-workstations-of-fear/

Glassman, J. K. (2008). Public diplomacy 2.0: a new approach to global engagement [Transcript]. Retrieved from https://2001-2009.state.gov/r/us/2008/112605.htm

Goode, L. G. (2009). Social news, citizen journalism and democracy. *New Media & Society, 11*(8), 1287–1305. Retrieved from http://journals.sagepub.com/doi/abs/10.1177/1461444809341393

Hall, S. (2001). Constituting an archive. *Third Text, 15*(54), 89–92.

Hardaker, C. (2010). Trolling in asynchronous computer-mediated communication: from user discussions to academic definitions. *Journal of Politeness Research. Language, Behaviour, Culture, 6*(2), 215–242. doi:10.1515/JPLR.2010.011

Hubbard, B. (2015, June 15). Offering services, ISIS digs in deeper in seized territories. *The New York Times.* Retrieved from https://www.nytimes.com/2015/06/17/world/middleeast/offering-services-isis-ensconces-itself-in-seized-territories.html?_r=0

Ingram, H. (2015). The strategic logic of Islamic State information operations. *Australian Journal of International Affairs, 69*(2), 729–752. doi:10.1080/10357718.2015.1059799

Jessee, D. D. (2006). Tactical means, strategic ends: Al Qaeda's use of denial and deception. *Terrorism and Political Violence, 18*(3), 367–388.

Kaufhold, K., Valenzuela, S., & Gil de Zúñiga, H. (2010). Citizen journalism and democracy: how user-generated news use relates to political knowledge and participation. *Journalism & Mass Communication Quarterly, 87*(3–4), 515–529. Retrieved from http://journals.sagepub.com/doi/abs/10.1177/107769901008700305

Kraidy, M. (2017, February 9). This is why the Islamic State shocks the world with its graphically violent imagery. *The Washington Post.* Retrieved from https://www.washingtonpost.com/news/

monkey-cage/wp/2017/02/09/this-is-why-the-islamic-state-shocks-the-world-with-its-graphically-violent-imagery/?utm_term=.379317b80eda

Lister, C. [Charles_Lister]. (2016, May 2). Good work by @ajaltamimi, providing detail & context missing from @SkyNews report on #ISIS, #Assad & #Syria: [Twitter post]. Retrieved from https://twitter.com/Charles_Lister/status/727266280009424901

Manovich, L. (2001). *The language of new media*. Cambridge: MIT press.

McLeary, P. (2015, December 24). Analysts, pentagon, debate authenticity of ISIS documents. Foreign Policy. Retrieved from http://foreignpolicy.com/2015/12/24/analysts-pentagon-debate-authenticity-of-isis-documents/

Melki, J., & Jabado, M. (2016). Mediated public diplomacy of the Islamic State in Iraq and Syria: the synergistic use of terrorism, social media and branding. *Media and Communication*, 4(2), 92–103. doi:http://doi.org/10.17645/mac.v4i2.432

Murthy, D. (2011). Twitter: microphone for the masses? *Media, Culture & Society*, 33(5), 779–789. Retrieved from http://www.dhirajmurthy.com/wp-content/uploads/2012/04/Twitter-Microphone-for-the-masses.pdf

Norris, W. (2017). Digital humanitarians: citizen journalists on the virtual front line of natural and human-caused disasters. *Journalism Practice*, 11(2-3), 213–228. Retrieved from http://www.tandfonline.com/doi/abs/10.1080/17512786.2016.1228471

Papacharissi, Z. (2015). *Affective publics: sentiment, technology, and politics*. New York, NY: Oxford University Press.

Ramsay, S. (2016, May 02). IS files reveal Assad's deals with militants. *Sky News*. Retrieved from http://news.sky.com/story/is-files-reveal-assads-deals-with-militants-10267238

RT. (2016a, March 24). *ISIS, oil & Turkey: RT obtains, analyzes trove of jihadist docs seized by Kurdish militia*. Retrieved from https://web.archive.org/web/20160324034019/https://www.rt.com/news/336967-isis-files-oil-turkey-exclusive/

RT. (2016b, March 24). *ISIS, oil & Turkey: What RT found in Syrian town liberated from jihadists by Kurds*. Retrieved from https://www.rt.com/news/336967-isis-files-oil-turkey-exclusive/

Semati, M., & Brookey, R. A. (2014). Not for Neda: digital media, (citizen) journalism, and the invention of a postfeminist martyr. *Communication, Culture & Critique*, 7(2), 137–153. doi:10.1111/cccr.12042

Sienkiewicz, M. (2014). Start making sense: a three-tier approach to citizen journalism. *Media, Culture & Society*, 36(5), 691–701. Retrieved from http://journals.sagepub.com/doi/abs/10.1177/0163443714527567?journalCode=mcsa&

Sienkiewicz, M. (2015). Open BUK: digital labor, media investigation and the downing of MH17. *Critical Studies in Media Communication*, 32(3), 208–223. Retrieved from http://nca.tandfonline.com/doi/abs/10.1080/15295036.2015.1050427

Sindelar, D. (2014, August 12). The Kremlin's troll army. *The Atlantic*. Retrieved from https://www.theatlantic.com/international/archive/2014/08/the-kremlins-troll-army/375932/

Skinner, A. (2016, March 14). *Grudge between Ankara and Moscow deepens in struggle for regional influence*. Retrieved from https://www.cnbc.com/2016/03/14/turkey-v-russia-grudge-between-ankara-and-moscow-deepens-in-struggle-for-regional-influence.html

Stern, J., & Berger, J. M. (2015). *ISIS: The state of terror*. New York, NY: Harper Collins.

Wall, M. (2015). Citizen journalism: a retrospective on what we know, an agenda for what we don't. *Digital Journalism*, 3(6), 797–813. Retrieved from http://nca.tandfonline.com/doi/citedby/10.1080/21670811.2014.1002513?scroll=top&needAccess=true

Warren, S. (2015, December 22). ISIL fighters ordered to dress as ISF and commit atrocities before fleeing Fallujah. [Twitter post]. Retrieved from https://twitter.com/OIRSpox/status/679323227387265024

Winter, C. (2015). Documenting the virtual "caliphate". Retrieved from http://www.quilliaminternational.com/wp-content/uploads/2015/10/FINAL-documenting-the-virtual-caliphate.pdf

Wright, R. (2016, December 12). After the Islamic State. *The New Yorker*. Retrieved from http://www.newyorker.com/magazine/2016/12/12/after-the-islamic-state

Index

Note: Page numbers in *italics* refer to figures
Page numbers in **bold** refer to tables
Page numbers followed by "n" refer to notes

Achilles 112
Adelman, Rebecca A. 3, 24
Adnani, Abu Muhammad al-, 55, 62
Adorno, T. W. 81
airstrikes 55
Aleppo Province Media Office 58n12
Allen, M. 16
Amaq News Agency 34, 36, 44–8, 57n2,n6,n8, 58n14
American Thinker, The 126
Angelus Novus (Klee) 132
animalization 14–15
annihilation 8, 14–15
anti-humanist critique 14–18, 19–20
anti-terrorism, digital 126
Arendt, Hannah 109, 110, 111
Artrip, Ryan E. 4, 77
Asad, Talal 35
Assad, Bashar al-, 4, 62, 66, 131
Assad, Hafiz al-, 63
assassinations 25
atrocity videos, ISIS 9, 10, 13
Ayalon, A. 10
al-Azm, Sadik, 100

Baath Party 62
Baghdadi, Abu Bakr al-, 43, 62–4, 67, 68–9, 70
Bannon, Steve 96
"Battle of Mosul" 37, 37
Baudrillard, Jean 2, 3, 18, 79–82, 87–90, 123
Bayan Radio 46, 58n10
Bayat, A. 71
beheadings 34, 37, 60, 86, 87, 108, 112; *see also* executions; immolations
Benjamin, Walter 132, 133
Berger, J. M. 43, 98, 124
Betancourt, Michael 27
Bilger, Alex 33, 34
Black Lives Matter movement 116
Boal, I. 11

Bockstette, C. 42
body: and horrorism 12; savaged 20–1
Bonnett, A. 65
Bowling Green Massacre 85, 86
Boym, S. 74n3
Brachman, Jarrett M. 124
breaching, acts of 112
British Broadcasting Corporation 128
Brookey, Robert Alan 130
Brown, Wendy 21n8
Brubaker, R. 109, 113

Caliph Ibrahim 64
caliphate 10, 64, 70, **72**, 95, 114–15; declaration of 41, 45, 62–3, 68, 114; currency of 67; as myth 71; nostalgic 65; propaganda of 49, 50–1, 55, 56; utopian life in 50–1, 61, 66, 73, 82, 84;
Cameron, David 13, 15, 21n1
Cantlie, John 38n3
Carr, David 10
Carter, J. A. 43
casualties 35, 57n1
Cavarero, Adriana 6, 8–9, 12, 30, 110, 112
censorship 84
Chouliaraki, Lilie 6, 8, 13
Clark, T. J. 11
Cold War 3, 92–103
communication: of horrorism 8–21; ISIS' death aesthetics 8–10; Islamic State 2, 42–6; strategic and political approaches 10–12
concentrated spectacular societies 61, 62, 67
conflicts, between Islamic State and the US 92–103
Connolly, W. 5
Conrad, Joseph 20
consumer marketing, and culture industry 81
Conway, Kellyanne 82, 85–6
Costa, C. 13, 20
counter-spectacle 67–74, 72–4
counterterrorism discourse 5

INDEX

"coxcomb" graphics, Florence Nightingale's 28
Crusaders 17–18, 49, 98
cyber warfare 55

Dabiq 6, 63, 66, 96, 98, 99
DAESH 111; *see also* ISIS
Dam Be She 69
dar al-harb (the domain of war) 95
dar al-Islam (the domain of Islam) 95
data-informed approach 56
data visualization 27, 28, 31
Dauber, Cori 29
Dawlat al-Khurafa (TV program) 61, 67–70, *68*, 71–2
death: and brutal killing 20; imaginations of 17; ISIS' aesthetics of 8–10; ISIS as cult of 41, 69; online videos of 8–21, 60; spectacles of 10–12; and subjectivity 13; violent 13, 18–19; Western visualities of 12, 13
Debord, Guy 4, 61, 62, 64–6, 72–4
Debrix, François 4, 77
defensive operations 53
Derrida, Jacques 133
détournement 72
Devji, F. 111, 114, 118
diffuse spectacles 4, 61
digital anti-terrorism 126
digital databases 132
digital media 32
dinar 61, 66, *67*
Diyala Province Media Office 58n11
"Documenting the Virtual 'Caliphate'" 42
dogs, in Islamic tradition 14
domination 88, 89
drift 73, 74n5
Drucker, Johanna 27, 33

Edarat al-Tawahhush (administration of savagery) 61
enemies 31, 34
Enlightenment 27
enmity, binary notions of 94–7
Erdogan, R. T. 14
eulogies, as propaganda 52
executions: mass battleground 9, 13; sequence of, ISIS's 14–16; *see also* beheadings; immolations

Facebook 124
"fact-checking" technologies 81
Fallujah, al- 43
Farwell, J. P. 10, 21
fear: and fun 71–2, **72**; and trembling 112
Featherstone, Robin 26
Fernandez, Alberto 122, 123, 125, 128
"fifth wave" terrorism 13
film, narrative pleasure in 66
Fisher, A. 43
Flames of War (Islamic State) 98
Fox News 96

Friendly, Michael 28
fun, and fear 71–2
Furqan, Abu Muhammad al-, 55

Galli, Carlos 26, 31, 33–4
Gehl, Robert 125
geopolitics 5; and ISIS media output 6
Giroux, Henry A. 11, 73, 125, 128
Glassman, James K. 122–5, 129, 133
global consumerism, with global militarism 11
global media 3, 79, 87
global space of appearance 110–14
globalization, violence of 84
gray zone 95
Gusterson, Hugh 33

Habermasian public sphere 111, 123
Hage, Ghassan 35
Hall, Stuart 133
Halpern, Orit 27
Hardaker, Claire 125
Hariman, R. 70
hashtag logics 124, 125
Hayat Media Center, Al 46, 127
hegemony, reversibility and 87–90
hijra (migration) 67
Hijri (Islamic) dating system 129
Himma Library 46
Hollande (President of France) 115
Horkheimer, M. 81
horrorism: abject 15–17, 19; analyzing 12–13; communication of 8–21; critique and savaged body 20–1; death spectacles 10–12; grotesque 14–15, 19; hybridity and moral narratives 19–20; and ISIS' death aesthetics 8–10; in ISIS videos 13–18; regimes of 6, 12, 13–18; spectacular thanatopolitics of 18–21; sublime 17–18, 19; and terrorism 6, 8–9, 112; against unthinkability 30
hudud punishments 51
Hughes, S. 84
Hussein, Saddam 4, 63, 66, 77
hybridity, and moral narratives 19–20
hypervisibility 31, 33, 63–4

Iconoclash 5; deflating 108–19
Ikhlas, al- 43
imagefare, strategic use of 10
images: fragments 87; phases of 79–80; virality of 79–85; virulence of 84
immolations 34, 60; videos of 12; *see also* beheadings; executions
"Impenetrable Fortress" video 17
implosions 81, 84, 85
improvised explosive devices (IEDs) *25*
infographics *25*: history of 27; ISIS 24–6, 30–7; news organizations utilized 31; production 32–5; as technology 3; visual practices 26–8, 34

INDEX

information: visualizations of 26, 27; warfare 55;
weaponization of 32–5
Ingram, H. 10, 124
Inspire 2
Instagram 124
insurgency 33, 42, 52
intelligence agents, shooting of 9, 13, 15
intelligence-led coalition operations 55
International Institute for Counter Terrorism 126
interpretive tier 4–5
invisible war 3, 97–100
Iraq 1, 61–2, 66
ISIS: arguing with 122–33; attacks 36, 86, 96; and
al-Baghdadi, 63; banality of 129–30;
communication strategies 10, 13, 28; "death
spectacles" as aesthetic practices 8–10; digital
communication 8, 60; execution sequence
14–16; glorification of 16; horrorism in ISIS
videos 13–18; infographics about 3, 24–6, 30–7;
instructions, from online sources 2;
interpretation of 125–9; Las Vegas shooting 1;
and media 3–4, 6, 82–5, 98, 110, 113; news
agency 36; nostalgic caliphate 65; online death
videos 8–21, 60; operating on basis of
"competitive systems of meanings" 12, 19; and
al-Qaeda, 123–4; realpolitik 6; as revolutionary
state 18; social media 2, 29, 122–33; spectacular
thanatopolitics 9; takeover map 65; terrorism
1–7; and U.S. media 3; viral images 83–4; visual
brutality 7; visual media 28–30; and al-Zarqawi,
77–8
ISIS Apocalypse, The (McCants) 83
ISIS: The State of Terror (Stern and Berger) 124
Islam 11, 31, 111, 118; protectionism 16
Islamic State (IS): brand 47–8, 49, 54;
communication 2, 42–6, 118; constructing as
global political entity 109; counter-spectacle
67–74, 72–4; currency 66; cybersoldiers 62; as
death cult 41, 69; deglobalization 45–7, 48;
Flames of War 98; iconoclasm 108–19; identity
forms 111; Internet ecosystem 55–6; media
offices 46; Nineveh Province Media Office 46;
official media 42; political and religious
dimensions of 118; productivity 45, 46–8;
religious and political motivations 108–19;
spectacle 61–7; swarmcast 43, 94; and the US
92–103; Utopia media 50–1, 50, 52; victimhood
media 48–9; wanted to become international
pariah 41–2; Warfare media 51–4, 53–4; *see also*
ISIS
Islamic State of Iraq and the Levant *see* Islamic
State (IS); ISIS
Islamic State of Iraq and Syria *see* Islamic State
(IS); ISIS

Jabado, M. 124
Jazeera, al- 102, 128
Jessee, Devin D. 124
jihad 17, 29, 51, 100; media 30; Salafi- 41, 42–3

Kaplan, J. 13, 20
Kellner, D. 11
Kerry, John 99
Khatib, Abdelhafid 65
"Khawarij, the" 97
Khayr Province Media Office 57n7, 58n13
Khouri, R. 21
Kierkegaard, S. 114
Kimmage, D. 43
King, G. 67
Kirkuk Province Media Office 57n4
Kissas, Angelos 6, 8
Kittler, Friedrich 5
Klausen, J. 43
knowledge, visuality and 27
Kraidy, Marwan 4, 60, 125
Kristeva, J. 16

Lami, Abu al-Harith al- 55
Las Vegas shooting 1
Latour, Bruno 117
Lia, B. 42
lies, truths and 82, 84
Lyon, Santiago 101

Maclean 35
Mahdy, Aliaa al- 67
Maher, S. 43
Management of Savagery, The (Naji) 88, 89, 100
Manovich, Lev 132
maps 32
martyrdom operations 35, 38
Marxism 61
Marxists 65
mass executions, battleground 9, 13
mass media 29
Matthews, J. 11
McCants, William 83
McLuhan, M. 109
media: analysis, Arendtian tradition of 118;
digital 32; global 3, 79, 87; and ISIS 3; of
jihad 30; mass 29; news 3–4, 113, 118;
oversaturation 78, 79, 89; reach and impact
100–2; and terrorism 10; terrorist strategy 90;
of victimhood 48–9; visual 28–30; warfare
51–4, 53–4; *see also* social media
mediation 78; and virality of image 79–85;
vulnerabilities 90
Medusa 9
Mekhennet, S. 82, 83
Melki, J. 124
Middle East Forum, The 126
Miladi (Gregorian) calendar 129
Miller, G. 82, 83
Miller, Steven 30
Milton, D. 43, 55
moral codes, puritanical 71
moral narratives, hybridity and 19–20
Morgan, J. 43

INDEX

Mosul, battle of 17, 37, 41, 46, 62
Moza, Shaykha 68
Mueller, Kayla 101
multi-modality, and recontextualization 12–13
Mulvey, L. 66
Murray, S. 6, 8
Muslims 31, 97, 111, 113; generic 118

Naba Newspaper 46
Naji, Abu Bakr 88–9, 100
narrativization 18
Neale, S. 62
neoliberal democracies 61, 73, 74
Neumann, P. R. 43
"new materialism" approach 5
New Yorker, The 123
news media 3–4, 113, 118
Nightingale, Florence: "coxcomb" graphics 28
nikah (matrimony) 69
Nimrud, Iraq 115
9/11 terrorist attacks 87, 100, 108
Nineveh Province Media Office 46, 57n9,n5
nostalgia, of caliphate 65

offensive operations 52, 53
O'Loughlin, Ben 5–6, 108
oversaturation, of media 78, 79, 89

Papacharissi, Zizi 124
Paris: attacks (2015) 86, 96, 101, 115; protests
    (1968) 61
Persian Gulf War, first (1991) 2
Pipes, Daniel 133
Playfair, William 27
pleasure 66, 67
polemical rejection 20, 21n8
political communication approach 10, 11
political strategy, primacy of 114–17
politics, as space of appearance 110
Popovich, E. 10
post-truth condition 78, 81–2
Powell, Colin 77–8
propaganda: of caliphate 49, 50–1, 55, 56; of
    deterrence and provocation 53–4; eulogies
    as 52
provocation, of global consternation 53
psychogeography 65

Qaeda, al- 2, 13, 29–30, 77, 83, 88, 109, 110, 118,
    122–4; *see also* Islamic State (IS)

radicalization 2, 28, 110, 118
Raqqa, Syria 1
Raqqa Province Media Office 57n3
re-mediation 86
re-territorialization 6
recontextualization: concept of 9, 12; hybridity
    of narratives 20; multi-modality and 12–13
religiosity, of Islamic State 109, 114–15, 117

religious communities 114
religious violence 113, 115
representation, image and 78, 79–80
reversal/reversibility: and hegemony 87–90; of
    media events, principle of 85–7
rise of Khilafah, The 66
Robinson, Mark 29
Rogers, Michael 101
Rumiyah 1, 6, 96, 98, 99

Saipov, Sayfullo 1
Salafi-jihadism 41, 42–3
Salazar, Philipe-Joseph 28
Semati, Mehdi 1, 130
Sheikh, J. 50
Sienkiewicz, Matt 4–6, 122, 127
Silverstone, R. 111, 112
simulation, Baudrillard's theory of 79, 87, 89
Situationists 61, 65, 66, 71, 72–3, 74
Situationist International 72
Sky News 131
Slate: Middle East Friendship Chart 31–2
Smythe, Dallas 93
social media 13; ISIS and 2, 29, 122–33
spectacle, defined 73
state, meaning of 5
Stern, Jessica 98, 124
strategic communication approach 10–11, 56
suicide bombing 24, *25*, 35, 69–70, 73
Sunni Muslims, victimization of 47, 49
superpower, Western 88–9
Sway, Mustafa Abu 133
Sykes–Picot agreement 63
Symbolic Exchange and Death (Baudrillard) 79
Syria 62, 66; Civil War 131; ISIS controlled 1
Szpunar, Piotr M. 1, 38n1

Tamimi, Aymenn Jawad al- 5, 123, 125–33;
    American tales 131–2; banality of ISIS 129–30;
    media rabbit holes and road blocks 130–1;
    theorizing and critiquing of 132–3
Telegram 44
Temple of Bel, in Palmyra 108, 112
territorial loss 55
terror, viral mediation of 77–8; hegemony 87–90;
    and reversal strategies 85–7; and viral images
    79–85
Terror Alert System 30
terrorism 112; acts of 8, 10, 30; and
    communication 10; "fifth wave" 13; and
    horrorism 6, 8–9, 112; and media 10; media
    strategy 90; threat of 30; viral mediation of
    77–90; *see also* ISIS
thanatopolitics 6, 8; of horrorism 18–21;
    spectacular 6–7, 9
Thompson, Clive 27
threat multipliers 35–8
Trump, Donald 82, 83, 85, 96, 99
truths, lies and 82, 84

INDEX

Turkey: airstrikes, in Al-Bab 14; as apostate 14; burning of soldiers 9, 13, 14; and Islamic State 115, 130
Twitter 44, 63, 84, 113, 124, 131

ultraviolence 60
Umah 13
unmanned aerial vehicles (UAVs) 35
unseen war *see* invisible war
U.S.: and ISIS media 3; military 28; power 86, 89
US–Islamic State conflict 92–103
us/other binary, use of 3
Utopia: media 50–1, *50, 52*; theme of 44, 51

Väliaho, Pasi 27
Vaneigem, Raoul 66–7, 73, 74n4
victimhood media 48–9
videos, ISIS: atrocity 9, 10, 13; horrorism in 13–18; online death 8–21, 60
Vidino, L. 84
violence: apocalyptic 10, 82; forms of 30; of globalization 84; religious 113, 115; ultra- 60
violent death 13, 18–19
virulence, digital 84
visual economy 108–9, 111

visual media 28–30
visual practices, infographic 26–8, 34
Vox.com 125

war, theme of 44
war on terror 30, 96, 113, 122
warfare media 51–4, *53–4*
Warren, Steve 131–2
Watts, M. 11
weaponization, of information 32–5
weapons of mass destruction 77
Web 2.0 strategy 122, 123, 125, 128
Weber, Cynthia 9
Wilson, Hugh 93
Winter, Charlie 6, 41, 129
Work, Robert 101
Wright, Robin 1, 123

Yaqeen Media 37, 38
Yarchi, M. 10
YouTube 125

Zarqawi, Abu Musab al- 29, 77–8
Zelin, A. Y. 43
Zelizer, Barbie 3, 6, 92
Zelizer, Echoing 9